THE FRANK SINATRA
SCRAPBOOK

For Scott,
All the best,
Frank Sinatra

THE FRANK SINATRA
SCRAPBOOK

His Life and Times
in Words and Pictures

by

Richard Peters

Incorporating
THE SINATRA SESSIONS
A complete listing of all his recording sessions, 1939–1982
by
Ed O'Brien & Scott P. Sayers, Jr.

St. Martin's Press
New York

Library of Congress Cataloging in Publication Data

784.5
P442f

Peters, Richard.
    The Frank Sinatra scrapbook.

    1. Sinatra, Frank, 1915-   . 2. Singers—United
States—Biography. I. Title.
ML420.S565P47   1983   784-5′0092′4 [B]   83-9659
ISBN 0-312-30337-8 (pbk.)

First published in Great Britain by Pop Universal Ltd.

First U.S. Edition

10 9 8 7 6 5 4 3 2 1

CONTENTS

the **Sands**

Las Vegas,

Nevada

Phone 735-9111

(Area Code 702)

This book is dedicated to
FRANK SINATRA

With admiration for his matchless talent
and respect for his humanity and generosity
****

Also, with special thanks to
The Sinatra Music Society (GB)
Sinatra Society of America

--without whose invaluable help
it would not have been possible

RICHARD PETERS
January, 1982

Introduction

Frank Sinatra is one of the true legends of our time, a man of formidable achievements whose face and voice are as familiar to a great mass of the world's population as those of members of their own family. His fame has grown and developed over forty remarkable years: years that have seen the most amazing developments in science and technology, the growth of television, the advent of the jet aeroplane, the computer and the micro-chip, and man's first voyages into space. Alongside this, and through all the changes in taste and fashion, Sinatra's musical genius has delighted and enraptured each successive generation without any compromise of style or quality. As the great Noel Coward once remarked, 'Putting it musically, Mr Sinatra has never sounded a wrong note.'

History tells us that Sinatra was the first American popular singer to achieve success as a *singer* rather than a band vocalist. How he came to fame through the incredible response of his early audiences—events that gave birth to the 'Era of the Bobbysoxers'—and how he has maintained this hold on the public ear through four eventful decades, is now an integral part of show business lore. He has earned his world-wide popularity not just as a singer—but as a supreme recording artist, a concert entertainer of unparalleled drawing power, an Oscar-winning film star, and a humanitarian of great dedication and generosity. That he is a complex man, a driven man, and a totally unique human being goes almost without saying. Those who have been in his company will vouch for the charisma that surrounds him: his sturdy, 5ft 11ins physique, his stylish and immaculate appearance, his courtesy, his craggy, unmistakable face and, above all else, his eyes—those direct, exceptionally sharp eyes, deep peacock blue in colour, which appraise an individual as effortlessly as they do an audience, and have earned him his most enduring nick-name, 'Ol' Blue Eyes'.

Despite the general impression that Sinatra's fame came to him in an overnight explosion of acclaim, the truth of the matter is that he had to work long and hard for the moment when the gods of fortune smiled upon him—and he has had to work equally hard in the intervening years to maintain his appeal. Indeed, when confronted with any pæan of praise about his talent, Frank will invariably put his achievements down to hard work; driving himself and those about him in the search for the kind of musical perfection he has come nearer to attaining than perhaps anyone else in his field. Several of the phenomena that surrounded him have been repeated in succeeding generations: but he was still the first of his kind in the music business. For example, a generation after him, Elvis Presley and The Beatles generated similar hysteria among their fans—but neither the rock n' roll singer nor the 'Fab Four' from Liverpool have survived their own particular age in anything other than nostalgia. Presley is dead, The Beatles disbanded: yet Sinatra goes on performing to this day. He too established records with the astronomical sales of his discs, by topping hit parades with almost monotonous regularity, and earning universal acclaim in a manner that is still the ambition of entertainers everywhere. He has also undoubtedly done more than any other American singer to raise the general standard of popular music by his integrity and dedication, and his profession as a whole owes him a large debt of gratitude. It is not without some justification that the American broadcaster, William B. Williams, has called him, 'the most imitated, most listened-to, most recognised voice of the second half of the twentieth century, and the number one favourite of the other pop singers.' And the columnist Earl Wilson has added, 'Music has been his life. He was born to it without any hereditary justification, he has the gift, he is naturally musical. His life is a series of flashbacks pointing to this undeniable talent. He is worshipped for it by his followers, and he no longer finds it curious that they revere him.'

Frank has similarly become something of a legend as a result of his fierce loyalties—a natural feature of his Italian heritage—and through his generous praise of others. Consider Bing Crosby, for instance, with whom he wrestled for musical supremacy in the early days of his career. (Bing, of course, was then known as 'The Crooner' and Frank 'The Swooner'.) On Crosby's death, a deeply moved Frank told the world's press, 'He was the father of my career . . . the idol of my youth . . . a dear, dear friend of my maturity. He leaves a gaping hole in our music and in the lives of everybody who ever loved him.'

Frank himself has earned the same kind of devotion

The three eras of Frank Sinatra. (Above) teenage idol, (below) Oscar-winning filmstar, (right) concert entertainer supreme (Annette Levine).

among *his* closest friends. Film star Gregory Peck calls him, 'One of the most noble, trustworthy and truthful men I have ever known . . . and one of the great performers of the century'. Actress Deborah Kerr, seeing him through a woman's eyes, puts it this way: 'There's a curiously tender and vulnerable quality about Frank. That's what touches the audience—and it wants to touch back.' And one of the closest of all, Sammy Davis Jr., expresses his feelings even more emotionally: 'He is one of a kind. He is just the best there is. And when he's gone there won't be another one . . . There's never been another performer who could phrase a note like him, who could do what he does with the microphone. And when's cookin', look out. He is simply the best there is. There is no other way to say it.'

Of course, anyone with even the most perfunctory knowledge of Sinatra's career will know that there has been another side to the man. Or perhaps I should say another side that some sections of the press have tried to foster. Writing about this 'bewildering Jekyll-and-Hyde public image' of Sinatra, the English music critic Benny Green has said, 'He is folk hero to some and a double-dyed villain to others. And there is no middle view; you're supposed to either worship him or detest him. Yet the man was never born who could be as black or as white as rival factions paint him. Which is the real Sinatra? The man who offers reporters a Henry Cooperish shot to the jaw, or the benefactor who goes 6,000 miles to visit an orphanage? Is he the man whose morals are a scandal, or the artist whose dedication is legendary?' Mr Green believes that the answer to this question lies in the fact that those who attack Sinatra are rarely ever his fellow professionals. He says that anyone who talks to other singers, actors, dancers and especially musicians gets 'an immediate impression of something close to hero worship.'

Of his own personal experiences with Sinatra, Benny Green has written, 'I have watched him mingling with musicians, hearing them run through each orchestration, cracking a wry joke with the musical director. I have watched this and then wondered how the legend of swaggering belligerence had ever started . . . One of the great clichés of all time is that a man speaks as he finds—well, I found a Sinatra totally unrelated to the loudmouth I had read about. I found that certain people expected some outrageous act—which never happened. I also found him an acutely understanding man with a marvellous sense of professionalism.'

I believe the truth of the matter is that Sinatra has become a prisoner of his own success. His musical achievements, his stature as a world famous personality, and the magic that surrounds his very name, have cost him his freedom: the choice to do as he

pleases and go where he chooses *at will* as you and I can do on any day of the week. Wherever he goes, there are people jostling to see him; whatever he does, however he reacts, there will be somebody—perhaps jealous or just mean-minded—ready to put on him the kind of pressure that would try the patience of a saint. And much as I and millions of others admire him, none of us would claim he was *that*! You can easily find some confirmation for this view of his character by consulting his horoscope. Frank was born on December 12, which makes him a Sagittarian, a person favoured by the stars. The characteristics of the sign are: a man of action, rebellious, sensitive to criticism,

Frank leaves his handprints outside Grauman's Chinese Theatre in Hollywood in 1964.

outspoken, generous, optimistic, annoyed at routine, never satisfied, and always racing against time. Could any description be *more* fitting than that?

For much of his public life, Frank has worn his celebrity with dignity and accepted the adulation with grace, even pleasure. But in return he has repeatedly asked for his privacy to be respected. As he declared emphatically in December 1957 when fighting a libel

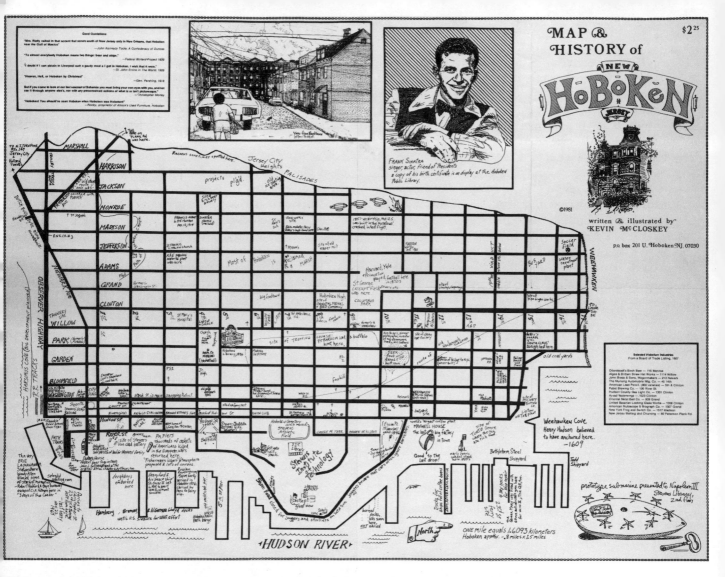

MAP & HISTORY of NEW HoBoKeN

©1981

written & illustrated by
KEVIN McCLOSKEY

p.o. box 201 U. Hoboken NJ. 07030

FRANK SINATRA
singer, actor, friend of Presidents
a copy of his birth certificate is on display at the Hoboken
Public Library.

Map and postcard view of
Frank's birthplace in Hoboken,
New Jersey.

10

suit against *Look* Magazine who he claimed had intruded into his private life, 'I have always maintained that any writer or publication has a right to discuss or criticise my professional activities as a singer or actor. But I feel an entertainer's right to privacy should be just as inviolate as any other person's right of privacy.'

Those are sentiments with which I wholeheartedly agree, and they have been my maxim throughout the compiling of this book. In a sentence, then, this is a work about Frank Sinatra the professional—professional singer, professional entertainer and professional actor. That it charts his rise to fame and subsequent career, as well as recording just a few of his endeavours as a charity worker and crusader against intolerance and racialism, is important in any assessment of the public man, I think. But there is no place in this book for prying into what Frank would quite rightly regard as his private affairs: in particular his personal relationships and his marriages. This scrapbook in fact sets out to record the amazing life of this man which now spans over sixty years: forty of them spent relentlessly in the public eye. It takes us to several American localities, all of which were important in his development and which range from one side of the Continent to the other. And the impact of his presence is to be found in all of them as I know from my own visits. In Hoboken, just across the Hudson River from New York, the neighbourhood restaurants and barber shops proudly proclaim that it was here that Frank Sinatra was born and began his singing career. In Hollywood, outside Grauman's Chinese Theatre, he has left his hand and footprints to mark the fact that here he developed his talent as an actor. In Las Vegas, the gambling and entertainment centre of the nation, he refined his skill as the supreme night club entertainer in the world. And, lastly, there is Palm Springs, where he now lives on a lavish complex in Rancho Mirage—sometimes called 'Frank Sinatra's Desert Kingdom'—basking in the love of friends and admirers. That he is a much honoured resident is evidenced by the fact that the road running by the complex is now called Frank Sinatra Drive, while some local people call him the 'Mayor of Cathedral City'. Frank, for his part, has endowed the city with a Medical Centre and High School named after members of his family.

Among the highlights of the book are special sections devoted to Frank's views on his life, his career, his music and his philosophy. There is the phenomenon of the Bobbysoxers era by someone who was there, and a detailed look at Sinatra the film star. As well, there is an in-depth study of his great concert performances, and a unique listing of every record he

has ever made. Most of the material—both text and pictures—has never been published in book form before. It makes, I think, for a fascinating and revealing portrait of the Greatest Entertainer of the Twentieth Century.

Of course, there have been attempts before to explain Sinatra and his appeal, but as a writer, the one that I consider the most convincing—as well as being closest to my own idea—is that made by the American journalist, Richard Gehman, a Sinatra-watcher for many years. This is what he wrote in 1961 and I think it remains every bit as true today: 'Sinatra has become a symbol to millions of us of all that we may never hope to achieve. The American ideal. He is a man who lives the way we are told those children who were our forefathers lived—in a terrain he established and bounded himself and fought to keep. In these grey and sour days, he has managed somehow to become a throwback: modern as he is, he epitomises a kind of jaunty and irreverent good humour that has vanished from American life. His is an approach to romance that disappeared when the cavalier writings of Rafael Sabatini, that supplier of swashbucklers for the talents of Errol Flynn, fell out of favour and were replaced by John Steinbeck's dusty, slogging tales of human courage.'

Despite his one attempt at 'retirement', Sinatra today gives every indication of wanting to continue entertaining, be it in night clubs or in the most prestigious concert halls in the world: seemingly compelled to go on proving to himself and us (as if we needed any convincing) that he is still The King. He also shows a determination to go on recording and acting—though again the need to prove himself in these areas has long since passed. No one, I suspect, save Father Time will ever get the better of him, and even that inexorable gentleman will find Sinatra no easy man to best. For as he says, 'You got to love living, baby, dying's a pain in the ass.'

Frank also clings tenaciously to his determination to be a mover and a shaker: a rebel to the core. As he says, 'I've always been a rebel, always fought to do what I thought right or best. I shall feel rewarded if some of what I've done musically rubs off on some youngster in the future.'

Could those of us who have enjoyed this amazing man and his superb music for more than four decades wish for anything more than that someday, well in the future, somebody, somewhere, might just be talented enough to take up his mantle?

As someone born when Frank Sinatra's career was just dawning, I did not discover his music until he was well into the second major phase of his life, as a film actor in Hollywood in the 1950s. Yet he spoke to my generation just as he had done to the previous one, and has gone on doing so ever since. The quintessence of what he sang about was the oldest of emotions, love, romantic love, love without lust and crudity, and it has been the increasing need of each successive generation to try and preserve the ideals of this kind of love in the face of a rising tide of promiscuity, pornography and moral decay that has probably been a major factor in his continuing popularity. Certainly, over the years he has been seen by a number of critics as a kind of 'Laureate of Love'—in all but the title America's 'First Poet Laureate'. He has made his mark on our ears, on our eyes and on our minds, and we all owe a little of what we have become to him.

Richard Peters

Palm Springs california

HOTEL DIRECTORY 1981-82

The Life and Achievements of Francis Albert Sinatra

1915

December 12, 1915. The birth of a son, Francis Albert Sinatra, to Natalie (Garavanti) and Martin Anthony Sinatra, at 415, Monroe Street, Hoboken, New Jersey, in the sixth year of their marriage. The baby, weighing a massive 13½lbs, undergoes a difficult birth and the doctor's forceps cause damage to his face and neck. The child also does not breathe until held under a cold water tap by his grandmother, Rosa Garavanti. Both parents are of Italian origin, Natalie (or Dolly as she was called) working as a nurse and later becoming involved in local politics, and Martin fighting as a bantam-weight boxer under the name of Marty O'Brien before taking over the running of a tavern. Later he becomes a fireman. Of her only child, Dolly Sinatra says, 'I wanted a girl and I bought a lot of pink clothes. When Frank was born, I didn't care. I dressed him in pink anyway. Later, I got my mother to make him Lord Fauntleroy suits.' As he grows, Frank's relatives tell him, 'God loved you, he saved you for something. You're meant to be somebody.' These words are to be the driving force of his life.

1928

1928. Teenager Frank, who is always well dressed by his devoted parents, is nick-named 'Slacksy' by his friends. He is keen on physical training, swimming and self-defence, and also develops a passion for fighting racial intolerance. He is generous to a fault. He recalls, 'In Hoboken, when I was a kid, I lived in a tough neighbourhood. When somebody called me a "dirty little Guinea" there was only one thing to do—break his head. When I got older I realised you shouldn't do it that way. I realised you've got to do it through education.' Frank attends the David E. Rue Junior High School, but shows no particular aptitude as a scholar. 'School was very uninteresting,' he said later. 'Homework . . . we never bothered with.'

1930

December, 1930. On his 15th birthday Frank is bought a ukelele by his uncle, Domenico Garavanti. For years he has enjoyed joining in family sing-songs. He is particularly impressed by his grandfather's singing, of whom Dom Garavanti says, 'All the talent Frank got, he got from my father. Pop had a tremendous voice, he was a great singer. I remember when Frank was just a kid, all the relatives used to come out from Brooklyn and New York on a Sunday. There'd be lots of food and wine and Pop would sing . . . Frank just grew up with a lot of music around him, good music, real music.'

1931

January 28, 1931. After graduating from David E. Rue at 15, Frank enters Demarest High School and furthers his interest in music by arranging bands for school dances—featuring himself as the vocalist! His growing ambition to be a singer makes him drop out of school

Frank's mother and father on their wedding day.

before the end of the year. To please his mother, he enrolls at the Drake Business School. 'Listen Frank,' Dolly Sinatra tells him, 'you're going to be something nice, like an engineer, and I don't want any more argument'.

December, 1931. As soon as Frank reaches sixteen, however, and can legally leave school, he quits Drake. Later in life he is to reflect, 'There are several things I think I would have done if I had the chance again. I would have been a little more patient about getting out into the world. I would have seen to it that I had a more formal education. I would have become an accomplished musician, in the sense that I would have studied formally, even if I never used it.'

1932

January, 1932. Young Frank begins to pursue his ambition to be a singer by offering his services to small bands and social clubs in the New Jersey area. A

Frank, circled, at his Junior High School. (Below) two early photographs of the embryo singer.

14

(Above) Frank as one of the Hoboken Four with Major Bowes. (Right) Bing Crosby—
Frank's idol.

neighbour, Nick Sevano, who later became Frank's road manager, recalls, 'His goals were much, much higher than anyone had ever dreamt of. When he made the announcement that he was going to be a singer, everyone was floored, and there was a lot of ridicule going around. Well, he started in. He sang at weddings, and at every kind of local function to get a chance to show what he had. He was a rough diamond and of course people were very slow to see his talent.' *March, 1932.* To earn a living, Frank takes a job at $11 a week delivering the local newspaper, the *Jersey Observer*, and is not long in discovering his attraction for women. 'Frank was always very big with the chicks, even as a kid,' Earl Wilson his biographer and friend quotes a Hoboken story, 'and he was a flirty little wolf when he worked on the delivery trucks of the *Jersey Observer*. He was something of a Romeo on that truck route with that spit curl down over his narrow brow.'

1933

March, 1933. With his girl-friend, Nancy Barbato, a plasterer's daughter from Jersey City, Frank visits the Loews Journal Square Theatre in New Jersey to hear the new singing sensation, Bing Crosby. Afterwards, Frank tells Nancy, 'I could do that. I could sing like Bing Crosby.' However, when he announces at home his intention to become a singer he receives a stinging rebuff from his father. 'My old man thought that anyone who wanted to go into the music business must be a bum,' he recalls. 'This particular morning my father said to me, "Why don't you get out of the house and go out on your own?" What he really said was, "Get out". And I think the egg was stuck in there about twenty minutes and I couldn't swallow it or get rid of it, in any way. My mother, of course, was nearly in tears, but we agreed that it might be a good thing, and then I packed up a small case that I had and came to New York. I was seventeen then, and I went around

15

the city singing with little groups in road houses. The word would get around that there was a kid in the neighbourhood who could sing. Many's the time I worked all night for nothing. Or maybe I'd sing for a sandwich or cigarettes—all night for three packets!'

1935

September 8, 1935. After two frustrating years singing wherever he could get a date—the monotony only relieved by winning an amateur concert at the State Theatre in Jersey City—Frank gets his first big break. He is teamed up with three other young singers, also from the same district as himself, as the Hoboken Four, to appear on a talent show called the Major Bowes Amateur Hour. This is a weekly radio programme broadcast by NBC from the stage of the Capitol Theatre in New York. Thanks to an enthusiastic audience in the theatre and at-home listeners who telephone their approval, the group takes first place. The quartet's success gets them a place in one of Major Bowes road shows. Though the touring proves extremely tough—Frank eventually parting company with the other members of the quartet—it does give him valuable experience. 'I worked on one basic theory,' he said later. 'Stay alive, stay active and get as much practice as you can.'

1936

April 26, 1936. Frank's mother and father are present when Frank plays a date at the Union Club, Hoboken, for a ball held by the Sicilian Cultural League of Hoboken, of which Mrs Sinatra is an important member. Frank manages to secure regular bookings at the Union, but leaves after a disagreement with the owner, and once more finds himself traipsing from club to club in order to find work.

1937

August, 1937. Frank finally lands his first permanent engagement at the Rustic Cabin, a roadhouse near Englewood in New Jersey. He sings with the Harold Arden band as well as doubling as headwaiter! Although poorly paid, Frank sticks to the job because the club is regularly featured on the radio and this gets his name before a wider audience. Recalling these days, Frank says, 'I got my job when some musician friends brought me to Harold Arden, then the bandleader at the Cabin. Arden gave me my first chance for $15 a week, a sum which I continued to be paid for almost a year and a half.' (As a matter of record, the roadhouse no longer exists, but on the site now occupied by a petrol station is a bronze plaque dedicated to Frank, erected in 1975, and reading, 'It must truly be said that he did it his way and it all started right here.')

Frank had ambitions to be a journalist . . .

1939

February 4, 1939. Nancy Barbato, the long-time girl-friend who has patiently supported and encouraged Frank (even subsidising him when times were really hard), becomes Mrs Frank Sinatra at the Catholic Church of Our Lady of Sorrows in Jersey City. Of his bride, the then 24-year-old would-be singer says, 'In Nancy I found beauty, warmth and understanding. Being with her was my only escape from what seemed a grim world.' Coincidental with his marriage, Frank got a rise in salary to $25 per week at the Rustic Cabin, and the couple moved into an apartment at 487, Garfield Avenue, Jersey.

June, 1939. While singing on WNEW Radio's 'Dance Band Parade' (to which he gives his services free) Frank is heard by Harry James, a former trumpeter with Benny Goodman's band, who is putting together his own outfit called Harry James and the Music Makers. James then visits the Rustic Cabin. 'I liked Frank's way of talking a lyric,' James said later. 'I went back the following night with Gerard Barrett, my manager, and we signed him for $75 a week.' James suggests to the young singer that he might change his name. 'Change it?' says Sinatra. 'You kiddin'? I'm gonna be famous.' The Harry James Band, plus their new singer, make their first appearance on June 30 at the Hippodrome Theatre in Baltimore.

July, 1939. During an engagement at the Roseland Ballroom on Broadway with Harry James, Frank gets his first press notice—a single line in *Metronome* which comments on the style of the band and 'the very pleasing vocals of Frank Sinatra whose easy phrasing is especially commendable'.

July 13, 1939. Another first for Frank—he cuts his first record as un-named vocalist with Harry James while in New York. The songs are 'Melancholy Mood' and 'From the Bottom of my Heart'. *Variety* magazine comments that 'the band still has a long way to go.' Although the disc sells only 8,000 copies, when it is re-released in 1943 it becomes a runaway best-seller.

December, 1939. Although still far from being a star, Frank is becoming better known in the music world and he is approached to join the enormously popular Tommy Dorsey Band. Trombonist Dorsey had been urged to listen to Frank by an executive of CBS who said, 'Go listen to the skinny kid who's singing with Harry's Band'. Despite having a two-year contract with Harry James, Frank is released by the generous-hearted bandleader. 'We dissolved with a handshake,' James said later. 'Frank's wife Nancy was expecting a baby and he needed the extra money. But I never did

Frank and Nancy with their daughter Nancy Sandra and son Franklin Wayne.

get around to tearing up the contract. If any of his managers had thought to come to me, Frank later wouldn't have had to pony up all that money to settle with Dorsey. Legally, he was under contract to me. Frank still kids about honouring our deal. He'll drop in to hear the band and he'll say something like, "Okay, boss"—he still calls me boss—"I'm ready anytime. Just call me and I'll be there on the stand."' Sinatra, for his part, leaves the band with real regret. He recalls: 'That night the bus pulled out with the rest of the boys at about half-past midnight. I'd said goodbye to them all and it was snowing I remember. There was nobody around and I stood alone with my suitcase in the snow and watched the tail-lights disappear. Then the tears started and I tried to run after the bus. There was much spirit and enthusiasm in that band. I hated leaving it.'

1940

January 26, 1940. Frank makes his first appearance with the Dorsey orchestra at Rockford, Illinois, as a member of the accompanying group 'The Pied Pipers'. His boss was, says Frank, 'like a god—the whole of the music business was in awe of him.' Jo Stafford, a girl vocalist with the band, remembers his debut. 'We were on stage when Tommy made the announcement

Frank with Harry James in the early days of his career and (below) re-united forty years on.

The famous Tommy Dorsey orchestra with Frank in the back row, right.

for Sinatra's first appearance,' she says. 'As Frank came up to the mike, I just thought, "Hmm—, kinda thin." But by the end of eight bars, I was thinking, "This is the greatest sound I've ever heard." But he had more. Call it talent. You knew he couldn't do a number badly.'

February 1, 1940. In Chicago, as a member of 'The Pied Pipers', Frank makes his first record with the Tommy Dorsey Orchestra, 'The Sky Fell Down'. He is already learning a great deal from Dorsey and has worked out a style for himself. 'I figured if he could do that phrasing with his horn, I could do it with my voice.' The arranger on this first disc is Axel Stordahl, the man who is later to play an important part in creating the 'Sinatra Sound'.

June 7, 1940. Their first child, Nancy Sandra Sinatra, is born to Frank and Nancy at the Margaret Hague Hospital in Jersey City. Frank nicknames her 'Miss Moonbeams' and she is later made the subject of one of his best-known songs, 'Nancy with the Laughing Face', with lyrics by comedian Phil Silvers. Nancy, after education at University High School in West Los Angeles and the University of Southern California, is to follow in her father's footsteps as a singer and actress, displaying considerable style and sex-appeal.

July 20, 1940. The Tommy Dorsey band reaches the number one spot on the *Billboard* best-selling records charts, with 'I'll Never Smile Again'—the vocals by an uncredited Frank Sinatra of 'The Pied Pipers'. Of it, the magazine says, 'A different, arresting record and one with great commercial as well as artistic appeal.' The disc stays at the top for a record seven weeks. The Band also becomes the summer replacement for the Bob Hope Radio Show.

August, 1940. Frank appears in his first film, a musical called 'Las Vegas Nights' which stars Constance Moore and Bert Wheeler with the Tommy Dorsey Band. Of Sinatra in the movie, George Simon says in *Metronome*, 'He sings prettily in an unphotogenic manner.' The band tour non-stop across America, and gradually Frank builds up a relationship with the aloof Tommy Dorsey. 'He became almost like a father to me,' Sinatra says, 'and this in spite of the fact that, being a John Rebel, I was always the guy who had to pass on the beefs of the boys in the band.'

1941

May 20, 1941. The annual College Music survey conducted by *Billboard* names Frank as the most outstanding Male Band vocalist in the United States. This rise in his popularity, despite only occasionally being named as the singer on the Tommy Dorsey records, is further confirmed in the *Down Beat* poll in December when he displaces Bing Crosby from the top spot. Crosby had won the accolade for the previous four years.

August, 1941. Tommy Dorsey publishes a book, *Tips on Pop Singing*, which names Frank Sinatra and a former Australian opera singer named John Quinlan as co-authors. Among the requisites for success it lists are 'good health, hard work and plenty of patience'. Sinatra later admitted to a great debt to Quinlan, 'If it hadn't been for his coaching when my voice was about done, I'd have had no career. He did it for nothing because I had nothing to give him at the time.'

1942

January 19, 1942. Frank cuts his first four solo songs for Bluebird Records with Axel Stordahl as arranger and conductor: 'The Night We Called It A Day', 'The Lamplighter's Serenade,' 'The Song Is You' and 'Night And Day'. Of this historic session, Harry Meyerson, the A and R Chief says, 'Frank was not like a band vocalist at all. He came in self-assured, slugging. He knew exactly what he wanted. He knew he was good.' Later, when he listened to the recording, says Stordahl, 'He was so excited, you almost believed he had never recorded before. I think this was the turning point of his career. I think he began to think then what he might do on his own.'

July 2, 1942. Now planning a solo career, Frank records what is to be his last song with Tommy Dorsey in New York, 'Light A Candle In The Chapel'. (Ironically, at the previous day's session he has cut 'There Are Such Things' which is to become a number one hit in December, three months after Frank has left the band!) Of his desire to go it alone, he says, 'What really put the clincher on my decision was when I heard that Bob Eberly was planning to break off with Jimmy Dorsey . . . Nobody had broken the ice since Crosby, and I thought that somebody is going to come along and do this any day. If Eberly got out ahead of me, I'd be in trouble.'

September 19, 1942. Frank and Tommy Dorsey part company, although the bandleader is to receive a percentage of his future earnings. (Sinatra was some years later reported to have paid $24,000 to break this deal.) Frank freely acknowledges his debt to the man who put him on the road to stardom. 'Tommy taught me everything I know about singing. He was my real education.' Dorsey also pays tribute to his former singer: 'I used to stand there on the bandstand so amazed I'd almost forget to take my solos. You could almost feel the excitement coming up out of the crowds when the kid stood up to sing. Remember, he was no matinee idol. He was a skinny kid with big ears. And yet what he did to women was something awful. And he did it every night, everywhere he went.' Dorsey's arranger, Axel Stordahl, also leaves to work with Frank, and he acquires a manager, Hank Sanicola, a

The young crooner and a pretty admirer.

former Broadway song plugger, who is to guide his career for twenty years until 1962.

December 30, 1942. Frank makes his first solo appearance as an 'Extra Added Attraction' on the 'King of Swing', Benny Goodman's New Year Show at the Paramount Theatre in New York. After being introduced simply by his name, something extraordinary takes place as the young vocalist himself describes: 'The sound that greeted me was absolutely deafening. It was a tremendous roar. I was scared stiff. I couldn't move a muscle. Benny froze too. He turned round and looked at the audience and asked, 'What the hell is that?' I burst out laughing and gave out with "For Me and My Gal".' The era of the Bobbysoxers had been born.

1943

January, 1943. 'Sinatramania' packs the Paramount Theatre until the end of Benny Goodman's four week engagement, after which Frank is contracted for another similar period. Only Bing Crosby has matched this record, and *Time* magazine comments, 'Not since the days of Rudolf Valentino has American womanhood made such unabashed public love to an entertainer.' Hundreds of column inches of newsprint are soon being devoted to the new phenomenon, and

Sinatramania!

Press agent
George Evans

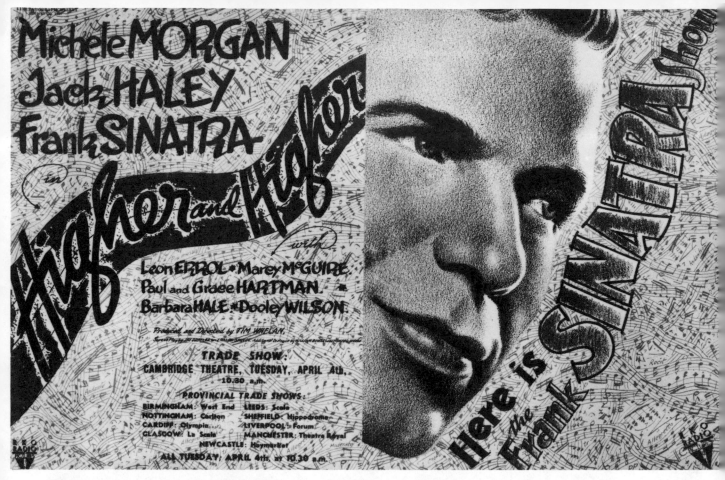

Frank is variously dubbed, 'The Sultan of Swoon', 'The Voice That Thrills Millions' and shortly thereafter just 'The Voice'. While the newspapers debate many and varied reasons for his sudden success, Frank has a simple and logical explanation. 'Psychologists tried to go into the reasons with all sorts of deep theories. I could have told them why. Perfectly simple: it was the war years, and there was a great loneliness. And I was the boy in every corner drug-store, the boy who'd gone off, drafted to the war. That was all.'

February 6, 1943. Frank gets his first sponsored show when he is signed to take over the top spot in America's most popular coast-to-coast radio programme, 'Your Hit Parade' presented by Lucky Strike, and the music magazine *Down Beat* describes him as the 'biggest name of the moment in the business.' He stays with the show for two years.

March 17, 1943. Frank makes his first nightclub appearance as a solo singer at the Riobamba Club in Manhattan. Although initially nervous, Frank charms his dinner-jacket audience, and the master of ceremonies, Walter O'Keefe, admits to his listeners at the end of Sinatra's four week engagement: 'When I came into this place, I was the star and the kid named Sinatra one of the acts. Then suddenly a steamroller came along and knocked me flat. Ladies and gentlemen, I give you the rightful star—Frank Sinatra!'

May, 1943. Columbia Records re-release 'All Or Nothing At All', the unsuccessful disc recorded by the Harry James Band with Frank as the anonymous vocalist. By July 10, with his name on, it is top of the Hit Parade, and he has signed a lucrative solo contract worth $360,000 with Columbia's A and R Chief, Manie Sachs, who is also to prove a big influence on his career.

June 7, 1943. Frank goes into Columbia's New York recording studios to cut his first three sides for them: 'Close To You', 'People Will Say We're In Love' and 'You'll Never Know'. Axel Stordahl is the arranger and Frank is accompanied by the Bobby Tucker Singers. The second and third discs both climb to number one on the Hit Parade and help him leap to the forefront in the record business.

August 14, 1943. Frank fills the giant Hollywood Bowl on his first concert there, and is nearly besieged by fans. 'They converged on our car,' he says afterwards, 'and practically picked it up. There musta been 5,000 kids jammed up behind the forty or fifty people mashed against the car. It was exciting—but it scares the wits out of you, too.' Frank is now receiving over a thousand fan letters a week, and the Sinatra Fan Club has two thousand branches in America, not to mention hundreds around the world.

September, 1943. The new singing sensation completes

work on his first starring part in a Hollywood movie, 'Higher and Higher', a Rodgers and Hart Musical which also features Michele Morgan, Jack Haley, Victor Borge and Mel Tormé. When released in January 1944, the *Hollywood Citizen News* says, 'He portrays himself so naturally that you catch yourself thinking, "He can act, too."'. One of his songs in the picture, 'I Couldn't Sleep A Wink Last Night', is an Academy Award nomination.

October 1, 1943. Frank opens a season in the Wedgwood Room of the Waldorf Hotel in New York, renowned as 'the classiest supper club in America'. Despite some initial worries that his style might not captivate the older, more sophisticated audiences, he achieves an unprecedented success. Columnist Elsa Maxwell, among the crowd of dignitaries and socialites, says admiringly, 'He has found a setting to show off the sweetness of his voice.'

October 22, 1943. Following a preliminary medical examination, Frank is declared 1-A and fit for military service in the Armed Forces. On December 9, however, he is called back by the authorities and, to the evident relief of hundreds of fans who camp outside the examination centre, is down-graded to 4-F because of a punctured eardrum. Frank himself is deeply disappointed at not being able to serve.

1944

January 2, 1944. Frank takes issue on the front page of the *New York Evening Sun* with classical musician Artur Rodzinski who claims that 'jazz is contributing to juvenile delinquency.' An Indiana University professor also maintains that Sinatra's popularity 'can be ascribed to a rebellion of many young people against the classical music training crammed into them at school.' Frank's defence of his music is supported by the renowned Leopold Stokowski as well as over 10,000 readers' letters.

January 10, 1944. A second child, a boy, Franklin Wayne Sinatra—named after President Roosevelt and later known as just Frank Jr.—is born in the Margaret Hague Hospital in Jersey City. He, too, is destined to be a singer like his father. Frank is busy making his second movie, 'Step Lively', which co-stars Gloria Haven to whom he gives his first 'screen kiss'. Reports journalist E. J. Kahn: 'This unprecedented bit of eroticism aroused so much interest that *Look*, America's Family Magazine, devoted four pages to it, and it was subsequently revealed that the fan mail of Gloria Haven, the actress granted the honour of receiving the historic kiss, had climbed from four or five letters a day to several hundred.' According to Gene Ringgold, Frank himself actually swooned on the set of 'Step Lively'—but that was when he heard he

An early British newspaper story on the new singing sensation, *Picture Show*, March 24th, 1945.

had become a father again!

September 28, 1944. Frank is invited to the White House for tea with President Roosevelt, the man after whom he had named his son, and is told by FDR, 'Fainting, which once was so prevalent, has become a lost art among the ladies. I'm glad that you have revived it.' The overawed young singer later tells the press, 'I felt as if I'd seen a vision. I thought, there is the greatest guy alive today and here's a little guy from Hoboken shaking his hand.' And he adds, 'He kidded me about the art of how to make girls faint. But he didn't ask me to sing!'

October 12, 1944. On a return engagement at the Paramount Theatre in New York, Frank's appearance leads to what the press calls 'The Columbus Day Riot'. (October 12 being celebrated as the day Columbus discovered America.) According to biographer Arnold Shaw, 'It brought on the mightiest demonstration of female hysteria that any entertainment star had until then been accorded.' Over 25,000 youngsters converge on the area of the Paramount, blocking the streets, holding up traffic and requiring several hundred policemen to handle the crowds. Similar scenes were to greet Frank when he appeared in other

Frank about to give his first screen kiss to Gloria Haven in 'Step Lively' (1944).

cities such as Boston, Chicago and Pittsburgh and of them, Earl Wilson wrote later, 'I was caught in the "swooning" panics or riots as they came to be, and can attest that Frank generated as much sexual excitement among those Bobby-soxers as the Beatles or Elvis ever did. Moreover, I think the teenage girls were more in love with their Frankie.'

October 31, 1944. To demonstrate his support for President Roosevelt, Frank appears at a Madison Square Garden re-election rally in company with Harry Truman. Apparently overcome by emotion when facing the massed crowds of FDR supporters, he tells them movingly of his idol, 'He is good for me and my kids and my country.' His contribution in campaigning for the Democratic Party undoubtedly played an important part in FDR's success.

November 14, 1944. After a dispute lasting a year between Columbia Records and the musicians' union which prevented any discs being made, Frank is at last able to return to the studio and cuts the classic 'Saturday Night (Is The Loneliest Night In The Week)' which remains high in the nation's charts for ten weeks.

1945

February 15, 1945. An evening of outrageous humour when Frank and an all-star cast record a radio parody of the popular comic strip hero, 'Dick Tracy In b Flat'. The show is for the Armed Forces Radio Service 'Command Performance Programme' with Bing Crosby as Tracy, Bob Hope the villain Flattop, Frank the despicable Shaky and Judy Garland as Snowflake. All the stars are the subject of jokes, including Frank who is referred to as a 'pipe cleaner in suspenders'. (Frank, in fact, appeared in a number of these war-time 'Command Performances', the first being in December 1943.)

April, 1945. Frank demonstrates his concern about racial prejudice by lecturing on the subject to a gathering of young people in Philadelphia. He also speaks at a Carnegie Hall Youth Rally where he urges his listeners to 'join with the youth of the United Nations so that we can live in peace with our neighbours across the sea as well as our neighbours down the street.' After the Harlem Riots he also declares, 'Every race produced men with big, strong muscles, and guys like me. There's no point in going around calling other kids names or indicating your racial prejudices.'

May, 1945. To celebrate the end of the war, Frank undertakes a six week world tour to entertain American troops abroad. He is accompanied by comedian Phil Silvers and song-writer Saul Chaplin. In Rome, he is granted an audience with the Pope. He

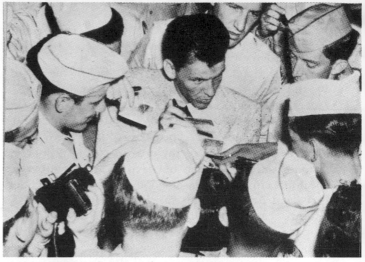
Frank mingling with American troops in 1945.

also 'adopts' 12 war orphans and jokes to the press, 'My wife will brain me!'

September 12, 1945. Start of a new CBS radio series for Frank, 'Songs by Sinatra', sponsored by Old Gold Cigarettes which runs for 30 minutes every Wednesday night. The resident orchestra is that of Alex Stordahl, and Frank is accompanied by the group to which he once belonged, the Pied Pipers. The show attracts many guest stars including Gene Kelly, Nat 'King' Cole, Peggy Lee, Benny Goodman and Tommy Dorsey.

November 17, 1945. In an emotional ceremony, Frank receives the annual American Unity Award of the Common Council for American Unity at a rally in Carnegie Hall, New York. The award is given for 'his work in advancing the cause of better Americanism' and in particular for his part in making the short film, 'The House I Live In' to which he, producer Frank Ross and director, Mervyn Le Roy gave their services free. In the picture Frank confronts a group of youngsters abusing a Jewish boy, remonstrates with them for their attitude, and sings the title song. All profits from the film go to organisations working on juvenile problems. The picture also receives several other citations, including the Bureau of Intercultural Education Award, the Council Against Intolerance in America 'Jefferson' Award, and the Newspaper Guild's Page One Award. The influential columnist, Harriet Van Horne, writes of Frank that 'here is a sincere, hard-working young man with a deep sense of his brother's wrong and a social conscience that hasn't been atrophied by money or fame.' Another important feature of the film has been highlighted by film historians, Gene Ringgold and Clifford McCarty, '"The House I Live In" is the harbinger which marks Hollywood's "coming of age". Within two years of its release, in 1945, many have forgotten Sinatra's pioneer film and credit the industry's brave and adult assault on racial intolerance to Darryl F. Zanuch and Elia Kazan for "Gentleman's Agreement", Dore Schary for "Cross-fire" and, later Stanley Kramer, for "Home of the Brave".' Frank's concern for racial equality has, in fact, remained just as enthusiastic all through his life. *December 5, 1945.* Frank demonstrates his versatility by deciding to make a record as a *conductor* rather than a singer. An admirer of the music of Alec Wilder, he cuts an album of Wilder tunes which greatly impresses the musician. 'What was so good about it,' says Wilder, 'was that it was so musical. Frank felt music and he listened carefully to the soloists and he built up a wonderful rapport with them and the other musicians.' Columbia Records recording chief, Manie Sachs, is even more impressed, 'By the time he was through, they were applauding him and hugging him and patting him on the back.' The year also closes with Frank winning the *Metronome* award as 'Act of the Year', and his first major film, 'Anchors Aweigh', co-starring Gene Kelly, being rated the year's best picture in *Screen Guide*'s Anniversary Poll. Hollywood columnist Louella Parsons says the box office smash film, 'moved Sinatra right up into the major star class.' It is also revealed that Frank has made his first million dollars, and Nancy declares, 'I can't believe it, only millionaires make millions. All I can think of is the time, six years ago, when we had spaghetti without meat sauce because meat sauce was expensive!'

1946

March 7, 1946. Frank and Mervyn LeRoy are awarded Special Oscars by the American Academy of Motion Picture Arts and Sciences for their contributions to 'The House I Live In.' Just prior to this Frank wins, for the third year in a row, the *Down Beat* award as America's Favourite Male Singer. During the Spring he also signs a new five-year film contract with MGM which guarantees him a million and half dollars a year! *June 22, 1946.* Lucky Frank! The following curious story about how luck can play a big part in an unknown's career appears in *Picturegoer*, entitled, 'How They Got Their Big Chance' written by Roland Wild. 'Frank Sinatra might still have been a clerk in a newspaper's circulation department if someone had not sent him upstairs on an errand. "I saw typewriters and knew what a Press Card does at a ball game," Frank told me. "And I said to myself—That's for me!" The end of it was an entry to the night clubs, a job singing in one, a radio engagement, Benny Goodman's Band, and his present position as Mother Superior of the Bobby-Soxers at 25,000 dollars a week—some weeks! But Frank agrees that the betting on a sports reporter becoming whatever he is today isn't encouraging.' *August 20, 1946.* While working on the G.I. film, 'It

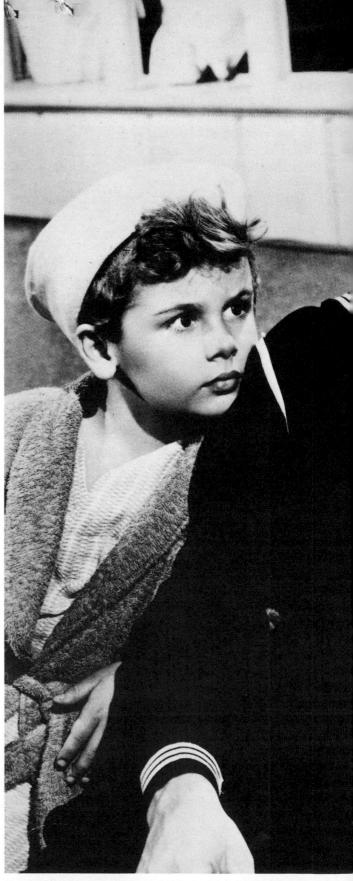

Frank with Gene Kelly who taught him to dance in 'Anchors Aweigh'.

Frank formed an outstanding comic partnership with Jimmy Durante in 'It Happened in Brooklyn' (1945).

Happened in Brooklyn', with Jimmy Durante, Frank hears of the death of his close friend, the night club comedian, Rags Ragland. He immediately flies to New York to stand in for the dead man and gives a sensational performance. The trade paper, *Variety*, writes, 'That appreciative gesture by Sinatra understandably sets him in a niche all his own in the big sentimental heart of show business.' And of his appearance in 'It Happened in Brooklyn', *The Los Angeles Examiner* says later, 'Frank, of course, thrills the customers with his vocalising, but it's his naturalness and easy-going charm that begets applause. . . . His comical duet with Durante provoked great whoops of approval from the boys and girls out front.'

October, 1946. Frank is voted the most popular screen star of the year by *Modern Screen* and at a celebration dinner held by the magazine he is presented with a bronze bust of himself made by the famous sculptor, Jo Davidson. Of his subject, Davidson says, 'His face has a curious structure. Those cheekbones! Those bulges around the cheeks! That heavy lower lip! He's like a young Lincoln.'

November, 1946. Publication of a major three part profile of Frank in the vastly influential *New Yorker Magazine*. Written by E. J. Kahn Jr., the articles were simply but graphically entitled 'Phenomenon'. Shortly afterwards the series was published in volume form as *The Voice*, and as the first objective study of Sinatra and his influence is now a much sought-after book.

1947

February, 1947. As a result of a brief holiday in Cuba, Frank on his return to America finds himself the target of abuse from several newspaper columnists, as well as becoming the centre of allegations that he has connections with the Mafia. He had already been attacked previously for his political campaigning on behalf of Roosevelt, and in some quarters he was even accused of being a Communist sympathiser! While his career has been checkered with skirmishes in one form or another with sections of the press, it needs to be said that many of the stories about Frank were deliberately orchestrated to show him in a bad light, and while he was certainly not above reproach on every occasion, his treatment has often been harsh and unjustified.

April 10, 1947. Despite the press hostility towards him, Frank attends a fund raising rally in Times Square, New York for the research fund of the American Cancer Society. An estimated 100,000 people gather for the event, many thousands of these quite evidently enthusiastic fans of 'The Voice' out to rebuff the charges made against him.

June, 1947. Long a boxing fan, Frank sponsors the heavyweight fight between Jersey Joe Walcott and Joey Maxim at the Gilmore Stadium in Hollywood. Unfortunately, the bout is badly attended and Frank loses approximately $50,000. It proves to be his first and last attempt at being a fight promoter.

August, 1947. Frank takes second place in a radio poll run by Jimmy Fidler of ABC to find 'The Most Popular Living Person'. The first position is won by Bing

Sculptor Jo Davidson at work on his bust of Frank.

Frank as a Catholic Priest in 'Miracle of the Bells' with Fred MacMurray and Alida Valli (1947).

Crosby, while Sinatra edges in just ahead of Pope Pius XII!

October 30, 1947. To mark his remarkable achievements, the civic authorities of Hoboken declare this 'Sinatra Day' and present Frank with a giant 'Key' to the borough. His mother is among the thousands of fans who attend the ceremony.

November 13, 1947. Frank appears for four weeks at the Capitol Theatre, New York, which is placarded with signs, 'First Aid Station for Swooners', and gets an ecstatic review from *Billboard*. 'Sinatra is showmanship personified.' During the course of the engagement, Frank forms what is proved a lasting friendship with one of the accompanying artists, Sammy Davis Jr, a member of the Will Mastin Trio. Sammy says later of this moment in his life, 'It was the most. And the build up he gave us when he brought us on stage! For me, it was really the beginning. All the great things happened after that. Now, can you help loving a guy like that?'

1948

March, 1948. To broaden his screen roles, Frank plays a Catholic Priest, Father Paul, in 'Miracle of the Bells' in which he only sings one song. He also decides to donate his fee to the Catholic Church. Although the film on its opening this month is greeted by mixed reviews, it does good box office business and Frank's performance is described as 'appealing'.

June 20, 1948. A third child, another girl, Christina, is born to Frank and Nancy at the Cedars of Lebanon Hospital in Hollywood. For the first time, Frank is present at the birth of one of his children. Christina, or Tina as she becomes known, proves to be the shyest of the Sinatra children, yet like her elder brother and sister enters the world of show business, though as an actress rather than a singer. She has said of her family, 'We're all little pieces of Daddy and I seem to follow his dramatic inclinations.'

August, 1948. Frank works on 'Take Me Out To The Ball Game' in which he co-stars with Gene Kelly again,

Frank in an off-duty mood on a film set.

songs he has to sing on 'Your Hit Parade', Frank leaves the show and on this day begins a new prime time radio programme, 'Light up Time', sponsored by Lucky Strike Cigarettes on the NBC network. He gets a higher salary and a three year contract. Among his guests is Ann Sheridan, famous as the 'Ooomph Girl', who says later, 'That guy still gives me goose pimples all over! The radio show I did with him was one of the zaniest and happiest times I had in Hollywood.'

November, 1949. 'The King of Swoon' is crowned King of the annual Tobacco Festival at Richmond, Virginia, and is featured on the front cover of *Billboard* singing to over 6,500 people from the roof of a department store!

December 8, 1949. Frank meets the ravishingly beautiful film star, Ava Gardner, at the New York premier of the new musical, 'Gentlemen Prefer Blondes' by Sammy Cahn and Julie Styne. She says of him, 'I think Frank is a wonderful person. I like him as a human being as well as for his talent.' Of their subsequent romance, Earl Wilson has said it was 'one of the wildest, weirdest love stories ever told about a show business couple.' The following day, Frank's new film about three sailors living it up on a furlough in New York, 'On The Town', attracts excellent reviews and draws enormous audiences. Says *Motion Picture Daily*, 'Never before has any motion picture

Frank relaxing with one of his records while filming 'The Kissing Bandit' (1948).

this time as a song-and-dance team who spend their summer months as members of a baseball team. Esther Williams provides the love interest as the pretty new manager of the team. Says *The Hollywood Reporter* of the picture, 'Frank Sinatra and Gene Kelly are not strangers to the jobs of sharing stellar honours, and the addition of Esther Williams makes their engaging talents seem that much brighter. Sinatra sings and gags his way through a most pleasant role, and Kelly steps out to knock the folks dead with his terrific dancing.'

1949

September 5, 1949. After a dispute over the type of

grossed as much on any one day in any theatre anywhere.' This same year also sees Frank awarded the Los Angeles Jewish Community 'Hollzer Memorial Award'.

1950

January 28, 1950. Death of Frank's long time press agent and friend, George B. Evans, who had been with him almost every moment of his meteoric rise to fame. Arnold Shaw said of Evans, 'The loss to Frank was incalculable. Whether or not he had planted swooning teenagers in the Paramount and squalling Bobby-soxers in radio studios, as *Variety* credited him with doing, he had been an imaginative drum-beater and a reliable friend. He has guided Frank skilfully through periods of controversy and helped him achieve a dimension that Sinatra could not have achieved as a mere warbler.'

February 14, 1950. Nancy announces that she and Frank have separated. 'Unfortunately my married life with Frank Sinatra has become unhappy,' she says. 'We have therefore separated and I have requested my attorney to work out a property settlement. I do not contemplate a divorce.'

April 26, 1950. Just as he is due to sing at the Copacabana Night Club, Frank loses his voice— 'nothing came out but dust,' he says later when explaining why he cannot perform, and Billy Eckstine takes his place. The loss is not for long, fortunately, although Frank makes light of the incident later by saying his doctor ordered him to remain totally silent for forty days to allow his famous vocal cords to recover!

May, 1950. Frank makes his television debut on a show with Bob Hope. (Curiously, Bing Crosby was also to make his first TV appearance with Bob Hope, but not until two years later.) As a result he is offered a five year contract with CBS, worth $250,000 a year.

July 12, 1950. Another first for Frank—he crosses the Atlantic to star at the London Palladium, the mecca of the British entertainment world. *The Guardian* on his opening night calls him, 'An Orpheus of Our Time' and adds that, 'Not to be outdone by their American sisters, a mob of respectable young women surged and moaned outside the theatre throughout the evening.' The paper continues, 'When Mr Sinatra at last appeared, pandemonium broke loose and (at the second house) it was often difficult to hear because of the barrage of comment, giggling, sighing and applause which punctuated the melancholy sounds proceeding from the stage.' Endeavouring to explain his appeal, the writer concludes, 'Just as Caruso was adored as the quintessence of every Mediterranean serenader, so Mr Sinatra is the incarnation of every love-sick G.I., the new myth, the new English dream.' Throughout the rest of his two months stay in England, Frank is subjected to similar mass hysteria wherever he appears, and is even dubbed, 'The Ambassador of Miserabilism' (the cult of loving misery.)

October 7, 1950. Frank's television series for CBS begins, highlighted by a musical take-off of Charlie Chaplin's film, 'The Kid', with Ben Blue as the Little Tramp and Sinatra as the child. *Variety*'s verdict is that Frank is a television performer 'with considerable charm, ease and the ability to sell a song.' He also works on the film, 'Double Dynamite' in which he co-stars with the comedian Groucho Marx and an almost demure Jane Russell in a comedy about an ill-fated get-rich-quick scheme.

1951

March 27, 1951. Deeply in love with Ava Gardner, Frank records a song he co-authored, 'I'm A Fool To Want You'. The critic George Simon declares it to be, 'the most moving song Sinatra has ever recorded.'

May, 1951. The month is designated 'Frank Sinatra Record Month', and 1,500 American disc jockeys invite their listeners to choose their favourite Sinatra tunes to be used in his new picture, 'Meet Danny Wilson.' Reporting on the outcome of the voting, *Picturegoer* says: 'With one exception the tunes that finally

topped the poll proved to be Tin Pan Alley "evergreens''. Evidently, enthusiasts still prefer the old hits from Frankie.' The final selection was: 'She's Funny That Way', 'You're A Sweetheart', Irving Berlin's 'How Deep Is The Ocean?', 'That Old Black Magic', 'When You're Smiling', 'All Of Me', George Gershwin's 'I've Got A Crush On You' and 'A Good Man Is Hard To Find' which Frank sang as a duet with Shelley Winters. The film 'Meet Danny Wilson' is based on a story by Harold Robbins, later to become internationally famous as the author of *The Carpetbaggers*.

October 30, 1951. Frank and Nancy are divorced. She is to receive one third of Frank's gross income up to $150,000 a year and ten per cent of his earnings above that. She is also granted custody of the three children. Despite parting, the two are to remain in constant touch and their friendship remains to this day. As Nancy says, 'If I hadn't held to friendship with Frank and made him welcome in our home, I couldn't have lived with my conscience. Children need two parents. Whenever there's some special problem of discipline, I've been able to call their father and say, "I think this is something you should handle. I can't be an ogre all the time." And always, Frank has come over.'

November 7, 1951. Frank marries Ava in a private ceremony at West Germantown, Pennsylvania, with Axel Stordahl as his best man. Says Ava, 'I was so excited and nervous . . . But as soon as I saw Frank standing there, I wasn't nervous any more. He looked so composed. But he told me he had a lump in his throat.'

December 1951. Frank and Ava return to London for him to appear in a Charity Performance at the Coliseum Theatre to raise money in aid of the National Playing Fields Association. The show is sponsored by the Duke of Edinburgh who tells the hundred American and British stars who appear, including Tony Curtis, Janet Leigh and Orson Welles, 'It was Mr Sinatra's idea that you should all come'. The show nets over $50,000.

1952

March 26, 1952. Frank returns to give concerts at the Paramount Theatre in New York where his phenomenal success began, and in the audience are a number of close friends including Phil Silvers, Jimmy Durante and Julie Styne. Earl Wilson, present at the opening night, describes the return as an 'emotional one'.

July 1952. In the *American Weekly*, Frank writes two remarkable articles under the title, 'Frankly Speaking' in which he talks openly about his life, his problems with the press and once again emphatically denies he is a communist. The cause of all his troubles, he says, is the fact that he is 'a high-strung, emotional person who

Frank and Ava Gardner on their wedding day, November 1951.

does things on the spur of the moment.'

October 27, 1952. Frank and Ava appear at a glamorous film stars' rally at the Hollywood Palladium in support of Governor Adlai Stevenson's presidential candidacy. Ava introduces Frank as 'a man I'm a great fan of myself' and he sings two outstanding versions of 'The House I Live in' and 'The Birth of the Blues'.

1953

January 9, 1953. After reading James Jones' best-selling novel, *From Here to Eternity*, about the attack on Pearl Harbour, Frank determines to get the part of the tough little soldier, Angelo Maggio, in the film which Columbia Pictures plan to make. He feels it is a part with which he can totally identify. 'For the first time in my life,' he declares later, 'I was reading something I really had to do. I just felt it—I just knew I could do it, and I just couldn't get it out of my head.' His belief and his persistence pay off and on this day he signs to co-star in the film with Burt Lancaster, Montgomery Clift and Deborah Kerr.

April 2, 1953. Frank joins the Capitol Record label and begins an association which is to last for seven years and see the development of the 'swinging' style of singing which has marked his later years. His first

A rare photograph of Frank at work on the set of 'From Here to Eternity' in 1953.

track is 'Lean Baby'. Although his long time associate, Axel Stordahl, arranges this particular session, it is to be his last. Thereafter for some years his arrangements are to be in the hands of Nelson Riddle, who also came from New Jersey and with whom his name has subsequently become inextricably linked. Of Sinatra, Riddle has said, 'There's no one like him. Frank not only encourages you to adventure, but he has such a keen appreciation of achievement that you are impelled to knock yourself out for him.' For his part, Frank later admitted, 'It was a happy marriage. Nelson had a fresh approach to orchestration and I made myself fit into what he was doing.'

May, 1953. A month-long tour of Europe begins with Frank giving concerts in several major cities including London, Stockholm, Naples and Rome. He then rests in London while Ava films 'The Knights of the Round Table'. Of the concert tour, the influential *New Musical Express* says, 'Sinatra is still the greatest male singer in pop music. His range and power seem greater than ever.'

October 27, 1953. MGM announce that Frank and Ava have separated and she will seek a divorce. Despite this unhappiness, he is about to enjoy a period of unprecedented success as an actor as well as a singer. *November, 1953.* In an in-depth study of Frank, George T. Simon, the noted *Metronome* critic, declares of one of his night club performances at this time, 'From the start to the end, it was all in magnificent taste, the songs, the incomparable Sinatra phrasing and the wonderful backgrounds. It was like a session of the best Sinatra records, with the visual charm of the man added.'

1954

March 12, 1954. Frank is back at the top of the Hit Parade for the first time in several years with 'Young at Heart', a song that had been turned down by several other leading singers including Nat 'King' Cole. *March 25, 1954.* At one of the most dramatic ever Oscar Award ceremonies, held at the Pantages Theatre in Hollywood, Frank takes the 'Best Male Supporting

Oscar winners Frank and Donna Reed in March, 1954.

Actor' award for his role in 'From Here to Eternity'. The previous evening, ex-wife Nancy and his three children had given Frank a special gold medallion of their own on which was inscribed, 'Dad, we'll love you—from here to eternity.' Deeply touched by both presentations, Frank tells the press after the Oscar ceremony, 'Its funny about that statue. You walk up on the stage like you are in a dream and they hand you that little man before twenty or thirty million people and you have to fight to keep the tears back. It's a moment. Like your first girl or your first kiss.' And *Time* magazine raves, 'Frank Sinatra does Private Maggio like nothing he has ever done before.'

July, 1954. Frank's follow-up film to 'From Here To Eternity' gives him another dramatic role—this time as a killer bent on assassinating the President of the United States. The movie is called 'Suddenly' and he gives an excellent performance opposite Sterling Hayden as the hostage trying to prevent his deadly mission. *Newsweek* is just one of many magazines that praises Frank: 'As the assassin in the piece, Sinatra superbly refutes the idea that the straight-role potentialities which earned an Academy Award for him in "From Here to Eternity" were one-shot stuff. In "Suddenly", the happy-go-lucky soldier of "Eternity" becomes one of the most repellent killers in American screen history. Sneeringly arrogant in the

beginning, brokenly whimpering at the finish, Sinatra will astonish viewers who flatly resent Bobby-soxers' idols.'

October 14, 1954. Frank is the subject of a 'This is Your Life' programme in which host Ralph Edwards presents a lively and somewhat elaborated biography of the man he calls 'The Pied Piper of Hoboken'. He also works on the hospital drama film 'Not As A Stranger' with Robert Mitchum, of which *The Hollywood Reporter* is to say later, 'Sinatra, who seems to become a better actor with each successive part, is simply terrific.'

December, 1954. A triumphant year for Frank ends with him winning a trio of awards in *Billboard*'s annual poll. He is named top male singer, his song 'Young At Heart' from the picture in which he co-starred with Doris Day, is the year's best disc, and his album 'Swing Easy' is voted No. 1 LP. As if to underline his great renaissance, *Down Beat* names him Most Popular Vocalist, and *Metronome* declares him 'Singer of the Year'.

1955

March, 1955. Frank turns in an outstanding performance as the gambler Nathan Detroit in the musical 'Guys and Dolls' co-starring Marlon Brando, although he is unhappy about the 'Method' style of acting. 'I don't buy this take and re-take jazz,' he said. 'The key to good acting on the screen is spontaneity—and that's something you lose a little with each take.'

April 21, 1955. Bela Lugosi, the famous Hollywood horror film star, voluntarily admits himself to the Los Angeles General Hospital as a self-declared drug addict. Aid comes from an unexpected source. 'Frank Sinatra was the only star I heard from,' he says later. 'I'd never even met him and it gave me such a boost for him to encourage me.' Fifteen weeks after admission, Lugosi is declared cured.

June, 1955. During the filming of his next picture, 'The Tender Trap', actor Lee J. Cobb suffers a heart attack, and is rushed to hospital. Thereafter Frank visits him almost daily. Said Cobb afterwards, 'In his typical unsentimental fashion, Frank moved into my life . . . He flooded me with books, flowers, delicacies. He kept telling me what fine acting I still had ahead of me and discussed plans for me to direct one of his future films.' Of this and many other anonymous acts of generosity, Father Bob Perrella, 'The Showbiz Priest', has written, 'When tragedy struck the lives of the Judy Garlands, the Ethel Barrymores, the unlucky ones never knew the identity of the man who paid their rents and bought their food.'

August, 1955. Accompanied by his elder daughter, Nancy, Frank flies to Australia for a twelve-day tour.

Mid-50's

The mid 50s were busy years for Frank, entertaining, recording and filming.

His four concerts are all record-breakers and earn him in excess of $40,000. Just prior to this trip he had sung with Nancy at her school concert in Santa Monica!

September 19, 1955. Frank gives a memorable performance as the singing 'stage manager' in the NBC-TV production 'Our Town' which also stars Paul Newman and Eva Marie Saint. The show has a musical score by Sammy Cahn and Jimmy Van Heusen and earns the rare distinction of launching a hit song, Frank's 'Love and Marriage'.

October, 1955. By way of complete contrast, Frank plays a drug addict in 'The Man With The Golden Arm' based on Nelson Algren's best selling novel. Although he is nominated for another Oscar for his role, the controversial nature of the picture causes him to be edged out by Ernest Borgnine (a co-star in 'From Here To Eternity') playing the title role in 'Marty'. The reviews are ecstatic, however, with *The Saturday Review* describing Frank's performance as 'truly virtuoso' and adding, 'His scene in the jail with a junkie screaming for a fix in the same cell, the scene of his own first fix in Louie's room—both played in huge, searching close-ups—and the terrible writhing agony of the 'cold turkey' treatment are conveyed with

clinical realism.' Early the following year, he is given a special award for this role by the British Cinematography Council of London.

December, 1955. Frank produces and stars in his first film as an independent, a Western originally titled 'The Loud Law' but eventually released as 'Johnny Concho'. His friend Don MacGuire directs the movie and Nelson Riddle writes his first score for the screen. For the opening of the picture the following year, Frank sings a special concert with Tommy Dorsey and his Orchestra at the Paramount Theatre in New York. It is to be the last appearance of the singer with his former employer: Dorsey dies later in the year.

1956

February, 1956. Frank works on the MGM musical, 'High Society' which also stars Bing Crosby, Grace Kelly and Louis Armstrong. Although Frank and Bing have long been in friendly competition for the position of number one American singer, they spark each other off wonderfully on the film set, and are nick-named 'Dexedrine' and 'Nembutal' respectively. *The Hollywood Reporter* later enthuses, 'This is slick, sure directing and great response from two unique stars. Miss Kelly is very good, and she plays with Crosby and Sinatra in a relaxed and delightful way.' Frank himself declares that the whole shooting of 'High Society' was 'a ball, a regular romp, the greatest.'

April, 1956. Frank flies to Spain to play the role of a peasant guerrilla fighter in 'The Pride and the Passion' based on C. S. Forester's dramatic novel, *The Gun*, co-starring Cary Grant and Sophia Loren. *Variety* reports on how hard Frank worked during the making of the picture, and says, 'Sinatra is the ''Passion'' vis-a-vis Grant is ''Pride''. One is the emotional, zealous, in-articulate Spaniard, driven by blind passion to destruction of the French bastion at Avila. The other is stiff, organised, disciplined—all Government Issue, British style. Sinatra looks and behaves like a Spanish rebel leader, earthy and cruel and skilled in handling his men in the primitive warfare. His is a splendid performance.'

July 31, 1956. Ava Gardner announces in Rome that she and Frank have signed the papers for a divorce. (They are not, however, finally divorced until July 5, 1957).

September 20, 1956. Frank sends a telegram to the Congressional Committee for Anti-Trust Action which is investigating charges that certain organisations have a stronghold on American music. He appeals to them to 'end the practices which deprive artists of creative freedom' and cites examples from his own career where he was forced to record what he considered inferior material. 'Rather than continue a frustrating battle I chose to take my talent elsewhere,' he says.

October, 1956. Frank plays the real-life character of Joe E. Lewis, a singer turned comic whose vocal cords were slashed by mobsters, in 'The Joker Is Wild'. Of the role, Frank says, 'Joe was a helluva singer before the punks heeled on him. Everyone who knew him then said he really had a voice. I wouldn't play just a singer in a movie—like Russ Columbo or a Rudy Valee. Joe's is a powerful story.' And Joe E. Lewis himself says, 'Frankie enjoyed playing my life more than I enjoyed living it.' One of the songs, 'All The Way', also won an Academy Award.

December, 1956. Metronome magazine invites 109 jazz performers to name 'The Musician's Musician' of the year. Frank tops the list, polling more votes than all the other nominees put together. His album 'Swinging

Bing Crosby scores a 'hit' with Frank in 'High Society', made in 1956.

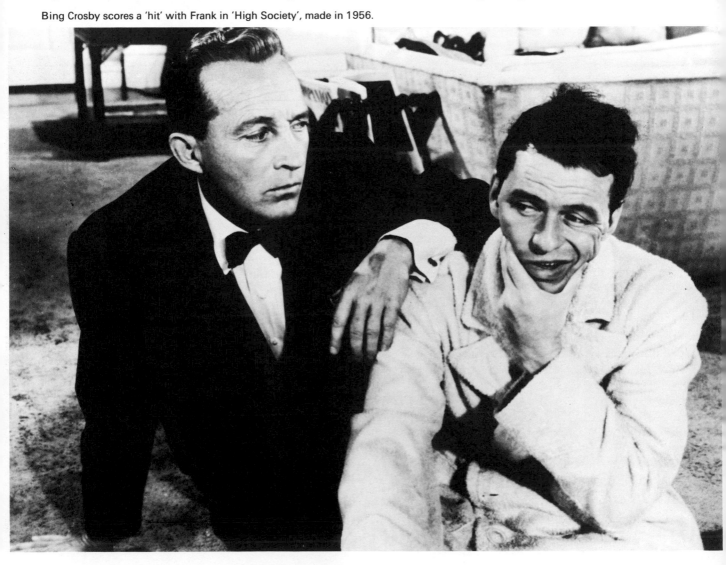

Lovers' is also named one of the best jazz albums of the year.

1957

January 14, 1957. In the early hours of the morning, Frank's close friend, the actor Humphrey Bogart, dies. He is deeply affected by the death and cancels his appearance at the Copacabana night club in New York, telling his agent, 'I can't go on. I'm afraid I won't be coherent.'

March, 1957. Frank begins work on another tailor-made film role—the lead part in 'Pal Joey' based jointly on John O'Hara's novel and the musical show written by Rodgers and Hart. 'It's the only role I've dreamed of doing for many years outside of Private Maggio', Frank says, and turns in an outstanding peformance as the smooth, fast-talking singer. He also gives memorable renditions of such tunes as 'My Funny Valentine' and 'The Lady Is A Tramp'. When author John O'Hara is asked later if he has seen Frank's performance, he replies, 'No, I didn't have to see Sinatra. I invented him.'

October, 1957. In a sudden outburst against the raging popularity of Rock 'n' Roll music, Frank tells the French magazine *Western World* that it 'fosters almost totally negative and destructive reactions in young

Frank compares his 'make-up' scars with the real ones on Joe E. Lewis, whom he portrayed in 'The Joker is Wild' (below), also made in 1956.

A smiling Frank gives evidence against *scandal magazines* in Los Angeles, February 1957.

be an opinion he later modifies drastically.

October 18, 1957. Start of Frank's 'anthology' series of TV shows for which he is being paid $3 million! These hour-long programmes consist of either musical variety shows or dramas which Frank introduces. He makes appearances in four of the dramas: 'The Hogan Man' (October 25) playing a New York cabbie raising two adopted children; 'Brownstone Incident' (November 11) in which he and Cloris Leachman are a couple agonising whether or not to get out of the big city jungle; 'A Gun At His Back' (November 29) as a cabbie once again, looking for his stolen taxi; and 'Take Me To Hollywood' (December 13) with a show business background. Of the first programme, a musical, the *New York Herald Tribune* enthuses, 'Frank was one hell of a performer and his first TV show a triumph in almost all departments.'

December, 1957. Another string of awards for Frank including *Playboy*'s 'Top Male Vocalist', *American Weekly*'s 'All-Around Entertainer of the Year' and *Metronome*'s 'Mr Personality'. The reader's poll run by *Metronome* also gives him such an overwhelming victory, that an Editorial comments, 'Sinatra literally devoured this one: there was no chance for anyone else.'

1958

people.' And he adds, 'My only deep sorrow is the unrelenting insistence of recording and motion picture companies upon purveying this most brutal, ugly, degenerate, vicious form of expression.' This proves to

March 23, 1958. Frank concludes a two week appearance at the Fontainebleau club in Miami which takes over a hundred thousand dollars and breaks all existing American night club records. *Variety* writes

Frank with Lee J. Cobb, whom he helped when Cobb was taken ill, seen here together in 'Come Blow Your Horn' (1963).

breathlessly that Sinatra was 'the hottest attraction ever to have played the area'. Despite all the acclaim, Frank also experiences the sadness at this time of losing another of his close friends, Manie Sachs. He acts as a pallbearer at the funeral in Philadelphia and says emotionally, 'What bothers me is that when I holler for help, he ain't gonna be there anymore.'

June 14, 1958. Frank attends the Monte Carlo premiere of his latest film, 'Kings Go Forth' which co-stars Tony Curtis and Natalie Wood. At a midnight gala he is introduced by Noel Coward, and also has to be formally presented to Princess Grace, his former co-star in 'High Society'. He also approaches Sir Winston Churchill, a man he has long admired, and asks, 'Sir, I have always wanted to shake you by the hand.' Charmed by his deference, Sir Winston introduces Frank to Lady Churchill who confesses herself an admirer of his records. The gala evening raises over $12,000 for the UN Refugee Fund, and of the film, about a white soldier's love for a young half-Negress, it is later claimed that it 'may well have contributed to some advanced thinking about mixed marriages'. The *Los Angeles Examiner* also writes 'The Thin Singer has never had a more difficult role and he has never more completely mastered a characterisation. Might as well admit it, he's a great actor.'

September 27, 1958. Huge crowds chanting 'We want Frankie' cause a massive traffic jam and block the roads around the Odeon Theatre in Leicester Square, London, where Frank hosts another gala premiere. The film is Danny Kaye's new picture, 'Me and the Colonel', and among the guests at the evening are the Queen and the Duke of Edinburgh. Frank confesses, 'I happen to love London more than any other city in Europe, and helps raise $70,000 for the British Cancer Fund.

November 1958. After months of negotiating by producer Raoul Levy, a project to bring together Frank and the French sex symbol Brigitte Bardot to film 'Paris By Night' falls through. The failure is recorded with some regret by *Playboy* magazine which has been eagerly debating what might happen when 'The Voice meets the Broad of Broads'!

December 1958. Frank's stature as a singer and entertainer is marked by the presenting to him of the Al Jolson B'Nai B'Rith Entertainer of the Year award for 1958.

1959

January 26, 1959. 'Some Came Running', the film Frank had shot the previous August about the crisis in the life of a devil-may-care writer, opens in New York with high praise for Sinatra from the *New York Times*: 'He is downright fascinating—or what the youngsters would

An eye for a well-turned ankle—Frank filming 'Can-Can' in August 1959.

call "cool" . . . He is beautifully casual with a bottle, bull's-eye sharp with a gag, and shockingly frank and impertinent in making passes at dames.'

April, 1959. Frank makes a short concert tour of Australia, meeting briefly with his ex-wife, Ava Gardner, in Melbourne, where she is filming the Nevil Shute story, 'On The Beach'.

May 8, 1959. In a recording session with Nelson Riddle, Frank cuts the engaging tune 'High Hopes' written by Sammy Cahn and Jimmy Van Heusen. It is to be the theme song of the Sinatra film, 'A Hole in the Head' in which he co-stars with Edward G. Robinson. Later 'High Hopes' wins the Academy Award for 1959.

July 25, 1959. Scenes of near-riot greet Frank's eight days of shows at the 500 Club in Atlantic City. Arnold Shaw says later that the appearances were 'so spectacular that police had to keep excited fans under control both at the club and his hotel. During his stay, more than two hundred women required hospital treatment. Reservations were re-sold at a 1,000 per cent profit.' Such is his evident appeal at this time that the *New York Post* dubs him 'The Love Voice of America'.

August, 1959. The Russian Premier, Nikita Khrushchev and his wife visit the 20th Century Fox film studios where Frank is filming 'Can-Can'. Khrushchev is apparently amazed at the dancing scenes he witnesses and later describes them as 'immoral'.

Frank, who loves baseball, at the Los Angeles Baseball Writers' Dinner in April 1959.

Frank explains a point from the script of 'Never So Few' to his lovely Italian co-star, Gina Lollabrigida, in October 1959.

October, 1959. Cast as the leader of a group of G.I.s and guerrillas fighting the Japanese in Burma in 'Never So Few', Frank also co-stars with the beautiful Gina Lollobrigida and a young actor on the verge of superstardom, Steve McQueen, who was previously only known as a television actor. Says the *Los Angeles Examiner*, 'Sinatra is in his element, swinging with the plot from tough soldier to teasing lover, and tossing off the smart dialogue in that casual, underplayed way of his.'

December, 1959. Frank rounds off the year with no less than two Grammy Awards—his song 'Come Dance With Me' is nominated as 'Best Solo Vocal Performance', and his LP of the same title takes the award as 'Album of the Year'.

1960

March, 1960. Elvis Presley, the Rock 'n' Roll idol, finishes his two years in the American Army and Frank

With Elvis Presley on Frank's television spectacular in March 1960.

WILLIAM BRADFORD HUIE
THE EXECUTION OF PRIVATE SLOVIK

The true story of the only American soldier executed for desertion in World War II

The book which public opinion prevented Frank from filming in 1960.

turns one of his TV spectaculars into a 'Welcome Home Elvis' show. Pre-recorded at the Fontainebleau in Miami where Frank is appearing, the event is billed by the press as 'the meeting of The Voice and The Pelvis—two generations of idolatry.' Screams from the live audience greet both entertainers and underline how little has changed over the years from the time of Sinatra's Bobby-soxers to Presley's Rock Generation. When the show is networked on television in May it is watched by over 40 per cent of the viewing population of the country and the *Hollywood Reporter* declares the figures to be 'the highest for any TV show in five years'.

March 21, 1960. Frank becomes embroiled in controversy over his plan to film a book called *The Execution of Private Slovak* by William Bradford Huie, the true story of the only American soldier to be executed by the American Army since the days of the Civil War. He wants to use a scriptwriter named Albert Maltz for the screenplay, but there is an immediate press reaction because in June 1950 Maltz had declined

41

to answer questions before the U.S. Congress's Un-American Activities Committee about alleged membership of the Communist Party, and as a result had received a $1,000 fine and a year in prison. A furore breaks over Frank's head involving journalists, entertainers and even people close to him.

April 8, 1960. After days of soul-searching, Frank makes a decision not to go ahead with the *Private Slovak* film. He releases the following statement in the form of an advertisement in *Variety*: 'Due to the reactions of my family, my friends, and the American public, I have instructed my attorneys to make a settlement with Albert Maltz and to inform him he will not write the screenplay for *The Execution of Private Slovak*. I had thought the major consideration was whether or not the resulting script would be in the best interests of the United States. Since my conversation with Mr Maltz had indicated that he had an affirmative, pro-American approach to the story and since I felt fully capable as a producer of enforcing such standards, I have defended my hiring of Mr Maltz. But the American public has indicated that it feels the morality of hiring Mr Maltz is the more crucial matter, and I will accept the majority opinion.'

April 12, 1960. After an absence of eight months from the recording studios, Frank cuts a new song, 'Nice 'N' Easy' which is to be the title tune for a new album as well as making the number one spot in *Billboard*'s chart by August 21.

July 10, 1960. Frank attends the Democratic Party's nominating convention at the Beverly Hilton Hotel, Los Angeles and declares his support for John F. Kennedy as President. He and Judy Garland entertain the guests. He also participates in later fund raising activities including a ball in New Jersey on October 18 at which so many people try to attend that over 20,000 have to be locked out of the Sussex Armoury in Newark. 'One of the most tumultuous meetings in New Jersey history', to quote one report of the event.

August 3, 1960. The world premier of 'Oceans Eleven', the first of a series of films in which Frank stars with his group of friends known as 'The Clan'—Dean Martin, Sammy Davis Jr., Peter Lawford, and Joey Bishop. The picture had been made earlier in the year in Las Vegas and produced marvellously colourful performances by the five men as a group of former Army veterans who raid five gambling casinos and steal ten million dollars. Of their acting on the set and partying afterwards, comedian Milton Berle declared, 'I've seen a lot of wild nights, but this was the greatest.' The picture also turns out to be a box office smash.

September 11, 1960. Daughter Nancy — she of the 'Laughing Face'—is married in Las Vegas to singer Tommy Sands, with Frank giving the bride away. Nancy says of her father, 'My brother and sister and I look up to him, respect him, and love him. My mother and father have refused to let their personal differences upset our lives. We're a family and we know it.' (Unhappily, Nancy and Tommy were divorced in 1965).

December 12, 1960. As he celebrates his forty-fifth

Frank and his friends of 'The Clan' who had such fun on stage, make their first film together, 'Oceans 11' (1960).

FRANK SINATRA

Among those appearing are Count Basie, Mahalia Jackson and Tony Bennett, with a closing appearance by Dr King himself, just released from a Georgia jail. *Variety* magazine enthuses afterwards that the show was 'one of the greatest ever seen in New York.'

February, 1961. Frank plays a spell-binding season at the Sands Hotel in Las Vegas, which he part owns. *Variety* applauds his performance and calls him 'the hottest star in Las Vegas—and probably anywhere else.'

April, 1961. Frank achieves another of his great ambitions—he sees the launching of his first album on the label of his own company, Reprise Records—'to play and play again'. The company has actually been formed the previous December because, says General Manager, Morris Ostin, 'Frank wanted to encourage other artists to join him in what he felt would be a freer, more creative atmosphere.' The first album 'Ring-A-Ding Ding' has also been recorded that month on December 19 and 20 in Los Angeles, with arrangements by Johnny Mandel. It is destined to become a Gold Disc. During 1961, he follows this success with two more albums, 'Sinatra Swings' released in July, and a tribute to the man who played such an important part in his early career, Tommy Dorsey, on 'I Remember Tommy' which appears in October. By December, the Dorsey tribute is in the LP Top Ten and substantiating Frank's claim, 'I really think it has some of the best work I've ever done. I feel sentimental over Dorsey . . . I tried to sing the songs as he used to play them on his trombone.'

October, 1961. Frank is guest of President Kennedy at the Compound in Hyannis Port where, according to Press Secretary, Pierre Salinger, discussions take place about a souvenir record of the Inaugural Gala being released to raise funds for the Democratic Party.

1962

January 9, 1962. Frank becomes engaged to Juliet Prowse, a South African dancer who appeared with him in the film 'Can Can'. The engagement lasts barely six weeks, however, the couple splitting on February 22 becuase of a 'conflict of career interests.'

February 17, 1962. The Philadelphia radio station, WING, declares this 'Frank Sinatra Day' and feasts its listeners with Frank's records. The New York station, WINS, also programmes only Sinatra records for a period of sixty-six hours, and the same idea is taken up in Baltimore and Sacramento where local radio stations launch 'Sinatra-thons'. This same month. Frank's Western comedy, 'Sergeants Three' with the other members of 'The Clan' opens in New York.

April 15, 1962. Frank sets off on a two month, round-the-world tour to raise money for children's charities.

birthday, Frank is voted 'Top Box Office Star of 1960' by the Film Exhibitors of America, and *McCall's* magazine lists him as one of the 'Most Attractive Men in the World'. He is also busy on a new film 'The Devil at Four O'Clock' with Spencer Tracy.

1961

January 19, 1961. Frank organises the Inaugural Gala for President Kennedy in Washington and draws a veritable galaxy of stars including Gene Kelly, Ella Fitzgerald, Nat 'King' Cole, Bette Davis, Harry Belafonte, Tony Curtis and many more. Despite a sudden snow blizzard which prevents some guests reaching The National Guard Armoury where the event is to be held, the pre-sold tickets guarantee a take of over a million and a half dollars for Democratic Party funds. Thanking the organiser, Kennedy says, 'We're all indebted to a great friend, Frank Sinatra. Long before he could sing he was pulling votes in a New Jersey precinct . . . Tonight we saw excellence.' Frank says later, 'I only wish my kids could have seen it. I can't find the words.'

January 27, 1961. A packed audience in Carnegie Hall sees a superlative tribute to the Civil Rights leader, Martin Luther King, staged by Frank and his friends.

Frank working with Robert Farnon and Co., during the 'Great Songs from Great Britain' sessions in London in 1962.

Because he says he considers himself 'an over privileged adult' he pays all the expenses of the tour—his own, his assistants' and those of the musicians—so that the money raised from the thirty concerts can go straight to charity. With the target of one million dollars in mind, he travels from Los Angeles to Tokyo, Hong Kong, Tel Aviv, Athens, Rome, Milan, Paris, Monte Carlo, London, New York and back to Los Angeles. Enormous crowds greet him in every city. In Tokyo he is presented with the Key of the City (the first non-military American to receive this award); in Israel he meets Prime Minister Ben-Gurion; in Italy he is given the Star of Solidarity Award; and in London he is a sensational success at the Royal Festival Hall before an audience including Princess Margaret. (While in London, on June 12–14, he also cuts an album, 'Great Songs from Great Britain'; and the Variety Club present him with a 'Silver Heart' trophy in appreciation of his 'magnificient efforts' for charity.) Frank returns to the United States on June 17, the tour having cost him over half a million dollars but having comfortably surpassed its target. Of his undoubted triumph, he says, 'I found out a lot of things I didn't know before. It was a revelation.' And of his most unforgettable moment, 'I was visiting a home for blind kids in London and one little girl asked me, "What colour is the wind?" I didn't know what to answer, so in the end I just said, "No one knows—because the wind moves too fast".'

October, 1962. With the release of 'The Manchurian Candidate', Frank once again proves his remarkable skill as a straight actor, giving a gritty performance as a Major in Army intelligence trying to track down the Communist 'sleeper' agent plotting an assassination. *The New Yorker* calls the film, 'A thriller guaranteed to raise all but the limpest hair,' and says that Sinatra 'in

his usual uncanny fashion, is simply terrific.' Frank himself thinks it is 'the best picture I've made since "The Man With The Golden Arm".'

1963

January, 1963. Release of an outstanding album featuring Frank and the great jazz musician, Count Basie and his orchestra. The 'Sinatra-Basie' album had been recorded the previous October in Los Angeles with arrangements by Neil Hefti, and such is its appeal that it becomes an instant best-seller. With this record, Frank assures himself of the reputation as a great jazz singer, according to many critics.

February 5, 1963. Frank takes part in a lengthy and revealing interview with *Playboy* magazine which describes him as 'the acknowledged king of showbiz'. Among his memorable quotes are, 'I'm for anything that gets you through the night, be it prayer, tranquillisers or a bottle of Jack Daniels.' And, 'I'm for anything and everything that bodes love and consideration for my fellow men'; 'What I've learned from my father is to abhor prejudice, to respect the other fellow, to be honest and uncompromising with principle.' And he says of his skill as a singer, 'It's because I get an audience involved, personally involved in a song—because I'm involved myself.'

February 10, 1963. Frank's mother and father celebrate their fiftieth wedding anniversary in New Jersey and

Long-time rivals, but always friends, Bing Crosby joins Frank's Reprise label.

he joins in the celebrations with other members of the family and friends. He also attends a benefit premiere of 'Come Blow Your Horn' in Palm Springs which raises $15,000 for the City of Hope Hospital. *Variety* says of the film, 'Sinatra's jaunty performance is his best in some time. The role is perfectly suited to his rakish image.'

July 27, 1963. Bing Crosby, Frank's one time rival for the affections of Young America, signs for Reprise Records. He tells the press, 'Let's face it, Sinatra is a king. He is a very sharp operator, a keen record chief, and has a keen appreciation of what the public wants. I'm happy to be associated with him after all these years.' Of the new addition to his label, Frank says, 'It is a proud moment for the whole organisation.'

August, 1963. Major three-part deal reputedly worth $10 million arranged between Frank and Warner Bros. 1. Reprise Records merges with Warner Bros. Records, Frank retaining one third ownership. 2. Sinatra Enterprises to produce a series of feature films, financed and distributed by Warner Bros. 3. Frank to act as special aide to Warner President Jack L. Warner, to advise on product and policy. Displaying the multi-million dollar cheque he receives for the deal, Frank, recalling his Hoboken days, says, 'This is what I call real pocket money. I always wanted to have a million bucks in my pocket!'

September 9, 1963. Frank's son, Frank Jr., makes his debut as a singer at The Royal Box in the Americana Hotel, New York, backed by the Tommy Dorsey Band. A music major at the University of Southern California, Frank Jr. earns high praise from the press, including *Life* magazine which features a picture of father and son on the front cover and a critique inside which says, 'He set off an uproar by simply walking on stage. The new Sinatra sound is an eerie, incredibly exact echo of Frank Sr.'s singing.' On September 12, Frank Sr. visits The Royal Box and declares, 'The kid sings better than I did at that age. He's way ahead of me because he's a studied musician which I am not.'

September, 1963. Release of 'Sinatra's Sinatra' album, Frank's second collaboration with Nelson Riddle, highlighted by new versions of 'In the Wee Small Hours of the Morning' and 'All The Way.' Arnold Shaw reports that the disc was 'a triumph commercially and remained on best-seller charts for almost a year.'

December 8, 1963. Frank Jr. is kidnapped at gun point shortly before being due to go on stage at Harrah's Casino at Lake Tahoe near Reno. Frank Sr. immediately flies to the scene and offers to negotiate with the kidnappers if they will contact him. 'I'd give the world for my son,' he says. When contacted, Frank agrees to a ransom of $240,000 and a place for the money to be 'dropped'. After an agonising wait, Sinatra Jr. is found blindfolded 480 miles away beside a road in Bel-Air, Los Angeles. The three men responsible for the kidnapping are later arrested by the FBI, the ransom money recovered, and Frank Sr. turns his December 12 birthday into a family celebration for his son's safe return. Says father Sinatra, 'Frankie showed plenty of guts. Credit must go to the FBI for a masterful operation.'

1964

January 2, 1964. Frank and Bing Crosby join together in Hollywood to record an album entitled 'America, I Hear You Singing' with Fred Waring and his Pennsylvanians. The album was conceived by Fred Waring who says that he and Frank and Bing wanted to impart through it their belief that 'America—you never had it so good.' The songs are recorded during several sessions in January and February, while Frank and Bing are also busy filming 'Robin and the Seven Hoods', the fourth of the Clan movies about a gang of Chicago gangsters, which parodies the legend of Robin Hood. *Life* magazine later comments, 'With this off-gait, off-beat film, Sinatra and the Clan have finally made their point.'

February, 1964. Frank flies to Tokyo to begin work on 'None but the Brave' with which he is to make his debut as a director. The story concerns a group of Japanese soldiers hiding out on an island long after the war has passed by and what happens when a damaged American plane, complete with a small force of soldiers, crash-lands in their midst. The theme of man's inhumanity to man caused by war particularly attracts Frank, and he believes the picture to be an ideal vehicle to satisfy his long felt desire to direct. 'Directing's my favourite medium,' he tells newsmen. 'It keeps me busier and I like that. I also like the sense of responsibility.'

May 10, 1964. While shooting 'None but the Brave' on Kauai, one of the small Hawaiian islands, Frank has a narrow escape from death when bathing in the ocean. Suddenly engulfed by a giant wave, he is rescued from drowning by an actor named Brad Dexter, and requires artificial respiration. Later he admits, 'Another couple of minutes and I wouldn't have made it.'

July 11, 1964. Frank flies to Tel-Aviv for the dedication of a youth centre to be named after him. Built almost entirely from the proceeds of the concerts he gave in Israel during his round-the-world tour in 1962, the magnificent centre in Nazareth is to serve as an inter-community home for Jewish and Arab youths. Says Frank, 'I'm not old enough to understand adults, but I think I know enough to understand kids. And I think if we can get the kids together, maybe we'll be able to keep them together when they get to be adults.'

Frank clowning with Dean Martin as he puts his footprints outside Grauman's Chinese Theatre in 1964.

Brad Dexter, the actor who saved Frank from drowning while they were filming 'None but the Brave' in May 1964.

August, 1964. Frank spends this month and the next in Rome filming 'Von Ryan's Express', another Second World War movie based on David Westheimer's best seller about a group of POWs who escape from an Italian prison camp and steal a train to get to Switzerland. His co-stars are Trevor Howard and Brad Dexter, the actor who saved him from drowning. *The Hollywood Citizen-News* later says of the picture, 'This is Sinatra at his best as an actor, and far removed from his image as a rollicking, elbow-bending song stylist.'

November 26, 1964. Thanksgiving Day, and Frank and Count Basie give their first public performance together at the Sands Hotel in Las Vagas before a specially invited audience. This is to prove the first of a series of joint appearances over the next two years. Earlier in the year the two musicians have also issued a second album, 'It Might As Well be Swing' which soon reaches number 13 in the *Billboard* charts and is declared by the magazine to be a 'gasser' with 'Sinatra swinging at his best'.

Frank jokes with Dean Martin, Sammy Davis and Johnny Carson at the Dismus House Benefit in St. Louis in 1965.

1965

February, 1965. President De Gaulle of France awards Frank one of the country's most prestigious decorations, *Commandeur de la Sante Publique*, for his humanitarian work, and in particular for raising £13,000 at his Paris Charity Concert.

April 23, 1965. Life magazine devotes much of its issue to Frank, his life and career, with a spread of pictures headlined, 'A Visit To His Private World'. Highlight of the issue, which becomes the biggest-selling number in the magazine's history, save that devoted to the assassination of President Kennedy, is an article written by Frank himself, 'Me and My Music'.

July 4, 1965. The annual Newport Jazz Festival is stunned by an outstanding performance by Frank along with the Count Basie Orchestra. *Variety* magazine declares Newport 1965 to be 'Sinatra's Festival', calls his performance 'over-powering, glamour showmanship,' and records that he left the stage to the 'biggest ovation of the night.' Thereafter Frank continues with performances at Forest Hills, Detroit, Baltimore, and Chicago taking over half a million dollars at the box office.

August 21, 1965. Frank's LP, 'September of My Years'

Frank takes his daughters Nancy and Tina to his 50th birthday celebration on December 12th, 1965.

is released and in this, the year of his fiftieth anniversary, proves an enormous hit, winning the Grammy Award as Album of the Year. Among the songs is 'It Was a Very Good Year' which also wins Frank a Grammy for Best Male Vocal Performance, nets another for Gordon Jenkins' arrangement (Best Accompaniment Arrangement), and sees Frank back in the nation's Top Ten for the first time in over ten years. Of his latest film, 'Marriage on the Rocks', in which he co-stars with Dean Martin and Deborah Kerr, *The New Yorker* says, 'Mr Sinatra is his usual, uncannily confident self.'

November 16, 1965. CBS TV presents a documentary, 'Sinatra', in which Walter Cronkite interviews Frank on his life and music, the conversation mixed with film of Sinatra at work and play. Of the production, Frank says, 'I enjoyed watching the programme tremendously . . . I was both pleased and honoured.'

November 24, 1965. Another TV spectacular about Frank on Thanksgiving Eve, 'Sinatra—A Man and His Music', this time presented by the rival NBC network. Largely made up of songs, the show reveals Frank at the height of his art, and the *American Weekly* declares it to be 'the best musical TV hour of the year.'

December 12, 1965. Frank celebrates his fiftieth birthday at a special party planned and hosted by his former wife, Nancy, at the Beverly Wilshire Hotel in Hollywood. Coincidental with this a de luxe double LP, 'Frank Sinatra—A Man and His Music' complete with a brochure on Sinatra's life, becomes a Top Ten best seller. It also wins Grammy, Emmy and Peabody awards. Frank ends the year—his 25th in show business—as No. 1 on the Publi-metrix Poll of 'Most Mentioned Personalities'. He declares, 'Life has been very good to me. Enough has happened to me, more than I deserve. I have everything I need for the rest of my life. Now I would just like to have a little peace of mind.'

1966

February 1, 1966. Frank's first album of concert recordings is made from ten shows he and the Count Basie Orchestra have performed at the Sands Hotel in Las Vegas between January 26 and this date. Included among the tracks are such classics as 'I've Got You Under My Skin', 'You Make Me Feel So Young', 'My Kind Of Town' and 'Come Fly With Me'.

April 11, 1966. In Hollywood, Frank records 'Strangers In The Night' with an arrangement by Ernie Freeman. By June 18 the album of this title has reached number one spot on the *Cash Box* albums chart, the first of his LPs to achieve this position. It remains for a record 35 weeks. The single also wins Grammys as 'Best Solo Vocal Performance' and 'Record of the Year.'

July, 1966. In a feature article, *Look* magazine invites Frank to talk about The Beatles, currently enjoying the same mass adulation and hysteria that had greeted his early years as a singer. 'I could never sing with them,' he declares. 'I wouldn't know how. They have completely different interpretations. I'm an optimist and a romantic. Yes, a romantic.'

July 19, 1966. Frank marries for the third time—to Mia Farrow, 21-year-old actress daughter of Maureen O'Sullivan. The ceremony takes place at the Sands Hotel in Las Vegas. Of their meeting in October 1964 when she had been appearing in the TV serial, 'Peyton Place' and he had been making 'Von Ryan's Express', Mia says, 'He asked me to the screening of one of his pictures, and of course I went. I liked him instantly. He rings true. He is what he is.'

September, 1966. Chorus of excellent reviews for 'Assault on a Queen', Frank's film about a fantastic scheme to hi-jack the 'Queen Mary' in which he plays the leader of the raiders, an ex-submarine officer. *The Hollywood Reporter* enthuses, 'Sinatra is excellent as the mainspring of the plot. It is the kind of role he does best, sardonic, masculine, sympathetic . . . he is eminently conceivable as a soft-spoken tough guy.'

1967

January 12, 1967. Frank throws a party for his friend Joe E. Lewis, the veteran comic he portrayed in the

Father and daughter Nancy recording 'Something Stupid' in February 1967.

Frank with Antonio Carlos Jobim and Claus Ogerman during the 'Francis Albert Sinatra Antonio Carlos Jobim' sessions in 1967.

Two legends meet. Frank with Duke Ellington during the 'Francis A & Edward K' sessions in 1967.

film, 'The Joker Is Wild.' Over 150 people attend the celebrations which mark Lewis' 65th birthday at Jilly's South in Miami Beach.

January 30, 1967. Another innovation for Frank, he makes a series of recordings with the Brazilian guitarist and composer, Antonio Carlos Jobim. Jobim himself lends vocal support on a number of the songs—most of which he has written—the arrangements supervised by Claus Ogerman. Says Frank of the beautiful melodies, 'I haven't sung so soft since I had the laryngitis.'

February 1, 1967. Back in the Hollywood studios for another session, Frank records a catchy ballad number, 'Somethin' Stupid' with daughter Nancy. This is to prove his eighth million-selling disc, and is to top the Hit Parades in both America and Britain.

May 3, 1967. Frank is named National Chairman of the American Italian Anti-Defamation League in honour of his work on behalf of racial tolerance.

June, 1967. Frank is deeply saddened by the death of his close friend, actor Spencer Tracy. He acts as a pallbearer at Tracy's funeral in Hollywood along with

Frank in 'The Naked Runner', made in 1967.

James Stewart and other luminaries of the film world. *June 25th, 1967*. Frank flies to England to star in 'The Naked Runner' based on Francis Clifford's tense thriller about a former Army marksman enveigled into the hunt for a British spy defecting to the Communists. A chilling film with a dramatic dénoucment, *Newsweek* gives particular praise to his performance as the ice-cool marksman who becomes a pawn in the murky world of espionage. His skill as a screen actor, it notes, had already earned him the nick-name 'One-Take Charlie'. *November 22, 1967*. Frank announces that he and Mia have 'mutually agreed to a trial separation.' She has been working on 'Rosemary's Baby' the film which is to become a box office hit, while he has made his first film playing a private eye, 'Tony Rome', co-starring

Jill St. John. *The Los Angeles Times* writes, 'What gives the movie its strength is that in Tony Rome, Sinatra is able to play a character much like himself, or part of himself: wisecracking, tough, mobile, romantic, world-bruised but idealistic.'

1968

April, 1968. Frank turns in another outstanding performance in a film about crime, 'The Detective' which has been filmed over the turn of the year. He plays Joe Leland, a tough New York detective, devoted to his job but sickened by the corruption of city life and tormented by the failure of his marriage. Praise for the picture is universal, lead by Ray Lynd of *The Hollywood Reporter*, who writes, 'Sinatra has honed his

Frank makes a dramatic arrest in 'The Detective' (1968).

Frank Sinatra in the recording studio with Tina and Nancy during the sessions for 'The Sinatra Family Wishes You A Merry Christmas' in 1968.

album made by Frank Sinatra and Duke Ellington. The record is highly praised as 'an album of pure, unselfconscious music-making by two masters of the popular form''

August, 1968. Mia completes divorce proceedings from Frank in Mexico, citing grounds of incompatability.

August 12, 1968. In a festive recording session in Hollywood, Frank cuts several Christmas songs with his children, Frank Jr., Nancy and Tina. The arrangements are handled by Nelson Riddle and among the songs are 'The Twelve Days of Christmas' and 'The Bells of Christmas.'

November, 1968. Frank becomes worried about the health of his much-loved father, Martin, who after his years as a boxer and tavern keeper has served with distinction as a Captain in the Hoboken fire department for twenty-four years. Now, as a result of suffering a heart attack, Frank sends his father to the famous specialist, Dr Michael DeBakey, in Houston.

December 30, 1968. In Hollywood, Frank records what is to become arguably his most famous song, 'My Way', with a Don Costa arrangement. The single eventually sells in excess of a million copies in both America and Britain, and although it strangely never reaches the number one spot on either side of the Atlantic, it remains for a staggering 120 weeks in the UK Top Thirty charts—the longest period ever achieved by any recording.

1969

January 29, 1969. After intensive care in Houston, Frank's father, Anthony Martin Sinatra, dies at the age of 74. Frank's long-time journalist friend, Earl Wilson, writes, 'Sinatra was shaken by the death even though it was expected. He was tight-lipped, tearful and grief-stricken at the funeral at the Fort Lee, New Jersey, Madonna Church. It was a requiem mass for the man who had wanted his son to be an engineer or a prize fighter.' The funeral is attended by a galaxy of stars, and local firemen and policemen escort the coffin to the

laconic, hep veneer to the point of maximum credibility, and his detective Joe Leland is his best performance and role since ''The Manchurian Candidate''.'

May, 1968. Release of the 'Francis A and Edward K'

A light hearted moment when Frank met Elvis Presley and his manager Colonel Parker in Las Vegas in 1969.

MY WAY FRANK SINATRA
ARRANGED AND CONDUCTED BY DON COSTA
MRS. ROBINSON
YESTERDAY
FOR ONCE IN MY LIFE
HALLELUJAH, I LOVE HER SO
WATCH WHAT HAPPENS
IF YOU GO AWAY
DIDN'T WE
ALL MY TOMORROWS
A DAY IN THE LIFE OF A FOOL
MY WAY

One of the most famous of all Frank's songs.

Holy Name Cemetery in Jersey City. Frank's wreath of red roses says expressively, 'Beloved Father'.

February 11, 1969. Frank records again with the brilliant Bosa Nova guitarist and composer, Antonio Carlos Jobin, cutting such fine tunes as 'One Note Samba', 'Desafinado' and 'Drinking Water'. Their backing is provided by an orchestra directed by Morris Stoloff.

July 14, 1969. Another busy recording session for Frank, in New York this time. Joseph Scott and Bob Gaudio provide him with fine arrangements of 'I Would Be In Love' and 'She Says', while Charles Calello arranges a lovely tune, 'What A Funny Girl (You Used to Be)'. Sinatra is unhappy with a version of the beautiful 'Lady Day' in memory of Billie Holliday and he re-records this again on October 13 and November 7 (this time with an arrangement by Don Costa) before declaring himself satisfied.

1970

May 7, 1970. Frank plays two 'Sinatra at Midnight' charity concerts at the Royal Festival Hall in London accompanied by Count Basie. Sinatra pays all the expenses himself, and is invited to special celebration dinners given by Princess Margaret and Walter Annenberg, the American Ambassador in London. Of his performance, James Green in the *Evening News* writes, 'This was his first London concert since 1962 and the result was never in doubt. Applause is one thing. What he experienced was near adulation. Where once Bobbysoxers squealed, dinner-jacketed socialites offered the loudest welcome since Winston Churchill took his V-Day tribute.'

September, 1970. Another total change of acting style for Frank when he appears in the title role of the Spoof-Western, 'Dirty Dingus Magee', based on the novel by David Markson. Sinatra as Magee is an unscrupulous robber pursued by both cowboys and Indians, and he romps through the picture with complete disdain for the consequences of his actions. Hal Shaper says of Frank, 'His perennial competitiveness kept him high, dry and happy while others, in the inevitable way of things when Sinatra is on-screen, duly or otherwise got theirs.'

November 2, 1970. Frank goes into the Hollywood recording studios to cut what are to be his last two songs for three years—both duets with daughter, Nancy, 'Feelin' Kinda Sunday' and 'Life's A Trippy Thing'. He rehearses a song, 'The Game Is Over' with Bill Miller, but decides against recording it.

November 16, 1970. Back in London for the second time in the year, Frank appears in two concerts at the Royal Festival Hall entitled 'Night of Nights'. Says *The Daily Sketch*, 'Here was the one-man Cup Final of show business, and you couldn't get into the Festival Hall to see him unless you had diamonds to swap for standing places in the aisles. . . . He was bathed in all the glory that comes from being the greatest entertainer the world has ever known.'

December 12, 1970. Daughter Nancy marries again, to television choreographer Hugh Lambert, in Cathedral City, California. It is also Frank's 55th birthday, and Nancy says she chose this day because, 'Daddy likes to give things away on his birthday.'

1971

January, 1971. Frank is a deeply moved observer at the dedication ceremony of the Martin Anthony Sinatra Medical Centre in Palm Springs. He donated over $800,000 to this building named after his father, and at the close of the ceremony is given an honorary medical degree. Among the guests at the opening are the members of his family, and two political friends, Vice President Spiro Agnew and Governor Ronald Reagan. (Frank has some months earlier become co-chairman of the committee to re-elect Reagan as Governor of California, declaring of him, 'We share the same desire for the welfare of the people of the state of California and the nation.')

February 11, 1971. Now 55 years old, Frank considers retirement from the hectic and demanding world of concerts, recordings, films and public appearances which have absorbed his time and energies for well over thirty years.

March 21, 1971. Frank announces that he is to retire. He says he is seeking 'breather time' for reflecting, reading, writing and 'perhaps even teaching.' He

Frank in Los Angeles on September 30, 1973 (Jim McNalis).

issues the following statement from his home in Palm Springs, California:

'I wish to announce, effective immediately, my retirement from the entertainment world and public life.

'For over three decades I have had the great and good fortune to enjoy a rich, rewarding and deeply satisfying career as an entertainer and public figure.

'My work has taken me to almost every corner of the world and privileged me to learn by direct experience

Frank in 'Dirty Dingus McGee' (1970).

how alike all people really are—the common bonds that tie all men and women of whatever colour, creed, religion, age or social status, to one another; the things mankind has in common that the language of music, perhaps more than any other, communicates and evokes.

'It has been a fruitful, busy, uptight, loose, sometimes boisterous, occasionally sad, but always exciting three decades.

'There has been, at the same time, little room or opportunity for reflection, reading, self-examination and that need which every thinking man has for a fallow period, a long pause in which to seek a better understanding of changes occurring in the world.

'This seems a proper time to take that breather, and I am fortunate enough to be able to do so. I look forward to enjoying more time with my family and dear friends, to writing a bit—perhaps even to teaching.' Echoing the thoughts of his millions of fans, *The New York Daily News* says, 'In a sense, Sinatra goes out in a blaze of glory, still very much in demand, still turning down movie scripts, recording dates, TV shows, night club engagements and magazine interviews. He retires as a champion whose name and voice are known in every corner of the world.'

April 15, 1971. Frank's outstanding work for charity through self-funded concert appearances and world tours is recognised when Gregory Peck presents him with the Jean Hersholt Humanitarian Award at the Oscar Ceremonies in Hollywood. The City of Los Angeles also give him their Humanitarian Award.

June 13, 1971. 'An epic evening of epic evenings'—to quote Earl Wilson—occurs at the Los Angeles Music Center when Frank makes his last appearance. The evening has ostensibly been organised for the Motion Picture and Television Relief Fund, but with the announcement of Frank's retirement, the demand for the $250 tickets is enormous. In paying tribute to Frank, actress Rosalind Russell says, 'This assignment is not a happy one for me. Our friend has made a decision. His decision is not one we particularly like, because we like him. He's worked long and hard for us for thirty years with his head and his voice and especially his heart. But it's time to put back the Kleenex and stifle the sob, for we still have the man, we still have the blue eyes, those wonderful blue eyes, that smile, for one last time we have the man, the greatest entertainer of the twentieth century.' Frank's performance is a resumé in words and music of his career, culminating in 'My Way' and 'Angel Eyes'. Earl Wilson records these climactic moments: 'He asked for the stage to be darkened, just a pin-point spot on him. Midway through the song, he lit a cigarette. The smoke wrapped him within it. He was in silhouette. He

53

came to the last line of the song: "Excuse me while I disappear". And he did.'

1972

June 7, 1972. After living quietly for a year, Frank visits London and discusses the possibility of filming a musical version of Antoine de Saint-Exupéry's classic fairy story, *The Little Prince*. He also spends a few hours relaxing at one of the great English sporting events of the year, the Derby, held at Epsom race course just outside the capital.

July 18, 1972. Frank appears before the American Congress Select Committee on Crime to answer questions about his position as vice-president of Berkshire Downs race track in Hancock, Massachusetts. After a heated exchange, listened to by some 500 spectators, in which he claims he was constantly

From *The New York Times*, July 24th, 1972.

---

1. There must be a willingness on the part of all trading nations to pre-

Leonard Silk is a member of the editorial board of The Times.

'We Might Call This The Politics of Fantasy'

By FRANK SINATRA

WASHINGTON—At one minute after 11, on the morning of July 18, I walked into a large hearing room in the Cannon Office Building in Washington to testify before a group called the Select Committee on Crime. The halls were packed with visitors; the rows behind me were sold out. And every member of the Congressional committee was present, an event which I'm told does not happen too often.

The details of what happened that day have already appeared: the tedious questioning about a brief investment I made in a minor league race track ten long years ago; whether or not I knew or had met certain characters alleged to be in the crime business; whether I had ever been an officer of the Berkshire Downs race track, etc. With my lawyer providing some details that had been lost in the passage of time, I answered all questions to the best of my ability. Assuming that the committee even needed the information, it was apparent to most people there that the whole matter could have been resolved in the privacy of a lawyer's office, without all the attendant hoopla.

But there are some larger questions raised by that appearance that have something to say to all of us. The most important is the rights of a private citizen in this country when faced with the huge machine of the central Government. In theory, Congressional investigating committees are fact-finding devices which are supposed to lead to legislation. In practice, as we learned during the ugly era of Joe McCarthy, they can become star chambers in which "facts" are confused with rumor, gossip and innuendo, and where reputations and character can be demolished in front of the largest possible audiences.

In my case, a convicted murderer was allowed to throw my name around with abandon, while the TV cameras rolled on. His vicious little fantasy was sent into millions of American homes, including my own. Sure, I was given a chance to refute it, but as we have all come to know, the accusation often remains longer in the public mind than the defense. In any case, an American citizen, no matter how famous or how obscure, should not be placed in the position of defending himself before baseless charges, and to Congressional

committee should become a forum for gutter hearsay that would not be admissible in a court of law.

Over the years I have acquired a certain fame and celebrity, and that is one reason why so much gossip and speculation goes on about me. It happens to a lot of stars. But it is complicated in my case because my name ends in a vowel. There is a form of bigotry abroad in this land which allows otherwise decent people, including many liberals, to believe the most scurrilous tales if they are connected to an Italian-American name. They seem to need the lurid fantasy; they want to believe that if an entertainer is introduced to someone in a night club, they become intimate friends forever. But it is one thing to watch a fantasy for a couple of hours on a movie screen and then go home. It is quite another thing when the fantasies are projected on real, live human beings, because it doesn't say "the end" when they are finished. Those human beings have to go on living with their friends, family and business associates in the real world.

We might call this the politics of fantasy. Sitting at that table the other day, I wondered whether it was any accident that I had been called down to Washington during an election year, a year in which Congressmen have difficulty getting their names into the newspapers because of the tremendous concentration on the race for the Presidency. It certainly seemed that way.

And I wondered if the people out there in America knew how dangerous the whole proceeding was. My privacy had been robbed from me, I had lost hours of my life, I was being forced to defend myself in a place that was not even a court of law. It wasn't just a question of them getting off my back; it was a question of them getting off everyone's back. If this sort of thing could happen to me, it could happen to anyone, including those who cannot defend themselves properly. I would hope that a lot of Americans would begin to ask their representatives, in the Government and in the media, to start separating fantasy from reality, and to bring this sort of nonsense to an end once and for all.

© 1972/Frank Sinatra

Frank Sinatra, singer and actor, is now retired.

---

being exploited by people he hardly knew, and that he has never been to the race track in question, he is exonerated of any suggestions of wrong doing. 'His victory was so complete,' says Earl Wilson, 'that two congressmen apologised. Rep. Charles Rangel, a Harlem democrat, offered his hand and told Frank, "You're still the Chairman of the Board".' On July 24, Frank responds in print to the accusations that had been laid against him by writing an article, 'We Might Call This The Politics of Fantasy' which is published in the influential *New York Times*.

October 20, 1972. 'The Voice' sings again! Frank reappears from 'retirement' to demonstrate his political beliefs by campaigning on behalf of Richard Nixon and Spiro Agnew for President and Vice-President. He flies to Chicago from Palm Springs and sings for a 'Young Voters For Nixon' rally. The songs include 'My Kind of Town' and a special version of 'The Lady Is a Tramp' with new lyrics by Sammy Cahn and retitled 'The Gentleman Is A Champ', featuring Spiro Agnew who is present in the audience.

November 1, 1972. Spiro Agnew returns the compliment to Frank by presenting him with a Medallion of Valor at a State of Israel Bonds dinner at the Los Angeles Century Plaza Hotel. The Vice-President calls Frank a 'legend in his own time, not only in the world of entertainment, but in the world of philanthropy.' And he adds, 'Frank is a man who has unselfishly used his blessings, the blessings bestowed by a God-given talent and hard work, to benefit his fellow men . . . He is a very personal as well as a very personable man. He's genuinely interested in individuals and what is inside them. He never holds himself aloof from liking or disliking, and he's even been known openly to love and hate.' The evening raises $6·5 million in bond pledges.

1973

March, 1973. At a ceremony in the Plaza Hotel, New York, Frank is presented with a 'Splendid American Award' by the Thomas A. Dooley Foundation. In making the presentation, William Lederer, vice-president of the Dooley Foundations says, 'Sinatra— the things he's done, they're endless! This is a man with a big heart!'

April 17, 1973. Frank attends a White House State Dinner held by President Nixon for visiting Premier Andreotti of Italy and sings for the 200 guests. Thanking him, President Nixon says, 'This house is honoured to have a man whose parents were born in Italy, but yet from humble beginnings went to the very top in entertainment. Replying, Frank reveals, 'When I was a small boy in New Jersey I thought it was a great boot if I could get a glimpse of the mayor. It's quite a boot to be here. I'm honoured and privileged.' It is Frank's first performance in the White House.

April 29, 1973. Although rumours have been circulating since March that Frank is planning to return from retirement, it is not until this day that he actually takes the step of going into the Goldwyn recording studios in Hollywood. However, although he cuts three songs, including 'The Hurt Doesn't Go Away', Frank deliberately has the masters of these discs destroyed.

June 4, 1973. Once again Frank returns to the Goldwyn studios, recording a number of sides including the previously rejected 'The Hurt Doesn't Go Away', with arrangements by Gordon Jenkins and Don Costa. By June 21—the hottest recorded day in Los Angeles at 106 degrees—enough songs for the new album have been cut, among them the brilliant 'Let Me Try Again' and, because of Frank's particular interest in them, 'Send in the Clowns.' A Sinatra aide reveals that he has made the album in response to over 30,000 letters begging, 'At *least* make an album again!' The collection will be released later in the year—when his 'return' becomes official—as 'Ol' Blue Eyes Is Back.'

September 30, 1973. Frank makes an unheralded appearance at the Dorothy Chandler Pavilion in Los Angeles for a benefit concert in aid of the Los Angeles Music and Art School. Of this event, which should by rights be considered as his first 'comeback' performance before a live audience, little mention is made in the press beyond a report by the noted jazz critic Leonard Feather who says that Frank sang four songs, 'World On A String', 'I Have Dreamed', 'Here's That Rainy Day' and 'I Get A Kick Out Of You'. Feather adds: 'He seemed to be reminding us that as long as there is a Sinatra to sing them, lyrics and melodies of this quality shall not perish from the earth.' Shortly after, the Song writers of America name Frank 'Entertainer of the Century'.

November 18, 1973. In a stunning one hour TV special called 'Ol' Blue Eyes Is Back', Frank appears to formally announce his 'retirement from retirement' to a specially invited audience. His repertoire ranges across many of the songs with which he had become associated over the years, and while Gordon Jenkins conducts the orchestra for the ballads, Don Costa takes charge for the upbeat numbers. *The New York Daily News* enthuses the following day, 'We thought we were through writing love letters to Frank Sinatra. Here we go again!'

1974

January 25, 1974. Frank returns to Las Vegas to star in a season at Caesar's Palace, and a galaxy of stars appear among the first night audience of 1,100 people. Bill Miller conducts the orchestra, and Frank's old friend,

the comedian Pat Henry, is his supporting artist. The programme declares, 'Caesar's Palace hails the Noblest of Resonant Romans'. Among the first night audience are Frank's mother, and his two daughters, Nancy and Tina, the latter of whom gets married the following day in Las Vegas to Wes Farrel.

March, 1974. The American Film Institute invites Frank to host its 'Salute to Jimmy Cagney' at the Century Plaza Hotel in Hollywood. Paying his own tribute to Cagney, he says, 'I drove my mother crazy doing my impression of him in "Public Enemy", I would ring the door bell and fall forward on my face. Come to think of it, I still do a lot of that today!'

April 8, 1974. Frank stars in a concert at Carnegie Hall to raise funds for the Variety Club International, and such is the demand for tickets that some are said to have changed hands for in excess of $1,000 each! *Variety*, along with the other newspapers, acclaims his performance: 'It was a phenomenon, a ritual, a mob ceremony. They shook, yelled, stomped, clapped together, stood up at least five times.'

May 22, 1974. Frank becomes a grandfather! Daughter Nancy and her TV director husband, Hugh Lambert, have their first child, a girl whom they name Angela Jennifer Lambert. When he hears the news, Frank is understandably overjoyed and toasts his first grandchild from the stage at Caesar's Palace with the words, 'I wish her one hundred times the fun I've had and one hundred times as many guys as I've had broads.'

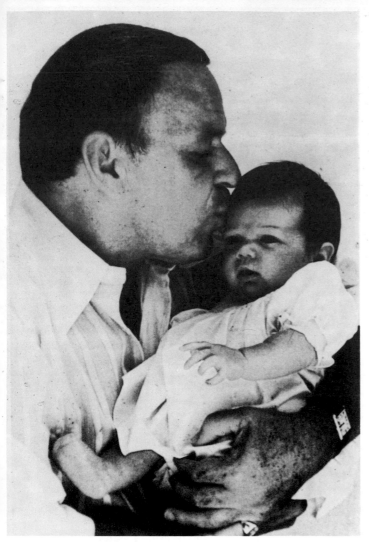

Frank becomes a grandfather—here with grand-daughter Angela in 1974.

July, 1974. Frank flies to Australia for a series of concerts in Melbourne and Sydney, a tour which is initially soured by a dispute with pressmen. Yet on stage in Melbourne he tells his audience, 'I like coming here and I like the people. I love your attitude, I love the booze and the beer and everything else. I like the way the country's going and it's a swinging place.' The five concerts he performs earn more money at the box office than any previous entertainer in Australian history.

September, 1974. In a delightful article in Ladies' Home Journal, Frank talks about his grandchild and expresses one fervent wish: 'All I ask is that Nancy never lets the child grow up and see "The Kissing Bandit", a picture I made some years ago (1948). I've been trying to change my name ever since!'

October 10, 1974. Death of Hank Sanicola, Frank's long-time business manager. Of his years with Frank he had said earlier in an interview with Hal Shaper, 'It was a fantastic era, and I loved it all. Frank was, and is, the greatest thing that ever happened to the music

business. He is a great man, and a great star. Probably the greatest phenomenon in the history of show business. I watched him for years doing things that no one has ever given him credit for . . . acts of generosity that he would regard as bad manners to discuss, and I won't demean those acts by discussing them now. Frank ended the band era. Fini. There will never be another one like him. He made the word "Star" really mean something.' In his tribute to Sanicola, Frank says emotionally, 'Of the five most important people in my life, Hank Sanicola was one. I couldn't have made it without him.'

October 13, 1974. Frank appears at the Madison Square Gardens in New York in a bonanza concert televised live and headlined as 'The Main Event'. Over 20,000 people pack the arena, according to Earl Wilson who says, 'Two hemispheres from Halifax to Rio de Janeiro, comprising the biggest television audience in history, so they say, watched transfixed as the "King" climaxed the evening by strolling happily around the stage, smiling and waving to the audience.' And Frank himself adds, 'I have never felt so much love in one room in my life.' Songs from this concert, plus earlier tunes recorded during a nine city tour with Woody Herman and The Young Thundering Herd, are assembled for his new album appropriately called 'The Main Event'.

1975

April, 1975. Although into his sixtieth year, Frank sets off on a gruelling concert tour across America which also takes in Montreal and Toronto in Canada. At the Maple Leaf Garden in Toronto he earns almost half a million dollars for two performances!

May, 1975. The North American tour is followed by a trip to Europe, with concerts in Munich, Frankfurt, Paris, Monte Carlo, Vienna, Brussels, Amsterdam and London. His May 29 and 30 concerts at the Royal Albert Hall are huge successes, and at the conclusion of the first show he tells his audience, 'This is one of the best nights of my career.' Among the rapturous crowd are three princesses, Princess Margaret, Princess Anne and Princess Grace of Monaco.

August 1, 1975. Frank teams up with young rock singer, John Denver, for a week of 'back-to-back' shows at Harrah's Lake Tahoe Hotel in Nevada. Pre-show advertising urges the public to make early telephone reservations for seats—and according to the management of the hotel this results in them receiving a total of 672,412 enquiries! Not surprisingly, they declare the double-billing 'the entertainment coup of the decade'!

September 5, 1975. Frank appears on Jerry Lewis's 'Labor Day' Telethon to raise money for Muscular

A family gathering of Frank with his son and daughter at Caesar's Palace, Las Vegas, 1975.

Dystrophy. Urging—and in some cases committing—friends to give donations, Frank himself donates $25,000 on behalf of his grand-daughter, Angela Lambert. He says, 'As soon as she starts talking, I would like her to know that she has given to this telethon.'

September 8, 1975. Frank follows up the Lake Tahoe triumph with another in New York—two weeks of concerts at the giant Uris Theatre on Broadway in company with Count Basie and Ella Fitzgerald. Playing to capacity houses, the concerts gross over one million dollars and show him once again to be 'the biggest attraction to play Broadway in modern times'—indeed no one has seen anything like the rapture which greets Frank's singing since he himself had appeared at the Paramount Theatre in 1943.

November 13, 1975. Frank brings his sixtieth year to a splendid conclusion with ten concerts at the London Palladium, accompanied by Count Basie and Sarah Vaughan. There are 350,000 orders for the 15,000 available tickets! From there he goes to Israel to give two charity shows for the Jerusalem Centre for Arab and Jewish Children. He also pledges $250,000 worth of State of Israel Bonds in memory of 'Mrs Goldberg who was my parents' neighbour in Hoboken' and also a good friend to him in his childhood. He in return is presented with the Jerusalam Medal by the City of Jerusalem. Back in America his year is completed by the award to him of the Cecil B. De Mille Golden Globe,

and the news that during 1975 he has given 140 performances in 105 days and been watched by over half a million people!

1976

March, 1976. The international show business organisation, The Friars Club, name Frank 'Top Box Office Name of The Century' and present him with the club's statuette in the shape of a friar. (Frank has subsequently been given the club's highest elective office, that of Abbot.)

May 23, 1976. The University of Nevada at Las Vegas confers an honorary Doctor of Humane Letters degree on Frank for his 'charitable endeavours which have raised millions of dollars for humanitarian causes and deeds that have frequently been done anonymously.' Frank telephones his mother in Palm Springs and says 'Ma, I graduated today!'

July 12, 1976. In Palm Springs, Frank marries the beautiful, blonde Barbara Marx, former wife of Zeppo Marx, at a ceremony attended by numerous old friends including Sammy Davis Jr., Gregory Peck, Kirk Douglas and the man destined to be President of the United States, Ronald Reagan. Among the members of Frank's family is his second grandchild, another girl, Amanda Catherine, who is just two months old. Afterwards he says, 'I really have found a new kind of tranquillity. Barbara is a marvellous woman and I have a different kind of life now.'

A delightful portrait of Frank and his wife Barbara.

September, 1976. Frank again appears on Jerry Lewis's Telethon programme to raise money for Muscular Dystrophy. Highlights of the show, which lasts 22 hours, are Frank's song sessions and appeals for pledges, and also the moment when he effects a reunion between Jerry Lewis and Dean Martin who had not been in touch with each other since their comedy partnership had broken up twenty years previously. At the year's end, he is presented with the Scopus Award of the American Friends of the Hebrew University of Israel. Sadly, for such a happy occasion, it is to prove to be the last award that Dolly Sinatra sees given to her famous son.

1977

January 6, 1977. The second great tragedy in Frank's life—the death of his 82-year-old mother, Natalie 'Dolly' Sinatra. The woman he had adored all his life had been flying from Palm Springs to Las Vegas to watch him perform when her plane disappeared. After two days of searching in the snow-bound San Bernadino mountains, the wreckage of the small jet aircraft and the bodies of the passengers are at last located. 'Her death was a terrible blow because of the way she died,' says Frank. 'She didn't fly more than five times a year. I couldn't understand something like that happening to *me*.'

January 13, 1977. After a quiet family service, Dolly Sinatra is laid to rest beside her husband in the New Jersey cemetery. At the funeral Frank is almost overcome with grief, leaning on his wife's arm. 'Sinatra remained in awe of his mother to the very end of her life,' writes John Howlett. 'She was insistently proud of his success and he, according to close friends, always in need or in search of her approval and praise.'

March, 1977. Another trip to London to appear in a week of concerts at the Royal Albert Hall, highlighted by the opening night which is in aid of the National Society for the Prevention of Cruelty to Children. This charity gala is attended by his great fan, Princess Margaret, and his ex-wife, Ava Gardner, and raises over £60,000. Says the *Evening Standard*, 'Once again the simple mastery of Francis Albert Sinatra triumphed. In just under two hours the years of experience mesmerized a breathlessly faithful and devoted audience.'

July, 1977. Frank again breaks new ground when he decides to appear in a three-hour television film, 'Contract on Cherry Street'. Prior to this he has always been reluctant to film TV movies, but decides to make this film as a tribute to his mother—for the book on which it is based, by Philip Rosenberg, had long been one of Dolly Sinatra's favourites. It is shot on location in New York and casts him as an ageing police inspector who becomes involved in a cops' vendetta against some local underworld characters. Later he says of it, 'We filmed "Cherry Street" entirely on location during two-and-a-half months of very hot

Frank demonstrates his culinary skills to an appreciative admirer.

Still the master of his craft—Frank photographed before the Sphinx in Egypt, September 1979.

weather in New York. When we were shooting in Little Italy, the neighbourhood people thought we weren't eating right. They sent us huge sandwiches!' The film, co-starring Verna Bloom, Henry Silva and Martin Balsam, is shown by NBC in November.

1978

February, 1978. Dean Martin hosts a TV special, 'Man of the Hour', in which Frank is 'roasted' by a large group of his friends. Millions of viewers hear tributes to him by people like George Burns, Telly Savalas, Orson Welles and Ronald Reagan who says, 'I'm pleased to be here tonight honouring my very dear friend, Frank Sinatra. I must say that when this television programme was being planned the producer hadn't decided what political figures would participate. It was a choice between me and Governor Brown, and I lost again. Seriously, this is Frank's night and I'm here out of gratitude. Frank worked for me in all my campaigns. He was with me all the way to the Governor's mansion. Without his help, who knows, I might have been President.'

April 9, 1978. A party of 150 stars, nick-named 'Frank Sinatra's Caravan', and including Frank and Barbara

Sinatra, visit Israel for the dedication of the Frank Sinatra International Student Centre at the Mount Scopus campus of the Hebrew University in Jerusalem. During the ceremonials Frank explains part of the reason for his donation, 'I had a street education, from the gutter to the curbstone. I am self-taught, but have learned a lot from listening to people with great knowledge. Education is what it is all about. I hope it will eventually wipe out the lack of tolerance, and that brotherhood and peace may spread throughout the world.' During the trip—which Frank later calls 'the most exciting of my life'—he and Gregory Peck meet Prime Minister Menachem Begin.

1979

March 22, 1979. Release of Frank's first new album in five years, the three disc 'Trilogy', which quickly climbs into the *Billboard* and *Cashbox* charts and is nominated for six Grammy Awards. The influential critic, Leonard Feather, says of the album, 'A new Sinatra record of any kind is newsworthy, like a volcanic eruption; you can't tell when it's liable to happen, but there can be little doubt it will make the headlines. In the case of "Trilogy", a better adjective might be historic.'

June, 1979. Former President Gerald Ford presents Frank with the 'International Man of the Year Award' in Denver. Shortly afterwards, he receives Italy's highest civilian decoration from Amadeo Cerchione, the Italian consul in Los Angeles.

September 27, 1979. Frank gives a unique concert in Egypt on an open air stage before the Pyramids in Cairo. The audience of 1,000 invited guests sit on Persian rugs and hear Frank say, 'It's the biggest room I've ever played—and the toughest act I have ever followed.' Writing the following day, James Bacon of *The Los Angeles Herald Examiner* says, 'Where Alexander the Great, Caesar, Cleopatra and Mark Anthony gasped in awe, Frank Sinatra sang his heart out last night. As a Sinatra watcher for 40 years, I can say flatly he was never better.' The three-day gala in Egypt raises over $500,000 for charity.

October 8, 1979. Columbus Day once again proves a red letter day for Frank. He is appointed grand marshal of the Columbus Day Parade in New York City, and the Columbus Citizens Committee present him with the organisation's Humanitarian Award.

December 12, 1979. Frank's 40th anniversary in show business is marked by a star-studded 'Black Tie Blast' at Caesar's Palace in Las Vegas. Hundreds of friends, associates and entertainers pack the lush building which is bedecked with souvenirs and photographs of Frank's remarkable career. The event is specially filmed by NBC-TV.

Frank attracts the largest live audience in the world in Brazil, in January 1980.

1980

January 26, 1980. Breaking new ground once more, Frank goes to South America for the first time, to give a concert in Brazil at the Maracana Stadium in Rio de Janeiro. Here he attracts the largest live audience ever recorded for a single performer when 175,000 people pack into the huge sporting arena. (This astonishing fact is now acknowledged in a special entry in *The Guinness Book of Records*.)

February 15, 1980. Over $2 million dollars are raised for the Palm Springs Desert Hospital by a gala at the Canyon Hotel Convention Centre, called 'Frank, His Friends and His Food'. One thousand guests are fed traditional Italian dishes which have been supervised by Frank and include 'Chicken Sinatra' made to a secret family recipe, and over 3,000 meat balls!

March, 1980. The Songwriters Hall of Fame present their first Johnny Mercer Award to Frank for his 'Lifetime Romance with the American Songwriter'. Shortly after, in Los Angeles, the Variety Clubs International present him with their Humanitarian Award for his fund raising efforts on behalf of their

needy and handicapped children's programmes.

September 8, 1980. Back in London, Frank gives two short series of concerts at the Royal Festival Hall and the Royal Albert Hall which play to capacity audiences. Says Derek Jewell in *The Sunday Times*, 'Sinatra has become the keeper of the flame for everyone from say 40 to 80. His songs distill the youth, the nostalgia of millions. He also happens to be the best at it: an artist of colossal stature. He swings, he speaks, he shapes songs like no one else. That's genius.'

October, 1980. Opening of Frank's latest film, 'The First Deadly Sin' in which he plays a New York Detective Sergeant stalking a psychotic killer. Filmed in New York, with Faye Dunaway as co-star, the picture is based on a best-selling novel by Lawrence Sanders. Frank is executive producer on the film. When the movie opens in Britain in May, 1981, *The Daily Mail* says it is notable for the performance by Sinatra 'who makes you wonder how great an actor he'd have become if he hadn't been able to sing.'

October 28, 1980. Frank is the narrator of 'Mission of Mercy' a documentary film about the work of the

World Mercy Fund in West Africa. He has been associated with the Fund since 1978 when he gave a benefit concert to aid its work, and in 1979 received their *Primum Vivere* (Life First) Award.

December 12, 1980. To celebrate Frank's 65th birthday, Barbara throws a surprise party, Western-style, in a huge tent near their home in Rancho Mirage, Palm Springs. Frank is unaware of the party until the 200 guests suddenly appear singing 'Happy Birthday'. He is given a huge train-shaped cake by his children (Frank is fascinated by antique locomotives) and Barbara fulfills what he had told her was a lifelong fantasy—'to sit undisturbed and luxuriate in having a top-drawer big band blow at me'. Barbara introduces the Bill Waltrous Band who then serenade him with vintage tunes for an hour.

1981

January 19, 1981. Frank produces and directs another spectacular Inaugural Gala, this one for his friend President Reagan, two hours of which are televised on ABC. Frank pays tribute to the new President and also his wife, with a specially written version of 'Nancy' which he directs at the new First Lady and leaves her very moved. He concludes the evening with the song 'America' and one observer writes, 'To describe the scene in print is impossible, but one could see just how much this country means to Sinatra in his expression and emotion during the song.'

July 10, 1981. Frank remembers his hometown, Hoboken, by making a donation to establish the Frank Sinatra Student Scholarship Fund. Says Hoboken Schools Superintendent, George R. Maier, 'I think this man who has gained world-wide affection in his field, will be forever remembered by his hometown and generations of high school students through this

Frank as a tough cop again in 'The First Deadly Sin' (1980).

scholarship. The words Hoboken and Sinatra always will by synonymous.' Earlier, the Board of Education had sent Frank an 'honorary' diploma from Hoboken High School, of which he says, 'I can't tell you what a thrill it was for me to receive it.'

July 24, 1981. Frank flies to South Africa to give a series of concerts to mixed audiences in Sun City, a huge entertainment centre, which is in the capital of Bophuthatswana. He regards singing in this black homeland as the latest round in his lifelong campaign against apartheid. 'I'll sing in South Africa,' he tells the

Frank and friends at his 65th birthday party on December 12th, 1980.

press. 'Why not? As long as there is no kind of segregation.' His concerts signal the opening of the new 7,000-seat Super Bowl, the biggest stage in Africa, and of Sun City he says, 'This is a wonderful place to come. I have never seen a development like this, not even in Vegas.' Frank is also given a singular honour by Lucas Mangope, the president of Bophuthatswana, who calls him the 'king of show business' and makes him an Honorary Chief, bestowing on him the country's highest honour, The Order of the Leopard. Frank follows these concerts with similar triumphs in Argentina (Buenos Aires) and Brazil (Sao Paulo).

Autumn, 1981. The circle turns full sweep with the announcement that Frank's life and career is to be the subject of a major motion picture. The movie is to be made by his own company, Artanis, and will cover the period from his youth in Hoboken to his 1953 Academy Award for 'From Here to Eternity'. An international search is to be made for a look-alike actor with blue eyes to portray Sinatra as a 25-year-old bobby-sox idol, and Frank himself promises full co-operation along with original recordings for the early sequences. The film will be shot in the locations where the most important events of his life occurred, New Jersey, New York and Hollywood, as well as introducing many of the celebrities who featured in his career. A budget of $10 million is estimated for the picture which has the working title 'The Frank Sinatra Story'.

1982

January 24, 1982. Frank sings a unique concert with the Italian opera singer, Luciano Pavarotti, at Radio City Music Hall in New York. The two singers draw on their common heritage for a number of duets including special versions of 'Sorrento', 'Vicin Al Mare' and 'O Sole Mio', and the evening is hailed by the *New York Times* as 'masterful'. Afterwards, Frank says he would like to sing more opera. 'It would be fun to be a tenor. They make such an exciting sound—a God-given, wonderful, big, bright sound.' Speaking of his life at the moment, he adds, 'I swim and do calisthenics. I walk fast, I don't jog. I don't believe in it—not at my age. And I lift weights and I've got a thing called a torture chair. It's for the abdomen. I do as much exercise as possible.'

SINATRA ON £1m TRIP TO SUN CITY

**From Ray Kennedy
Johannesburg, July 23**

Frank Sinatra arrived tonight in South Africa to the sort of reception reserved in most countries for visiting royalty.

South Africans may not see much on their television screens of next week's royal wedding because of a ban by Equity and the Musicians Union on their members appearing before South African audiences. Mr Sinatra, however, for a considerable fee, is prepared to ignore Equity bans and the possibility of being black-listed in a campaign being mounted through the United Nations to dissuade entertainers and actors from visiting South Africa.

He will display his talents at Sun City, the Las Vegas-type entertainment centre that has been built in the Bophuthatswana Bantustan, two hours' drive from Johannesburg and Pretoria.

The fee is said to be 1.8m rand (more than £1m).

Mr Sinatra flew from New York to Johannesburg on board a South African Airways jumbo.

South Africans will be paying from £50 a seat to watch the Sinatra show at Sun City.

The Times, July 24, 1981

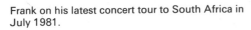
Frank on his latest concert tour to South Africa in July 1981.

The Slaves of Sinatra

by

E. J. Kahn, Jr.

First published in *The New Yorker* November 1946

Frank Sinatra has an extremely pleasant voice, but often, when he uses it professionally, his most ardent fans are so overcome by the sight of him that they drown out the sound of him by emitting ecstatic little yelps of their own. According to George Evans, who likes to say that his association with Sinatra has brought him, Evans, more publicity than most other singers' press agents get for their clients, there are forty million Sinatra fans in the United States. Evans estimates that there are two thousand fan clubs, with an average membership of two hundred, and he has further estimated (by means of logarithms and a press agent's intuition) that only one per cent of the Sinatra fans have yet bothered to join a club. These calculations may be imprecise, but there are unquestionably millions of Sinatra fans, mostly young women in their middle teens. The adulation they have been pouring, like syrup, on their idol since early in 1943 is not without precedent. When Franz Liszt played the piano, every now and then some woman listening to him would keel over. Women kissed the seams of Johann Strauss's coat and wept with emotion at the sight of Paderewski's red hair. In 1843, when the Norwegian violinist Ole Bull, who had long, golden hair and a striking build, gave some recitals over here, his feminine followers unhorsed his carriage and pulled it around town themselves. Then there was Rudolf Valentino's funeral. The astonishing affection lavished by some women on men to whom they have never even been introduced is, as a rule, not entirely platonic. Few of Sinatra's fans, however, seem to have designs on him. Of the five thousand letters they send him every week, not many are as amorous as one from a young lady who wrote, on stationery smeared with lipstick, 'I love you so bad it hurts. Do you think I should see a doctor?'

Because it was in 1943 that Sinatra caught on, his popularity has often been called a by-product of the war, the theory being that young women turned to him as compensation for the absence of their young men. Some of his ill-wishers have even blamed him for the wartime increase in juvenile delinquency. A great many psychologists, psychiatrists, psychopathologists, and other experts on the psyche have tried to define the relationship between Sinatra and young womanhood. 'A simple and familiar combination of escapism and substitution, to be expected in times of high emotional stress,' said one. 'Mass frustrated love, without direction,' declared another. 'Mass hysteria,' said a third; 'mass hypnotism,' said a fourth; 'increased emotional sensitivity due to mammary hyperesthesia,' said a ninety-seventh. One of the editors of the *New Republic*, a journal of opinion, went on a safari to the Paramount Theatre in New York while Sinatra was in season there and reported that in his opinion many members of the audience had seemed to find in the man on the stage a 'father image,' and added, 'Perhaps Frankie is more important a symbol than most of us are aware.' A romantic psychologist attributed Sinatra's eminence to 'a sort of melodic strip tease in which he lays bare his soul. His voice,' he continued, 'haunts me because it is so reminiscent of the sound of the loon I hear in the summer at a New Hampshire lake, a loon who lost his mate several years ago and still is calling hopefully for her return.' Sinatra's appeal to his fans, whether they think of him as a father, a hypnotist, or a widowed loon, can probably be ascribed simply to the desperate chemistry of adolescence. Some of his more rabid admirers have conceded guiltily that they may cast off a tiny bit

The first issue of the British fan magazine.

of the love they bear for him when they get married, and it is perhaps significant that when the president of a Sinatra fan club in New Zealand became engaged, she resigned her office, and that when she broke her engagement, she applied for reinstatement. In Detroit, early last summer, a radio station conducted a 'Why I Like Frank Sinatra' contest. Among the fifteen hundred essays submitted was one that read, 'I think he is one of the greatest things that ever happened to Teen Age America. We were the kids that never got much attention, but he's made us feel like we're something. He has given us understanding. Something we need. Most adults think we don't need any consideration. We're really human and Frank realises that. He gives us sincerity in return for our faithfulness.'

Sinatra has male fans, too, including twenty members of the crew of a navy vessel, who, just before their departure for the atom-bomb tests at Bikini, asked him for a photograph to pin up on a bulkhead. For a while, there was a Sinatra fan club whose membership requirements were nearly as exacting as the Union League's; you not only had to be male and to admire Sinatra, but you also had to be named Frank yourself. His fans are, however, overwhelmingly young women. Their versions of the effect he has on them are, on the whole, more daintily phrased than the callous judgments of the psychologists. 'I shiver all the

way up and down my spine when you sing,' a girl wrote Sinatra, 'just like I did when I had scarlet fever.' 'After the fourth time I fell out of a chair and bumped my head,' said another, 'I decided to sit on the floor in the beginning when I listen to you.' And when a local radio station held an essay contest to find out 'Why I Swoon at Sinatra,' the prize-winning answer, which could readily serve as the basis of a song lyric, was 'If lonesome, he reminds you of the guy away from your arms. If waiting for a dream prince, his thrilling voice sings for you alone.'

Sinatra is skilled at giving each of his listeners the impression that she is the particular inspiration of, and target for, the sentiments he is proclaiming. While singing to an audience, he rarely gazes abstractedly into space. Instead, he stares with shattering intensity into the eyes of one trembling disciple after another. Though his fans usually greet his appearance with loud acclaim, occasionally they are hushed as if they were in church, and in some fan-club publications all pronouns of which he is the antecedent are reverently capitalised. Sinatra handles the kids, as he calls them, with artful skill. 'I never saw anything like the way he milks 'em and kicks 'em around,' one Broadway theatrical agent said as he emerged, in a daze, from a Sinatra show at the Paramount. Experienced comedians appearing as guests on Sinatra's weekly radio programme have been so perplexed by the antics of his studio audiences that they have lost all sense of timing and gone up in their lines. Sinatra, on the other hand, is unperturbed when his chaotic fans are screaming, shivering, and falling off chairs. Never was a man more attuned to the discord of his accompaniment.

Sinatra fans express their devotion to him in odd ways. They sign letters 'Frankly yours' or 'Sinatrally yours,' and they begin postscripts not with 'P.S.' but with 'F.S.' They try, as nearly as is feasible for young women, to dress as he does. Once, after he had absent-mindedly appeared in public with the sleeves of his suit coat rolled up, thousands of other coat sleeves were tortured out of shape. The fans pin club buttons not only over their hearts but also on their socks, and they inscribe his name on sweaters and coats. One of them painstakingly inked the titles of two hundred Sinatra songs on the back of a beer jacket. Another braided her hair and tied up one braid with a ribbon labelled 'Frankie' and the other with one labelled 'Sinatra.' A girl whose arm he had accidentally brushed while trying to escape from a pack of fans wore a bandage over the spot for two weeks, to prevent anybody else from brushing it. Another became the envy of her gang when, after Sinatra had checked out of a hotel room, she got into it before the

SCHOOLGIRLS' HEART-THROB, Frank Sinatra, American crooner, has only to close his eyes and croon into a mike to send teen-age girls from coast to coast into æsthetic trances. He also provides a new target for cartoonists' wit

SWOON CROONER

FRANK SINATRA's popularity is a mystery. All he does is to close his eyes and croon softly into a microphone. But girls all over America love it. His voice is weak; he makes every song sound like the last one, but he's evidently got what it takes, for his fans have formed clubs; call themselves "The Slaves of Sinatra" or "Sighing Society of Swooners."

Counting on the fanaticism of his admirers to help balance their budget, the New York Philharmonic Orchestra invited him to appear as soloist at one of their concerts. "The Slaves" turned out *en masse* to scream and sigh at their idol.

Frankie started singing at school, but went to work as a copy boy, then cub reporter on a New Jersey newspaper. In 1937 he appeared in a quartet in a radio competition; won first prize. After a tour he sang over five New York radio stations on eighteen programmes a week for nothing.

Next he became head waiter and singer in a roadhouse at £3 a week. He was discovered in 1939 and six months later went to Tommy Dorsay and recorded "I'll Never Smile Again." It was a smash hit. Sinatra, making £1,000 a week, has been smiling ever since.

WHEN SINATRA PURRS his own particular brand of song into a mike, tenderly held, the audience sits tensely in reverent silence. Some wriggle rapturously as if it were difficult to bear. All bring the roof down with frenzied applause

HE WEARS a wedding ring, is married and has a daughter. But still the girls everywhere fall for him

Just one of many British magazine features on Frank—from *Illustrated*, December 18th, 1943.

Frank often needed wire fences to keep him safe from his fans! A still from 'Step Lively', 1943.

maids did and escaped with a cigarette butt and a half-used packet of matches, both of which she assumed he had touched. After he had left a restaurant, an equally lucky girl got to his table ahead of the bus boy and managed to polish off a bowl of cornflakes he had unquestionably touched. To the dismay of various municipal health departments, girls have eagerly and stickily pressed kisses upon pictures of Sinatra on display in theatre lobbies. The only reported instance of an attempt to do away with this promiscuous practice was that of a porter employed by the Capitol Theatre in New York, who—while *Anchors Aweigh*, starring Sinatra, was on the screen there, and numerous likenesses of Sinatra, framed and protected by glass, were scattered around the lobby—smeared ipecac on the glass and thus discouraged many girls from indulging in more than one kiss. Girls have plucked hairs from Sinatra's head and, at somewhat less trouble to him, have collected clippings of his hair from the floors of barber-shops. One Sinatra fan carries around in a locket what she insists is a Sinatra hangnail. Souvenir-hunting young ladies broke into his Hasbrouck Heights, New Jersey, house after he had moved out of it in 1944 and incestuously made off with a discarded bundle of old fan mail, some of which they had doubtless written themselves. So that some girls could get his autograph, others have momentarily immobilized him by throwing themselves sacrificially beneath the wheels of his car.

Most prominent entertainers who appeal to young people have one or two fan clubs; Sinatra has two thousand, among them the Subjects of the Sultan of Swoon, the Bow-tie-dolizers, Frankie's United Swooners, the Hotra Sinatra Club, the Our Swoon Prince Frankie Fan Club, the Bobbie Sox Swoonerettes, and the Frank Sinatra Fan and Mah Jongg Club. Some fans belong to several dozen clubs. Dues generally run around a dollar a year, and business meetings amount to little more than convening around a phonograph or radio and listening to The Voice. Some of the clubs have elaborate constitutions; the preamble to that of the Society for Swooning Souls of the Sensational Sinatra, a Pittsburgh organisation, says that 'We will never believe anything awful about Frank unless we hear him verify it.' A few dozen of the clubs are affiliated with the Modern Screen Fan Club Association, run by *Modern Screen* as a circulation device. This magazine also conducts an annual contest to find out what movie actor is most popular with its readers. Sinatra won the contest in 1944, Van Johnson in 1945, and Sinatra again last year. (At the same time, however, he was edged out by General Eisenhower in a poll conducted by some Boston schoolgirls to determine 'The Most Exciting Man of 1946.') Sinatra's eminence is at least in part a result of the feverish letter writing of his fans. They are as diligent a bunch of correspondents as any older pressure group, and, at the instigation of their leaders, they keep bombarding people in the radio, movie, and recording business with demands for more of Frankie.

Most of Sinatra's fans are insatiable for information about him and find that the sustenance provided by movie magazines—articles with titles like 'That Old Sinatra Magic,' 'Sweet Sin-atra,' and 'Sinatra—Prophet of Peace?'—is, like chop suey, filling enough but of little nutritive value. Their fan-club publications, mostly mimeographed affairs, which deal exclusively, and often lengthily, with Sinatra, provide more nourishment. Nearly every issue contains sentimental poems and an account of a dream in which the author met the singer. (Any club member who does meet or even see him can be counted on for two thousand words about the experience.) The club papers carry no advertisements, but many of them ask their subscribers to buy products with whose manufacturers Sinatra is or has been professionally associated. The text is usually laced with the slang Sinatra uses. Two recurrent words are 'fave' and 'natch,' for, respectively, 'favourite' and 'naturally.' The fans' fave adjectives are 'cute,' 'sweet,' and 'smooth,' most frequently employed in modification of Sinatra. (Often, to tease his fans, Sinatra sticks his tongue out at them, and one fan-club correspondent

A typical photograph of the type fans snapped up from Kier's Book House in New York.

black and white polkadot bow tie, light grey jacket, and a white carnation. Sharp, natch!!').

A conscientious Sinatra fan carries at least half a dozen snapshots of him in her purse wherever she goes and is always ready to trade with other Sinatra fans. No one can say how many pictures of Sinatra repose in how many homes, but one girl is known to have four hundred and twenty-four in hers; this was discovered when she wrote to Mrs Diven (of the Sinatra Press Office) requesting a four-hundred-and-twenty-fifth. Fans who can afford cameras take shots of Sinatra whenever he comes within range. (He carries a camera, too—a miniature the size of a cigarette lighter—but he never photographs fans.) Often, in their eagerness, they make the mistake of photographing someone who looks like him, but they usually manage to trade the resulting pictures off, in a dim light. The fans are so anxious to get any new pictures of Sinatra that when the Columbia Recording Corporation distributed to its dealers a handsome, almost lifesize likeness of him, several unscrupulous retailers made a nice profit by selling them to well-heeled fans at ten dollars apiece. The fans also buy plain, normal-size photographs of Sinatra. Kier's Book House, a cramped bazaar on the Avenue of the Americas in New York, is one of their favourite shops. Kier's publishes a catalogue which lists the more than three hundred entertainers for whose likenesses there is a more or less steady demand. Sinatra's name is the only one followed by any remark; after it appears the notation '35 Poses.'

who got a close-up view of this spectacle disclosed to her circulation that his tongue was smooth, too.) The fave utility word is 'hey,' which Sinatra occasionally uses, as if it were a period, to end his sentences. 'If you're old enough to smoke, try an Old Gold hey,' the fans tell each other, or 'Now please send in your dues hey.' The word has even been incorporated into one of the most popular Sinatra cheers, which goes 'H and a U and a B, B, A; Hubba, Hubba, Frankie Hey.' The club papers contain social notes ('Our president is a very fortunate girl. Her brother-in-law met a soldier who knew Frank'), political notes ('Frankie for President in 1956'), contests ('An 8 × 10 glossy action pose of Frankie for completing the sentence 'Frank is an average American because . . .' in less than fifty words'), and fashion notes ('He was wearing dark grey trousers, white shirt, black sleeveless sweater, a floppy

The Bobbysoxers

Sinatra's young fans earned their nick-name from the white socks which some used to wear during the early days of his fame. Later, it became evident that by far the majority wore nylon stockings or leg paint—but the nick-name persisted and became the term applied to a whole generation of popular music fans.

Marjorie Diven, who worked in Sinatra's New York Press Office in 1946, gave this composite picture of a typical Bobbysoxer:

'She's a fourteen-year-old girl living in a small town. She never gets to see anybody except her family, who haven't much money, and her schoolmates. She's lonely. On the way home from school, she stops at a drugstore for an ice-cream soda and picks up a movie magazine. She reads about Frank's life and it sounds wonderful: a pretty wife, two children—a boy and a girl—plenty of money, a home in Hollywood near the other movie stars. She writes him a letter. She imagines he gets about six or seven letters a day, and she visualises him at his breakfast table, with her letter propped against the toaster. She calculates how long it will take for his answer to her to come back. When the time arrives and she hears the postman coming, she runs down the lane to her mailbox, one of those wobbly rural boxes. She keep this up for three weeks, while her family makes fun of her. It's the thought of that fourteen-year-old girl running down that lane to that wobbly mailbox that makes me sympathetic to the fans.'

At this time, Mrs Diven was handling in excess of 5,000 fan letters a week, and had helped organise Sinatra fan clubs in virtually every nation of the world. Argentinian fans were the most excitable, she felt, and English the most reserved.

A Fan's Vocabulary

A word play using 'Sinatra' and 'Swoon'. The word swoon means a fainting fit and is believed to have derived from the Middle English word 'iswowen'. Its revival was due almost entirely to Frank Sinatra.

SCREENATRA
SINATRANCE
SINATRACEPTIVE
SINATRACTIVE
SINATRAPHILE
SINATRATION
SINATRALTITUDE
SWOONHEART
SWOONATRANCE
SWOONERY

STRIPATRA
SINATRITIS
SINATRAMANIA
SINATRALESS
SINATRAPHOBE
SINATRAISH
SINATRAING
SWOONOLOGY
SWOONATIC
SWOONITIS
SWOONAPHILE

SONATRA
SINATRALATING
SINATRICK
SINATRISM
SINATRADDICTION
SINATRABUGS
SINATROOPS
SWOONATRA
SWOONSTER
Etc.

Frank Sinatra himself also became known by the following 'titles':

THE MOONLIGHT SWOONATRA
THE PRINCE OF SWOONING
DOCTOR OF SWOONOLOGY
THE GREAT SWOONDOGGLER
THE SULTAN OF SWOON
THE SWOON PRINCE
THE SWING-SHIFT CARUSO
THE LARYNX
PRINCE CHARMING OF THE JUKE BOXES
THE SVENGALI OF SWING

THE LEAN LARK
THE CROON PRINCE OF SWING
THE SWOONLIGHT SINATRA
THE BOUDOIR SINGER
THE SWOON KID
THE GROOVEY GALAHAD
THE SWAMI OF SWOON
MISTER SWOON
THE BONY BARITONE
FRANKIE YOU-KNOW-WHO

The Rat Pack

Frank Sinatra's closest friends are united in their respect and loyalty to one another—and Frank in particular. For many years this group has been widely referred to in the world's press as 'The Clan' or 'The Rat Pack' and while there is certainly nothing formal about their organisation, they are undeniably an integrated group of like minds dedicated to fun, cameraderie and the occasional tilt at authority and pretentiousness. Though not formalised, the members do have their own titles within the group, Viz:

The Leader (or alternatively, The Chairman of the Board): Frank Sinatra

The Admiral (or Dino): Dean Martin

The Court Jester (or Tummler): Sammy Davis Jr.

Liaison Man: Peter Lawford

The Needler: Joey Bishop

Keeper of the Royal Exchequer: Jimmy Van Heusen

Court Wholesaler: Sammy Cahn

Mascot: Shirley MacLaine

There are other friends of this group who have, from time to time, shared their intimacy, participated in their practical jokes and night club entertainments, as well as enjoying the special language or argot which Frank played a major part in creating. As his long-time friend, Earl Wilson, has explained, 'Frank has never picked up any phoney affectations. His talk is plain, frequently earthy, and filled with some slang that he himself created and popularised.'

'The Broad Dictionary' printed on these pages contains definitions of the most popular words in this vocabulary, and has been compiled from newspaper and magazine sources, as well as from explanations provided by the members themselves, and an interview Frank gave on the subject to Art Buchwald, the columnist of the *New York Herald Tribune*.

According to biographer Arnold Shaw, Sinatra's group grew out of an earlier informal band of friends formed in 1955 by Humphrey Bogart, and named after the Hollywood locality where he lived—The Holmby Hills Rat Pack. It had been christened by Bogart's wife, Lauren Bacall, who seeing him lounging around with these friends one day, remarked, 'I see the rat pack is here.' Bogart later said the group's intention was 'the relief of boredom and the perpetuation of independence' and it was open to 'free-minded, successful individuals who don't care what anyone thinks of them.'

Among the group was Frank Sinatra, who was dubbed 'Pack Master or Chairman', and following the tragic death of Bogart, the members disbanded. Later, Sinatra formed a new group around himself with the same ideals. Arnold Shaw has explained what went on:

' "The Clan" or "The Rat Pack" (Sinatra's preference when he admitted to its existence) was the embodiment of the Swinging Years, and the so-called

Summit Meeting became its most vivid manifestation. The *en masse* appearance of "The Clan" at an important club engagement of one of its members and the staging of an improvised, unbuttoned show, proved the peak point of night-clubbing for many customers, an offence to some, and a matter of adverse comment by others. But despite criticism, which eventually rocked Sinatra himself, the antics of "The Rat Pack" fired the public imagination and caught the fancy of magazine editors, some of very sophisticated publications, intrigued at first by what Richard Gehman, in writing of Bogart, described as a "frig you" attitude.* A news magazine referred to this facet in more elegant fashion when it wrote, "They spit in the face of custom".'

Although rarely prepared to talk about 'The Rat Pack', its members have doubtless taken amused satisfaction from the comments of such enthusiastic supporters as journalist John McLain who wrote, 'They are certainly liberal to a fault, insanely generous and public spirited. They are a crazy and wonderful part of America.'

When these members are pressed for comments, their replies have been as flip as their unwritten charter demands:

Sammy Davis jr: 'The Clan? Why, that's just a little group of ordinary guys that get together once a year to take over the entire world.'

Dean Martin: It's silly to call it anything like The Clan or The Group. If anything, it's more like the PTA—a Perfect Togetherness Association.'

Peter Lawford: 'We're just a lot of people on the same wave-length. We like each other. What's wrong with that?'

Joey Bishop: 'Clan? Clan? Clan! I'm sick and tired of hearing things about The Clan—just because a few of us guys get together once a week with sheets over our heads.'

For his part, Frank has more than once denied that The Clan ever existed, asserting that it was just an invention of the press. 'There's no Clan,' he said on one occasion. 'How could there be with Sammy Davis Jr. as a member?'

But it was a different story when the famous Hollywood columnist, Hedda Hopper, tackled him on the matter:

'"I hate the name Clan," Frank said.

'"Did you ever look the word up in a dictionary?" I said. "It means a family that sticks together, like the Kennedys you're so fond of. They're the most clannish family in America. I don't like Rat Pack, but there's nothing wrong with the name of Clan."'

On another occasion, talking about some of the 'Summit Meetings' at which he, Dean Martin and several of the others had got together and given truly

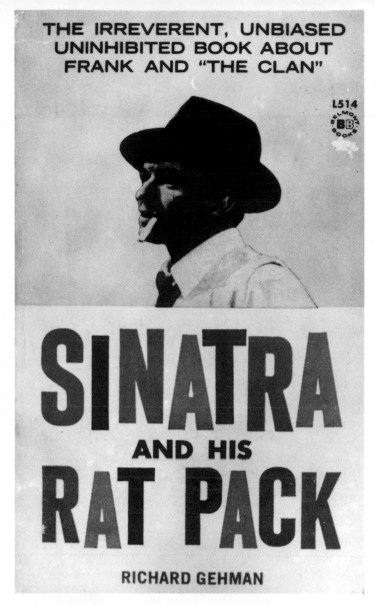

THE IRREVERENT, UNBIASED UNINHIBITED BOOK ABOUT FRANK AND "THE CLAN"

L514

SINATRA
AND HIS
RAT PACK

RICHARD GEHMAN

uproarious performances, he said, 'We never hurt anybody and don't intend to . . . I've never yet seen an audience dislike what we do. What we do is a rib—a good natured kind of rib. Really, we rib ourselves!'

Apart from the night club and concert appearances, the Pack members have also appeared together in four movies, 'Oceans Eleven', 'Sergeants 3', '4 For Texas' and 'Robin and the Seven Hoods' which have given enormous pleasure to an even larger, world-wide audience.

Today, the group are as informally linked and free-wheeling as ever. And it is no doubt true to say that anywhere else but in Show Business such a group would be regarded as just—friends. But when the people in question are headliners like Frank Sinatra, Dean Martin, Sammy Davis Jr., *et al*, the public and the media demand a label for them. Yet, because of the achievements of each and all of them, I say: Long may their friendship continue!

*Richard Gehman was the author of a now-rare paperback, *Sinatra and his Rat Pack* (Belmont Books, New York, 1961), which tells in a somewhat lurid style the 'history' of the group and its members.

A Broad Dictionary

BAG—as in 'my bag', a person's particular interest.

BARN BURNER—a very stylish, classy woman.

BEARD—a male friend who acts as a 'cover', usually for extramarital affairs.

BEETLE—a girl who dresses in flashy clothes.

BIG-LEAGUER—a resourceful man who can handle any situation.

BIRD—a 'suitcase' word sometimes used in reference to the pelvic section.

BOMBSVILLE—any kind of failure in life.

BROAD—affectionate term for a girl or woman with sex appeal.

BUM—a person who is despised, most frequently linked to people in the media.

BUNTER—a man who fails in almost everything he does, the opposite of GASSER.

CHARLEY—a general term for anyone whose name has been forgotten. See also SAM.

CHARLIES—admiring word for a woman's breasts.

CHICK—a young and invariably pretty girl.

CLYDE—a word used to cover a multitude of personal observations: viz 'I don't like her clyde' means 'I don't like her voice', etc.

COOL—a term of admiration for a person or place. An alternative word meaning the same thing is CRAZY.

CREEP—a man who is disliked for any reason whatsoever.

CRUMB—someone for whom it is impossible to show respect.

DAME—a generally derogatory term for a probably unattractive woman. The word DOG is also sometimes substituted.

DIG—a term of appreciation for a person or thing, as in 'I dig her'.

DYING—as in 'I'm dying' which means 'I'm slightly upset'.

END—a word to signify that someone or something is the very best.

ENDSVILLE—a term to express total failure, and similar to BOMBSVILLE. See VILLE.

FINK—a man who cannot be relied upon, whose loyalties are suspect.

FIRST BASE—the start of something, usually applied in terms of failure when someone has failed to reach it.

FRACTURE—as in 'That fractures me', meaning 'That's an amusing joke'.

GAS—a great situation as in 'The day was a gas'.

GASOLINE—a term for alcohol, more specifically Frank's favourite drink, Jack Daniel's Bourbon Whisky.

GASSER—a man or woman highly admired, considered to be the best or 'The End!'

GOFER—someone who does menial jobs or runs errands, as in 'go for drinks', etc.

GOOD NIGHT ALL—a term of invective to change the subject of conversation.

GROOVE—as in 'in the groove', a term of admiration or approval.

HARVEY—a man or woman who acts in a stupid or naive fashion; sometimes shortened to a 'Harve'.

HACKED—a word used to describe someone who is angry, as in 'He's hacked off'.

HELLO!—a cry of surprise to no one in particular when a beautiful woman is seen.

HUNKER—a jack-of-all-trades rather like the GOFER.

JOKES—a term used to describe an actor's lines in a film script.

LET'S LOSE CHARLEY—a term used among intimates who want to get rid of a bore in their company.

LOCKED-UP—as in 'All locked-up', a term for a forthcoming date or engagement, private or public.

LOSER—anyone who has made a mess of their life, drinks too much, makes enemies, etc.

MISH-MASH—similar to LOSER but refers specifically to a woman who is mixed up.

MOUSE—usually a small, very feminine girl who invites being cuddled.

NOWHERE—a term of failure, usually applied to a person, viz 'He's nowhere'.

ODDS—used in connection with important decisions, as in 'The odds aren't right', meaning not to go somewhere, accept anything or buy something.

ORIGINAL LOSER—a man or woman without talent; sometimes more fully expressed as 'He (she) is the original Major Bowes Amateur Hour loser'.

PLAYER—term for a man who is a gambler by nature, who makes friends easily, and never gives up trying.

PUNKS—any undesirable, in particular mobsters, gangsters or criminals.

QUIN—derisive term for any girl or woman who is an easy pick-up.

RAIN—as in 'I think it's going to rain' indicating that it is time to leave a dull gathering or party.

RING-A-DING—a term of approval for a beautiful girl, viz 'What a ring-a-ding broad!'

SAM—used in the same way as CHARLEY for a person whose name has been forgotten, most often applied to females.

SCAM—to cheat at gambling, as in 'Hey, what's the scam?'.

SCRAMSVILLE—to run off.

SHARP—a person who dresses well and with style.

SMASHED—a word used to describe someone who is drunk. On occasions it has been replaced with 'pissed'.

SQUARE—a person of limited character, not unlike a HARVEY.

TOMATO—as in 'a ripe tomato' a woman ready for seduction or even marriage.

TWIRL—a girl who loves dancing. An alternative word with the same meaning is a 'Twist'.

VILLE—a suffix used to indicate changes in any given situation. See ENDSVILLE, etc.

Frankly Speaking

'I'm not copping a plea for sympathy, but you know, there's no one I can turn to except myself. Take a fellow who works in business, makes a product. *I'm* my product.

'Every time I go on a sound stage or into a recording session, I've got nothing working for me except myself. I get sick, I'm out of business. I cut a few bad records, I'm out of business. And after going it alone all day I have to go it alone afterwards. Loneliness is pretty much forced on me.

'I can't walk into a restaurant and order dinner and sit by myself—I'd never get to finish. People feel I belong to them. I have to eat dinner in my hotel room or at home. I just can't go some place without it being a public appearance.'

(To Richard Gehman, 1961.)

ON HIS CAREER:

'Even as a youngster I thought about what I would do when I grew up. It was a tough neighbourhood. Many of my childhood friends grew up to serve sentences of from 10 to 15 years in jail. If I hadn't broken away I might have ended up like them, too.

'I got interested in music at 13—perhaps it soothed the savage breast. I knew then I would be a singer. I used to set a time-limit on everything that I decided to accomplish. I never failed. Usually I had time to spare. But I only moved from one phase to another when I knew I was ready and I had the experience.'

'People think when they see a singer stand up there that he just opens his mouth and out it comes. I wanted a certain type of voice phrasing without taking breath at the end of a line or phrase. I studied the violin playing of Heifetz to see how he moved his bow over the fiddle and back again without seeming to pause. I applied it to singing.

'When I joined Tommy Dorsey I watched how he took his breath when he played. He never seemed to open his mouth to draw breath at all. I learned to control my breath by swimming the length of an Olympic pool under water. I increased my lung power by pacing myself on a running track every day—first walking a lap, then running, then walking again. I did exercises and press-ups. It was hard work, but the hardest thing, when I could sing, was to pick the songs that meant something.

'And even when the words didn't mean much—and most of them don't—to sing them in such a way that they seemed to. I had to learn to read every song the right way and make a contact with the audience. And all the time I knew the audience was saying, "How does the guy get the breath to do it?"

'The reason why Perry Como has had such a lasting career is that when he sings it is $2+2=4$ and the

74

(Above) With Shirley MacLaine in 'Some Came Running', 1958. (Right) Serenading an unresponsive audience in 'Come Blow Your Horn' in 1963.
(Below) A gathering of the Sinatra and Martin families.

Frank with Dean Martin and Bing Crosby in 'Robin and The Seven Hoods' (1964).

audience can see it and the audience thinks it can do the same. My success has been more specialised because no one in the audience can sing my way. I'd love to hear a good imitator—a good mimic of Sinatra. But where is there one?'

(To David Lewin, 1964.)

'There's no teacher like experience. And singing with a band is like lifting weights. You're conditioning yourself.'

(To Hedda Hopper, 1968.)

ON HIS SINGING:

'It's just like reading poetry. And that's odd because poetry bores me. It always has. I'm one of the worst readers of poetry in the world. But when I do a song, I find that I enjoy it, and I find that I understand the distance necessary per phrase.'

(To *Life* magazine, 1965.)

'I use all the colour changes I can get into my voice. The microphone catches the softest tone, a whisper. I sing love songs and mean them.'

(To Arnold Shaw, 1968.)

'You must pace yourself even when you feel strong . . . Concentrate on the music, on the people around you. Every song holds a special meaning for someone and you can't think of yourself.'

(To Earl Wilson, 1976.)

'I get an audience involved, personally involved in a song—because I'm involved myself. Whatever else has been said about me personally is unimportant. When I sing I believe I'm honest . . . You can be the most artistically perfect performer in the world, but the audience is like a broad—if you're indifferent, endsville.'

(To *Playboy* magazine, 1963.)

'Every time a new song comes along, you have a whole new excitement again. That's what makes entertaining an interesting business.'

(To Fergus Cashin, 1970.)

'I love "Send In The Clowns". I like it because it's an unusual song. When have we had a song like that written? It's been years since Porter or one of those guys put together that kind of sophistication in the lyric. Do you know people still say to me, "I play that record 15–20 times and I don't quite understand all the words." And I just tell them one word: circus. It's two people who have a wonderful life and suddenly its a circus. The guy runs out on the dame and she says, "It's gonna be funny, send the clowns in because I'm gonna cry any minute." I've talked to singers who shall be nameless who've said to me, "I don't understand the words." I said: "Because you don't read them. For Christ's sake read the words" . . .'

(To Eliot Tiegel, 1975.)

ON RECORDING:

'Turning out a good record really lights my candle. It warms me all over with the pride and satisfaction of individual accomplishment. I feel like a little kid who makes his own mud pie with his very own mud and his very own fingers. I made a few muddy records in my day, too!'

(To Earl Wilson, 1976.)

'You know, I adore making records. I'd rather do that than almost anything else. You can never do anything in life quite on your own, you don't live on your own little island. I suppose you might be able to write a poem or paint a picture entirely on your own, but I doubt it. I don't think you can ever sing a song that way, anyway. Yet, in a sort of a paradoxical way, making a record is as near as you can get to it—although, of course, the arranger and the orchestra play an enormous part. But once you're on that record singing, it's you and you alone. If it's bad and gets criticised, it's you who's to blame—no one else. If it's good, it's also you . . . I myself can't work well except under pressure. If there's too much time available, I don't like it—not enough stimulus. And I'll never record before eight in the evening. The voice is more relaxed then.'

(To Robin Douglas-Home, 1962.)

ON SELECTING A SONG:

'It depends on whether I'm recording a single or an album. If I find a song I like, I'll record it as a single. For an album, I like to keep all the songs in the same genre—swing, love songs, etc. Once I decide what type of music I want for the album, I make up a list of song titles I'd like to record, and my associates (arranger, etc) suggest songs. When we actually get down to the point where arrangements have to be done, I go through the list again and pick out 8–10 songs and go with them.'

(The Main Event Concert, 1974.)

'I have a good memory for learning songs. I used to know the words of 300 songs at a time.'

(To Hedda Hopper, 1968.)

ON HIS CONCERTS:

'Naturally, I'm very flattered that people still want to see me perform after having been doing this for 40 years. It is truly a great personal high to have the public turn out like that.'

(The Main Event Concert, 1974.)

'Being nervous before a show never stops. I still am. That's why this going on the road, singing every night, all kinds of songs, to all kinds of audiences, is the best thing.'

(To *Life* magazine, 1963.)

'I have absolutely no desire to do a Broadway show, which is the only thing I haven't done. It's physically arduous when I sing now. I sometimes get sick before an engagement, worrying I'll forget the words . . .'

(To Roderick Mann, 1971.)

'Before I give a performance I have to go into training and cut down on smoking and drinking, and I play golf and do press-ups.
'I don't sing for the kids now—I never did, really. They have their special types of music, and that is good. But their music doesn't have to be mine.'

(To David Lewin, 1964.)

'There are only two of us left who do these songs—Tony Bennett and me. I think they're a great part of the English language. About the chick who has split . . . songs that tell a story.'

(London Concert, 1980.)

'Real singing is acting. I sang so well because I felt the lyrics here and here and here (touches his forehead, his heart and his stomach). Whatever the man was trying to say in the song—I'd been there. And back. I *knew* what it was all about.

'Then I developed into an actor and really in many ways it was the same as singing. You have to care and to sell yourself to an audience and make them care, too.'

(To David Lewin, 1963.)

ON HIS INSPIRATION:

'When I started singing, Bing Crosby was my inspiration. I didn't try to copy him, but his style—so relaxed and easy—encouraged me. It's nice to be told that I may have inspired other singers, but I'm sure that after me, there'll be others who'll have this same effect.'

(The Main Event Concert, 1974.)

'With few exceptions, every major pop singer in the US during her generation has been touched in some way by her genius. It is Billie Holiday whom I first heard in 52nd Street clubs in the early thirties who was and still remains the greatest single musical influence on me.'

(To *Ebony* magazine, 1958.)

ON HIS CONTEMPORARIES:

'For my money, Tony Bennett is the best singer in the business, the best exponent of a song. He excites me when I watch him—he moves me. He's the singer who gets across what the composer has in mind, and probably a little more. There's a feeling in back of it.'

(To *Life* magazine, 1965.)

'Nelson Riddle is the greatest arranger in the world. A very clever musician, and I have the greatest respect for him. He's like a tranquilliser—calm, slightly aloof, Nothing ever ruffles him. There's a great depth somehow to the music he creates.'

(To Robin Douglas-Home, 1962.)

ON WORK:

'When I'm working I want to get on with the job. When I'm playing I want my friends around me, and play hard.'

(To David Lewin, 1964.)

ON HIS GREATEST PRIDE:

'My children. I love them. I'm proud of them—Frank, Nancy, and Tina are fine kids. There is a great love in our family. I hate to cite myself, but in a family

that split early we are still closer than most. Every time I touch anywhere, I ring to say okay.'

(To Fergus Cashin, 1970.)

ON CHILDREN:

'I love children—anybody's children. Most often, they don't know who I am (whatever that means) and they look upon me as just some adult who's taken an interest in them, who'll stop to talk to them, or even play with them. They have no hang-ups and are completely honest in their reactions to me. I also think that there are many things we can learn from children, if we'd only stop to take the time.'

(The Main Event Concert, 1974.)

'I'm not old enough to understand adults, but I think I know enough to understand kids. And I think if we can get the kids together, maybe we'll be able to keep them together when they get to be adults.'

(To Earl Wilson, 1976.)

ON RACIAL DISCRIMINATION:

'I believe any form of discrimination is intolerable. People should not be judged by their race, religion or mode of living, but should be judged for the kind of person they are. And I also feel people should be judged as they relate to you, individually, and not how they relate to others.'

(The Main Event Concert, 1974.)

'Kids normally like other kids. They get along pretty well together until some misguided person finds out that their little boy is playing with another little boy named, maybe, Sammy Levine. So, a couple of days later her little boy tells Sammy they can't play together any more because his mother won't let him play with Jews. This is a terrible thing. Nobody's got any right to break up a friendship, because that's the kind of friendship that's important to the future of America and the world. What kind of a set-up would that be in a country that was founded by Pilgrim Fathers who went there in pursuit of religious freedom and happiness?'

(To Liberal News, 1950.)

ON HIS HOBBIES:

'Usually when I stop working I take off my watch and read until I can't see any more. Sometimes I play golf or watch baseball. I've dabbled in oil painting, and I

ABC Film Review

SEPTEMBER 1964

6D

Put me among the girls—Frank in a publicity still for 'Robin and the Seven Hoods' (1964)

like photography. In fact, hard as it may be to believe, I was actually a member of the working press. *Life* magazine had assigned me to cover the first Muhammid Ali (his name was Cassius Clay then)—Joe Frazier fight at Madison Square Garden in 1971, the fight that Ali lost by decision in the 15th round.'

(To Roderick Mann, 1971.)

ON LUCK:

'People often remark that I'm pretty lucky. Luck is only important so far as getting the chance to sell yourself at the right moment. After that, you've got to have the talent and know how to use it.'

(To Tom Pryor, 1968.)

ON MONEY:

'It doesn't thrill me. Never has. You gotta spend it. Move it around.'

(To Fergus Cashin, 1970.)

ON HAPPINESS:

'As I've told my audiences all over the world, I have more than my share of all the good things and I only wish the same for everyone.'

(The Main Event Concert, 1974.)

ON MODERN MUSIC:

'The music written today is nowhere near as good as it was 10 or 20 years ago. But it's a whole new world. I have no complaint with the youngsters and their kind of music because we must stop and think that 25 years ago we made the music of our era. We liked a certain kind of music, and that's what they wrote and played for us. Kids want identity and they find their own identity. Like my daughter Tina—she's 16 and she appreciates what I do, but she prefers the other, and I never put her down for it. Sure there are bad songs that the kids have. They're poorly written and they have no melody, but it's another kind of music. There's certainly no harm in it.'

(To *Life* magazine, 1965.)

ON HIS GENEROSITY:

'Since I've been exceptionally fortunate to "sing for my supper" and get paid for it as well, I feel it's almost an obligation that I have to help out those who are less fortunate.'

(The Main Event Concert, 1974.)

ON HIS CRITICS:

'I don't mind criticism so long as the people doing the criticism know their stuff, their facts. What infuriates me is that most of the so-called "music critics" have nothing in here (points to his head). No, worse still—in here (points to his ear). What I've forgotten about music they haven't learned yet.'

(To Robin Douglas-Home, 1962.)

ON WOMEN:

'I'm supposed to have a Ph.D. on the subject of women. But the truth is I've flunked more often than not. I'm very fond of women. I admire them. But, like all men, I don't understand them.

'I like intelligent women. When you go out, it shouldn't be a staring contest. The first thing I notice about a woman is her hands. How they're kept. Grooming is so important. I don't like walking perfume ads. Several colognes drive me right out of the room. First of all I've got an allergy to them. I begin to sneeze, which is not very romantic—and this certainly might annoy a woman.

'I don't like women to smoke a lot either—that drives me batty. It's unfeminine and dangerous—burn up the whole damn house, you know. I like a woman's clothes to be tasteful and subtle. I don't go for topless. Or for extreme cleavage. I like women to be women.

'I don't like excessive make-up. I know that a woman must have a little, but I think that women—generally—have enough beauty without doing the circus tent type make-up.

'I live my life certain ways that I could never change for a woman. I am a symmetrical man. I demand everything in its place. In some respects I'm a hard man to live with.'

(To Roderick Mann, 1971.)

ON PRIVACY AND PUBLICITY:

'In my films, on my records, in my concerts I have always given all of myself to the public. All of myself—all I have. Every fibre. If they like what I give, O.K. if they don't, I've failed.

'But I think any star like any other human being is entitled to make his own decisions about the private life when he is not, so to speak, on show. I guard my privacy jealously. Because if I didn't I would have no privacy left.

'I am not some bosomy starlet. I don't *need* to fall in with the demands of the ritual publicity machine. I want to be judged on what I do artistically.

'If the public don't like what I give them professionally, then I accept their judgement. But I don't have to give interviews or pose for pictures to get the public to like me. The public are more intelligent than that.

What can I say in an interview that could possibly increase my stature as a singer and actor? As I say, leave it to the public to judge. They know, they are not deceived by phoney publicity pictures. Or by show business people airing their views on everything from Vietnam to Birth Control.'

(To Robin Douglas-Home, 1966.)

ON RETIREMENT:

'I think if I stop singing, it would drive me mad. Fortunately, people like to hear me sing.

'I once tried to give it up. I was really tired, and I didn't have any plans. But, after a year, my kids were on my back and my gardener complained that I was barking at him too much—so I went back to work.

'Now, I am feeling really well. I have two grandchildren and I am hoping for more. At the moment there's little possibility of me retiring.

80

Frank, dressed for the part, on 'Opening Day' at the Dodger Stadium in April 1977.

'I would quit if I found a certain tremolo in my voice. But if I did quit, it would be because of that, not because of fatigue.'

(To Patrick O'Neill, 1981.)

The Sinatra Favourites

It is the mid-1970s. The setting is a small, private party in New York City. Sinatra is sitting at a table in a separate room talking to a friend. They are discussing Sinatra's music. Eventually, the friend asks Sinatra the one question few ever get the chance to ask: 'What is the best work you ever did? Sinatra answers quietly, but firmly, 'Only The Lonely.' His companion starts to protest. He cites other works, other moments. Sinatra insists. He reaches down and squeezes his friend's knee, and says, 'No . . . No . . . "Only The Lonely," I know.'

'Only The Lonely' is an album for losers. It was recorded in May and June of 1958. Nelson Riddle arranged and conducted the work. He had replaced Gordon Jenkins who had to bow out because of a conflict in schedule.

In this album, Sinatra comes as close to being a perfect singer as is humanly possible. His breath control, phrasing, diction and vocal reach are impeccable.

The title song is a hymn to loneliness. The pain in Sinatra's voice sets the mood for the entire project. 'It's A Lonesome Old Town' conveys a sense of total desolation. 'Angel Eyes' and 'One For My Baby' are two of the greatest saloon songs ever written. The bar-room mentality of these two songs is raised to a new level of despair by Sinatra. 'What's New' becomes a plaintive cry. 'Spring Is Here,' 'Willow Weep For Me,' and 'Gone With The Wind' are all masterfully understated. 'Goodbye' is a lament of utter regret. 'Blues In The Night' is a statement of extreme condemnation. It is sung with such conviction by Sinatra that it creates a paradox for the listener.

'Guess I'll Hang My Tears Out To Dry' is one of Sinatra's greatest recordings. His reading of the verse is absolutely perfect. The emotions that this recording elicits are almost unbearable.

'Ebb Tide' is an enigma. It is a beautiful song and Sinatra gives a powerful vocal performance. But, it doesn't belong on this album. It is a song of affirmation on an album that expresses complete anguish.

Is it Sinatra's greatest album? It may very well be. Sinatra was at his vocal peak. Riddle's arrangements are superb. As far as musical technique is concerned, it is without question his finest. Ed O'Brien.

THE 25 FAVOURITE SINATRA SONGS

In 1980, Frank's public relations firm, Solters & Roskin, conducted a poll to establish the singer's most popular recordings. A total of 7,600 fans from more than 11 countries were polled, and replies came from Britain, Canada, Australia, America, Japan, Brazil, France, Sweden, West Germany, Holland, as well as various other places. In all, 587 individual Sinatra titles were selected by fans, but the eventual winner proved to be a 25-year-old recording, 'I've Got You Under My Skin' with words and music by Cole Porter, released by Capitol in 1956! (Note: It has been suggested that the number 3 song on the list given as 'Chicago' should, in fact, be 'My Kind of Town'.)*

The list, with dates of recording, is as follows:
1. 'I've Got You Under My Skin' (January 12, 1956)
2. 'The Lady Is A Tramp' (November 26, 1956)
3. 'Chicago' (August 13, 1957)
4. 'My Way' (December 30, 1968)
5. 'Send In The Clowns' (June 22, 1973)
6. 'Nancy' (August 22, 1945)
7. 'Here's That Rainy Day' (March 25, 1959)
8. 'All The Way' (August 13, 1957)
9. 'It Was A Very Good Year' (April 22, 1965)
10. 'Night and Day' (November 26, 1956)
11. 'Come Fly With Me' (October 8, 1957)
12. 'I Get A Kick Out Of You' (November 6, 1953)
13. 'All Or Nothing At All' (August 31, 1939)
14. 'Angel Eyes' (May 29, 1958)
15. 'You Make Me Feel So Young' (January 9, 1956)
16. 'In The Wee Small Hours' (February 17, 1955)
17. 'Ol' Man River' (December 3, 1944)
18. 'All Of Me' (November 7, 1946)
19. 'Witchcraft' (May 20, 1957)
20. 'Put Your Dreams Away' (May 1, 1945)
21. 'One For My Baby' (June 25, 1958)
22. 'Where Or When' (January 29, 1945)
23. 'Violets For Your Furs' (November 5, 1953)
24. 'Strangers In The Night' (April 11, 1966)
25. 'September Of My Years' (May 27, 1965).

*In a 1982 poll Sinatra fans indicated that 'New York, New York' would now be number one on their list of favourites.

Frank Sinatra's Great Concerts

by

Stan Britt

September, 1975

' . . . As a singer of songs, we all know he has brought happiness to people all over the world. Not only because of his light, charming voice and his incomparable technique, but because when he sings he sings from the heart. . . .'

The late (Sir) Noel Coward, introducing 'mon vrai ami', Frank Sinatra, at a special charity concert by the latter, in Monte Carlo, in 1958

Frank Sinatra has been, in one way or another, the master of practically everything he has essayed, during a career of unusual distinction and one that has encompassed all the most important areas of the show business production belt.

Films, radio, TV, recordings—all of these media he has conquered, and many times over. Yet, if there is one specific section of the world of entertainment which singles out Sinatra's uniqueness as one of the great voices of this century more than any other it must surely be that of live performance. The area where any kind of entertainer—musical and otherwise—discovers whether or not he or she can communicate, both personally as well as artistically, to all manner of audiences.

While it is true that Frank Sinatra's talent has continued to be finely honed in nearly 45 years of singing, even his earliest live appearances, one is

reliably informed, evidenced a kind of less extrovert charisma which drew audiences to him. The appeal of Sinatra, then, was more laid-back, yet assuredly hypnotic to his fans. And whether he has performed in august concert halls, or in outdoor amphitheatres, or at football stadiums or in plush nightclubs, his reputation has long since become one of the omnipotent performer. His unparalleled achievements in live performance have continued to draw from his fellow singers and musicians, even the hardest-to-please critics, and certainly the more discerning pop-music lovers, the kind of praise reserved almost exclusively for those select few whose talents place them in a world far removed from the norm.

Without a shadow of doubt, it is in the context of performing before a live audience that more often than not Sinatra's vocal artistry is showcased at its ineluctable best. The same context in which he has—literally—sung before kings and queens, dukes and duchesses and presidents and prime ministers—and, of course, his most important audience of all: the millions of 'ordinary' folk who comprise, overwhelmingly, his real, and certainly his largest section of admirers. The millions who not only make all kinds of sacrifices—often, too, performing the most extraordinary feats of ingenuity—to ensure possession of tickets for his concerts. And, of course, those who religiously purchase each succeeding Sinatra album release, watch his latest TV show, or visit their local cinema to catch a re-run of one of his movies.

There have been many, many other vocal artists—emanating from all kinds of popular music of this century—who have continued to grace the entertainment platforms of the world. Any list of all-time greats might well include the following: Edith Piaf, Billie Holiday, Ethel Waters . . . Nöel Coward, Maurice Chevalier, Ray Charles . . . Judy Garland, Marlene Dietrich, Cleo Laine . . . Paul Simon, Johnny Cash, Mel Tormé . . . Shirley Bassey, Janis Ian, Ella Fitzgerald . . . Louis Armstrong, The Beatles, Nat Cole . . . Joan Baez, Dionne Warwick, Bessie Smith . . . Elvis Presley, Stevie Wonder, Perry Como . . . Tony Bennett, Rod McKuen, Billy Eckstine . . . Aretha Franklin, Gladys Knight, Mildred Bailey . . . Bing Crosby, Dick Haymes, Jimmy Witherspoon . . . Dinah Washington, Joni Mitchell, Peggy Lee . . . Al Jolson, Lena Horne, Sarah Vaughan, Sammy Davis Jr., Nina Simone . . . and more. . . . Each of these stylists has given, in their own individual way, distinctive qualities of interpretation in their live performances, with varying degrees of excellence and/or originality.

But in truth, not too many of even the greatest of these distinguished vocal artists can claim to have equalled Sinatra as an in-person performer, and it is even less doubtful if any one has actually surpassed him. To anyone who has attended a Sinatra concert during, say, the past 20 years, any such claim that he remains the most gifted live vocal entertainer is neither far-fetched, nor in any way outrageous.

Naturally, in analysing the overall qualities of any artist in this field, the ability to *sing* superbly well, and in a mostly consistent manner, is the *sine qua non* consideration. Sinatra's vocal consistency in live performance is legendary. Of course, there have been occasions when his vocal powers—for one reason or another—seemed to have deserted him; times when, perhaps, his vocal cords have let him down. That is an understandable, if (for the listener) an unsatisfying, situation. Less easy to comprehend have been those occasions when, apparently, his heart has not been in his work. Much rarer still—indeed, quite astonishing, when one remembers his usual immaculate, sensitive, intensely musical appearances—are the seemingly inexplicable lapses in taste.

For there have been occasions when Sinatra has changed a lyric, some would say in a less-than-desirable way, neither embellishing it to any real advantage nor improving it in any specific way. And certain 'hip' word substitutions sometimes tend to diminish the impact of a lyric; sadly, perhaps, also marring an otherwise impressive performance.

One other puzzling manifestation of less than good taste—this time of the strictly non-musical kind—has been his use of the concert stage, usually occurring during his 'rest period', as a kind of personal soap-box, in order to vent his feelings against a person or persons, for one reason or another. However deeply-felt his opinions might be, even firm Sinatra fans have often declared, such invective is rather out of place during a concert performance—even at best, an unnecessary intrusion . . .

Thankfully, these temporary aberrations are few and far between—certainly, one cannot recall a Sinatra concert-goer complaining that either an unsuccessful lyric-change, and/or an odd moment of verbal abuse, had ruined an entire performance, lasting from anywhere between 30–90 minutes.

From a purely vocal standpoint, what is Sinatra's uniqueness—that precious quality that sets him apart from his contemporaries?

Firstly, it is no exaggeration to say he has an especially distinctive vocal timbre, one that registers with immediacy, is instantly identifiable. Yet, other great singers have had this quality—Bessie Smith, Louis Armstrong, Piaf and Eckstine spring quickly to mind. Even after exhaustive exposure to his singing, there seems to be no explanation other than that the Sinatra timbre is *different*. So different, in fact, as to defeat even the voice-reproduction gifts of the finest impressionists who include singers as part of their repertoire. (Sammy Davis Jr., a long-time admirer and friend of Sinatra's, is an impressionist of exceptional qualities; yet, despite an obvious ability to walk and talk uncannily like Sinatra, Davis' attempts at reproducing Sinatra's singing voice remain his only unconvincing impersonation amongst an otherwise amazingly realistic catalogue of distinguished—and wholly distinctive—vocalists).

Stagecraft has long since been an important aspect of the live Sinatra. In his early—band-singing—days, his stagecraft was restricted mostly to using a stand-up microphone. Those embryonic dates with James and Dorsey enabled him to learn how to use his hands to further illustrate a certain point in a song's lyric. Additionally, he used the stand-up mike in a definite audience-baiting manner, often bending it in the same direction his swaying body moved—and the basically all-female, teen-age members of the audience responded in prescribed bobbysox fashion.

His deliberate accenting of certain words, the slightly over-exaggerated (yet never distasteful) way of using *glissandi* with a nevertheless blatantly sexual bias, rarely if ever failed to elicit from his youthful fans an immediate response—and a collective barrage of screams that could be, we are told, extremely unnerving to any non-participants also present. Same with the seemingly innocent act of shrugging his slender shoulders, or with a variety of hand gestures— all engendered instant audience reaction. This kind of hysterical reaction—something that was to continue for several years after leaving the Dorsey aggregation— was, in the early-1940s, a new phenomenon in pop music history. Even pre-Sinatra idols like Rudy Vallee, Bing Crosby and Gene Austin, and their contemporaries, had scarcely caused such a positive expression of unbridled emotion.

From the very earliest part of his singing career, when he hustled strongly for work—on local stations, and involving his spell as lead vocalist with the Hoboken Four, and later at roadhouses and clubs— Sinatra also took a keen interest in how other singers of the period handled themselves onstage. He noted their attributes, as well as ensuring that he would not repeat their mistakes and deficiencies.

When it became obvious that for singers like Sinatra a hand microphone was to become an essential part of their onstage act, it didn't necessarily follow that all the best vocal artists would use what is basically a sensitive piece of apparatus to the best advantage. Peggy Lee is but one world-class singer who was never able to convince herself she could use a mobile microphone in live performance. She agrees, though, that if someone like Sinatra can enhance his delivery of a song by skilful use of such an appendage, then, so be it. But: not for her.

'Yes, I tried . . . but I became too aware of the microphone, whereas it should have been like driving a car, or swimming—you don't think of all the different things you're supposed to do once you've learnt. With a hand mike, too, I'd feel responsible for tripping over the cord . . . that takes away from the music, for me. No, I prefer to work with the mike resting in the stand . . .'

Frank Sinatra has, at all times since his band-singing days, attached enormous importance to using a mobile microphone in a correct, yet always subtle manner. As he has said: 'Many singers never learned to use one. They never understood, and still don't, that a microphone is their instrument . . . It's like they were part of an orchestra, but instead of playing a saxophone they're playing a microphone . . .'

The use of a microphone is so important to Sinatra that he even makes sure that this essential piece of equipment is near to identical in colour to the black dinner jacket he invariably wears for his live appearances. For anyone who takes a more-than-casual interest in such matters, it is instructive to note, at all times, the degree of subtlety with which he uses his hand mike. Not only because of the way he holds it— close to his face for a *pianissimo* passage in a gentle ballad, or how he draws it away again for a powerful finale—but even when performing the apparently innocuous task of holding it, especially when walking from one side of the stage to the other. Everything is accomplished in a suitably unostentatious fashion. A part of his every performance which, when observed at first-hand, can convince his audience that the instrument is indeed a part of him.

Amongst other leading pop vocal stylists—past and present—only Johnny Mathis comes near to Sinatra's perfect use of a hand microphone. Again, when perceived at close quarters, it is absorbing to watch how Mathis projects *his* most unusual singing voice, and to the maximum advantage. Both Sinatra and Mathis are very much the leaders in this area, presenting an object lesson to many other top-class vocalists—Ella Fitzgerald and Tony Bennett spring instantly to mind—who seemingly have not the desire to improve their demonstrably poor microphone techniques.

Another hallmark of any Sinatra performance is the sensitive use of his hands—especially during a ballad. Seated atop a stool, the microphone in one hand, he uses the free hand to trace an invisible pattern in the spotlight, emphasising a particularly point in the lyric. Overdone—or clumsily executed—it is more often embarrassing, sometimes even laughable. Where Sinatra is concerned, this use of the free hand is never less than discreet and is, ultimately, an attractive enhancement to his singing.

Last but not least, Sinatra's personal charisma makes him not only one of the most visually exciting performers but also one who easily communicates with all kinds of audiences. The kind of charismatic performances Sinatra has delivered during the past 25–30 years differ greatly from those of the bobbysox days. Those early years are remembered mostly because of the teenagers' hysterical reactions to an apparently shy as well as gangling singer whose image and appeal to the other sex was far removed from that of the top box-office movie stars of the period, like Clark Gable, John Wayne, Robert Taylor and Gary Cooper.

The post-1940s Sinatra, however, has been just the opposite. The charisma, by this time, has changed to match a newly-found dynamism in his singing. All of which has resulted in a personal style that appeals to both sexes; a charisma that generates an electricity which fills even the cavernous concert palaces like London's Royal Albert Hall or New York's Carnegie Hall—and even roofless establishments such as the Hibiya Park Outdoor Theatre, Tokyo, and The

Stadium, Sydney.

But whatever period during his career one cares to choose, Sinatra's live appearances have demonstrated, at all times, just how deeply immersed he is in his music. Whatever happiness he has found through the years in other areas of his full life, it is doubtful that he can have too often attained the kind of fulfilment he obviously gets when singing in front of a band—large or small—in front of an appreciative assembly.

Probably the first most important live appearance Sinatra undertook in his immediate post-Dorsey period occurred right at the end of 1942. The venue: the Paramount Theatre, New York City. The date: December 30th. Appearing on the same bill: The Benny Goodman Sextet and Orchestra, plus the clarinettist's attractive young vocalist Peggy Lee.

The booking followed the visit to the Mosque Theatre, in Newark, New Jersey, one evening a month before, by the Paramount manager Bob Weitman and Harry Romm, Sinatra's personal representative with General Amusement Corporation (the agency with which the singer had signed when leaving Dorsey). Weitman and Romm were amazed after watching the reaction of a predominantly young—and female— audience to Sinatra, both during his actual performance and on his very arrival onstage. They agreed at once they might well get the same kind of reaction at the larger New York venue.

How right they were! Following Goodman's simple announcement—'And now, Frank Sinatra . . .'—came an almost terrifying loud and shrill response from the audience. Goodman stood, open-mouthed, in front of the mike, as if nailed to the stage. Half out loud, half to himself, he asked, with justified incredulity: '*What the hell is that?*' The mike picked up the gasp of amazement, amplifying it both to the audience and to Sinatra. It acted like a nerve-relaxer to the latter. Reports were unanimous in declaring the concert an overwhelming triumph—with the youthful audience claiming 50% at least of its success.

For Sinatra, the result of the December 30th appearance was twofold. First, his engagement was extended to eight weeks—longer even than the King of Swing, whose band was succeeded by other, much less important outfits. Second, it was a standard-setter for future live performances by an obviously out-of-the-ordinary talent. The crowds continued to pack the Paramount for all the eight weeks. Reactions tended to become, if anything, more emotive. The girls screamed and moaned at Sinatra's every move. Some even waved a variety of panties and such for his attention. Many a Paramount seat, too, was left moist—and on more than one occasion, claimed staff at the theatre—during that unforgettable two-month period. In fact, New York

SINATRA IN CONCERT
SEPTEMBER 25-26 · 8 PM
Prices—$25, $20, $15, $10.
Tickets on sale at the Hartford Civic Center
Box Office and all Ticketron Outlets.
Charge tickets to Mastercard/Visa
by calling CHARGELINE: 727-8010
For more information: 727-8080
Presented by Mel Rich Productions in association with
Thomas S. Perakos for H.S.R., Inc. and
The Hartford Civic Center C

was experiencing the first bout of genuine mass hysteria, the kind of reaction that at certain times through the succeeding years was to become a little more frequent—and which, by the advent of the 1960s, was to become even commonplace.

Sinatra's return visit to the Paramount, five months later, was not as support to Benny Goodman, but as the headline act, and as a star in his own right. By which time, his asking rate had risen by a cool $1,000 to an impressive $3,100. Again, the audience response was extraordinary.

In between these Paramount gigs, Sinatra had played a prestigious one-month stint at the Riobamba Club, also in New York. Not only did he once again confound the sceptics, but through his own vocal excellence, together with an ever-improving stage deportment, offered conclusive proof that he was fast becoming one of the upper-league artists in his branch of music.

His soaring career was assisted further by a shrewd switch from GCA to the giant Music Corporation of America agency. Later the same year, came additional first-time successes—at the Hollywood Bowl, accompanied by the famous California Auditorium's own Symphony Orchestra, then at the Wedgwood Room of the Waldorf Astoria, back in New York City. A jam-packed Bowl had given him a tremendous ovation; the usually stuffy Wedgwood Room habitués also succumbed to his personal charm and his uniformly fine singing.

Almost exactly one year after the Waldorf appearance, Sinatra returned to the Paramount. And this

time even the previous engagements paled into near-insignificance in respect of mass appeal. Sinatra fans more or less took over the Times Square district of New York, on and around the Columbus Day period. Such was the clamour for tickets—or even, for the unlucky kids who failed to get entry to the Paramount when the box office sold out in record time, just a glimpse of their idol—that the show's star was forced to make a 6 *am* arrival for rehearsal on October 11th (the day before Columbus Day itself).

Even by then, it was estimated that around 1,000 girls, attired appropriately in bobbysox apparel, had gathered to make homage. Some had been there since the day before. At 8.30 am, the theatre was open for business—and the three-and-a-half-thousand-plus seats disappeared almost faster than the box office could hand over the tickets.

Columbus Day, a national school holiday, was something else. All roads to and from Times Square and the Paramount were blocked by a total number of fans estimated seriously as being in excess of 30,000. Traffic—including pedestrians—ground to a halt on all sides. Thus were the so-called Columbus Day Riots

born. Scenes, hitherto never witnessed, helped build the 'riot' legend, fanned by dramatic commentary from the news media. Various reports spoke of broken shop windows, a succession of fainting females, and an overworked, and ultimately helpless, police force (reckoned to be over 500 strong). Not forgetting an almost non-stop barrage of hysterical cries and screams for the focal point of attraction to show himself. It was, altogether, an event that the Big Apple was not to witness again until four mop-headed young Liverpudlians first arrived in the city, over 20 years later.

No complaints from 99% of the Paramount audience, needless to say. Except for one male youth who narrowly escaped an early demise when a screaming mob of girls descended upon him after his well-thrown egg had created a crazy new colour design on Sinatra's jacket. It took the combined efforts of theatre staff and police, also present inside the Paramount, to rescue the terrified culprit.

Apart from the national newspapers, the respected music magazines were beginning to react favourably in their coverage of this exceptionally-popular phenomenon. Including *Metronome* and, in particular, its leading scribe, a certain George T. Simon. Even so, the basically music-reporting Simon could hardly refrain from commenting on the 'social' aspects of Sinatra's Columbus Day appearance, thus: 'On Frank's first number of the show, 'There'll Be a Hot Time In the Town of Berlin,' the girl next to me squealed so I couldn't hear too well. There were a few more songs, but I'm not too sure just what they were because the girls on either side of me, and the one in back and the one in front of me, squealed so much that I couldn't hear too well. . . . P.S. I finally heard Sinatra—on his two CBS (radio) shows. To me the guy's still tremendous!'

During the remainder of the 1940s Sinatra's reputation as a live performer continued to grow. Sadly, however, and following the disintegration of his first marriage, his hitherto enviable status as a recording artist began to tail off at the end of a decade. Then, came that horrifying night at the Copacabana—another swank New York nightspot which in previous times had echoed to the applause he was by then accustomed to receiving there—when his throat gave out and he was forced to rest for a while completely. . . .

It was not until 1950 that Frank Sinatra paid his first visit to Britain. Even though his records weren't selling anywhere near as handsomely as in previous years, and his name didn't figure too often at the top of music polls in 1950, the loyalty of his British fans ensured that his first-ever season at the London Palladium would be a box office success. Outside the Palladium, there were nightly demonstrations of affection. And his reception inside that mecca of British entertainment for each appearance wasn't exactly limp.

Certainly, the singing Sinatra produced during his first British shows was not that of a has-been, or a talent in comprehensive decline, a fact testified many times over in more recent times and certainly by those who paid to see him at the Palladium—some as much out of curiosity as anything, as they readily admitted. The local critics, too, seemed pleasantly surprised at what they heard and saw. The reviews overall were praiseworthy—albeit sometimes grudgingly so. The music paper *Musical Express*, for example, called him 'a superb performer and a great artiste'. Sinatra himself, most observers thought, seemed relaxed and happy—and any lack of ability to produce first-rate singing in this so-called period of decline seemed absurd to those who remember that inaugural season at the Palladium.

Despite the personal and professional ups-and-downs of the late-1940s/early-1950s the latter decade was to prove an almost unbelievably significant one—a decade that saw one of the most—if not *the* most—astonishing comebacks in showbiz history. When, following an Academy Award-winning role in the celebrated dramatic movie, 'From Here To Eternity'—all acting, no singing—the career of someone who many thought was well and truly over, suddenly took on a new and vital quality. Not only had Frank Sinatra become, almost overnight, a tremendously efficient screen actor, but his singing had acquired a more electric, more visceral quality. Now, without question, his singing communicated readily to males as well as the females. And thus he was attracting an additional and important audience: one that might well have passed by his vocal work of earlier times.

Rhythmically, Sinatra had improved exceptionally—previously, he had hinted, but only hinted, at what was to come, with recordings such as 'The Birth of the Blues', 'Bim Bam Baby', and 'Sweet Lorraine'. Now, on the non-ballad numbers that had become an essential part of his in-person and recording repertoire, he really swung. Or put another way, his singing had become unquestionably jazz-orientated.

This vocal metamorphosis was more easily discernible during his live performances. Apart from the maturity and all-round improvement in his singing, the shy nice-boy-next-door entertainer of the 1940s had changed to one of a sharp, finger-snapping extrovert—sometimes arrogant, more overtly sexual, more instantly communicative to concert and club audiences of all types and ages. Well before the end of the 1950s, Sinatra had acquired an even stronger reputation as the most potent in-person vocal entertainer of all.

This hard-earned reputation has continued, up to and including the present. No matter in which concert hall he sings, no matter in which country, and irrespective of how important or otherwise the occasion might be, the name Sinatra is synonymous always with the highest of artistic achievement. The times Sinatra has peaked in concert performance since his legendary comeback are too numerous to recall. But, without a doubt, there have been those extra-special occasions since the early-1950s when he has attained peaks of excellence even he has rarely, if ever, surpassed.

With the rapid growth of more proficient tape-recording equipment since then, the chance to evaluate (and re-evaluate) a wide selection of Sinatra concert material has, not surprisingly, increased. The majority of this offers copper-bottom evidence of Sinatra's preeminence—worldwide—in this field.

With his pre-occupation as a movie star, both in musical productions as well as in strictly acting-only productions, together with a busy record-making schedule, the rest of the post-*Eternity* decade meant that his live appearances were not nearly as frequent as one might be forgiven for believing. Not nearly as often, say, as during the 1970s-into-the-1980s. True, he did play almost obligatory seasons, annually, at top Las Vegas entertainment houses such as Caesar's Palace and the Sands, but actual *concerts* were much less frequent events and, therefore, something rather special. . . .

By 1957, the partnership of Frank Sinatra and arranger/conductor Nelson Riddle had long since become a potent force, one of international repute, established mainly through the medium of a succession of highly-successful—artistically as well as commercially—recordings. It was in the same year that Riddle was asked to conduct a studio-size orchestra for a Sinatra concert held at the Civic Auditorium, in Seattle, Washington. It was appropriate that he should conduct, for all but three of the 17 numbers heard on that June evening were Riddle-orchestrated.

Listening to a tape of that concert 25 years later is most instructive (especially for those familiar with his live performances of the past decade). For example, the repertoire is interesting, insofar as it reflects—comprehensively so—Sinatra's emergence as a rhythm-conscious vocalist. Indeed, almost three-quarters of the Seattle material is a positive confirmation of his by now full-time involvement with emphatically swinging arrangements. Material which, not surprisingly, comprised standards Sinatra had recorded for Capitol Records, with Riddle as his musical director. All the rhythm items bar one emanate from standard-setting albums whose titles alone are sufficient to signify their right to be called classics in their field: 'Songs For Young Lovers', 'Songs For Swingin' Lovers', 'A Swingin' Affair'.

Sinatra's vocal range at this time was greater—especially at the top. (The more youthful quality in his singing voice needs no explanation. It simply had greater flexibility at that time, something which manifests itself both in ballads and the more rhythmic songs).

The post-*Eternity* Sinatra had added a definite jazz-hipness to his singing that he had rarely shown before. Typifying this aspect of his singing at Seattle is Sinatra's re-writing of a stanza from 'Just One of Those Things', (which re-appears thus: '. . . turned out to be one of those mutharee nights . . .!') No doubt the sometimes tetchy Cole Porter, the song's author, would have voiced his disapproval at this lyric-change, in typically trenchant, po-faced style, if and when he'd heard Sinatra's version at the Seattle concert.

Yet even if one objects to this kind of liberty-taking, most pop-vocal music-lovers can nevertheless find much elsewhere to admire in Sinatra's highly-personal treatment of an accepted classic standard such as 'Things': the undisguised sexuality in its overall feel, together with a genuine, non-artificial excitement engendered by an exhilarating freewheeling approach, not forgetting the accent being on a decidedly rhythmic concept, with the performance proceeding at a positive medium-fast tempo. Somewhat different, in fact, to the way in which he'd recorded the number in his Columbia days, or indeed how he'd interpreted it during the film 'Young At Heart', a mere three years previously.

Buoyancy is the hallmark of Sinatra's interpretations of such as 'You Make Me Feel So Young', 'Oh! Look At Me Now' ('This song helped me a lot', he informs the audience, '. . .it brings back such wonderful memories for me'), 'The Tender Trap', and 'I've Got You Under My Skin'. When Sinatra is as relaxed as during this concert, his singing of the rhythmic numbers lends credence to claims by those who consider him to be a jazz vocalist. Like 'Under My Skin' and 'Just One of Those Things', there is a definite red-blooded, sexually-motivated approach by Sinatra to another Porter song, 'At Long Last Love', although here it is projected in a more subtle manner. With 'At Long Last Love', too, one is accorded another Sinatra trademark—an effortlessly executed hang-over phrase, that stretches the word 'McCoy' ('*McCoy-oy-oy-oy* . . .!') into the beginning of the following phrase, without taking a breath in between. Never at any time exaggerated or over-used, it provides the listener with an additional musical bonus.

For the '57 concert, Riddle sensibly retains the familiar small-combo setting for numbers such as 'A Foggy Day', 'I Get a Kick Out of You' and 'They Can't Take That Away From Me' (all arranged by George Siravo, not Riddle, although the former received no name-check on the 'Young Lovers' LP from which most of the audience must have remembered them). Sinatra's control in 'Foggy Day' allows him to play with time in an ultimately beneficial way. It is questionable whether Sinatra's introduction to 'Hey! Jealous Lover'—a 'B'-side Stateside single release, an 'A'-side issue in the UK—is either ethical, or indeed does very much for its commercial aspirations: 'I absolutely and unequivocally detest this song!' There are several other interruptions, mid-song, plus a 'false start' that doesn't come over as humorously as was the obvious intention. But, whatever, the audience seems to like it . . .!

Only four ballads at Seattle—although each a classic Sinatra ballad, and each from classic Sinatra albums. However, it is true to say that the singer doesn't sound altogether as totally committed as with other concerts

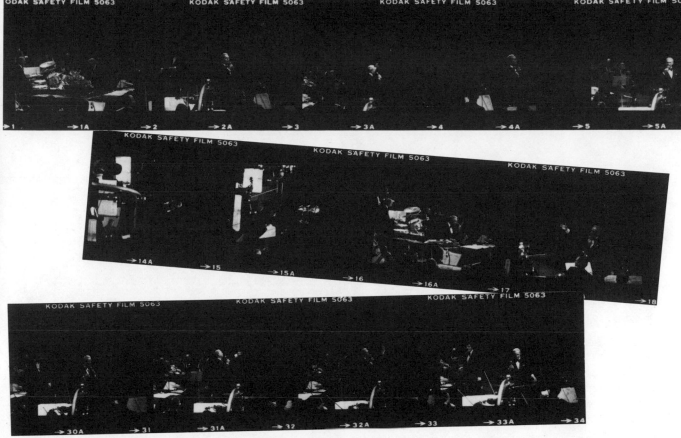

Sinatra in concert—various moods and moments captured by Roy Palphryman.

from this period, and indeed thereafter. But there is no doubting Sinatra sings them well. Best of the quartet is 'Glad To Be Unhappy', with archetypal Sinatra phraseology the most important ingredient of 'Violets For Your Furs'. ('When Your Lover Has Gone' and 'My Funny Valentine' are the other ballad selections). Curious aspect of this quartet: each is performed at tempos slower than the recorded versions. Curious, only because almost inevitably live recreations tend to emerge at *faster* tempos.

Seattle, Washington is several thousands of miles away from Monte Carlo. But it was in the Principal's Sporting Club that Frank Sinatra participated in a memorable concert, almost exactly one year after Seattle. This time, though, the orchestra is conducted by Quincy Jones, at that time living and working in Paris*. The generous—and obviously sincere—introduction to the evening's star guest is delivered by Noel Coward, bi-lingually, his French as impeccable as his English. The concert's distinguished hosts: Their Serene Highnesses, Prince Rainier and Princess Grace of Monaco.

*It would seem that Sinatra wasn't, then, too familiar with this supremely gifted writer/conductor, as he refers to him during the concert as 'Richard Jones'. Jones, of course, was to work with Sinatra on more than one occasion—both in the recording studio and in actual live performance—during the 1960s. They became very close, and Sinatra usually referred to Jones affectionately as 'Q'.

At the Sporting Club, Sinatra is in obvious high spirits. Singing-wise, too, there is little or nothing at which to complain. Certainly, the midnight gala—a charity event, which ultimately benefited the United Nations Refugee Fund to the tune of $12,000—offers substantial proof that Sinatra's concerts often find him sounding better as they unfold. Yet, there is very little wrong with the opening three numbers—'Come Fly With Me', 'I Get a Kick Out of You' and 'I've Got You Under My Skin' (with Sinatra adding a lightning quip in one place—'*We may all get arrested tonight!*')

'Come Fly With Me', a fairly new Cahn-Van Heusen addition to the ever-growing Sinatra discography, and already a favourite track from the eponymous LP, was to become increasingly popular at Sinatra concerts the world over in the next two decades. Also included in the Monte Carlo programme, and also part of the 'Come Fly With Me' album—'Moonlight In Vermont', 'April In Paris', and 'Road To Mandalay'. Both the two ballads had been, since the Capitol recording of both (in the previous October), almost automatically elevated to the pantheon of the greatest Sinatra interpretations. The $50-a-head audience is treated to two well-nigh flawless renditions of both with the already legendary hang-over phrases (*Paris—'. . . tree-ee-ee-es . . . April in Paris . . .*'; and *Vermont—'ee-ee-v'ning summer breeze . . .*')—thrillingly in evidence. 'Road To

Mandalay'— is completely different, and something of an oddity in the Sinatra discography. Basically, it is a glorious send-up of the staid Rudyard Kipling opus, swung with a vengeance and with Sinatra transforming large chunks of the lyric into more personal, basic language (e.g. '. . . *come back you mother soldier*!' . . . and '*there's a Burma broad a-sittin' and I know dat she waits fo' me . . .*') Sinatra's own broad sense of humour responds willingly to one of the most creatively humorous orchestrations by Billy May, the prince of fun-in-music amongst all arrangers. Predictably, Sinatra cannot resist a dig at the Kipling Estate's succesful ban in Britain on his recording of 'Mandalay'. After the Sporting Club audience has responded enthusiastically to the parody, he snarls, in friendly fashion: 'Kipling's daughter had the nerve to ban that in England. How *dare* she! She drinks a little bit, so we'll forgive her for that . . .'

Also included in the Monte Carlo programme are several songs recorded after Seattle, '57. Including 'Bewitched', 'All the Way' (no Riddle orchestration, unlike the Capitol recording: simply Miller's sensitive keyboard accompaniment, a format that was to become automatic for future concert performances), 'Where Or When' and 'Monique'. The inclusion of 'Where Or When' is interesting.* The treatment is unusual, with Miller's piano the only instrumental support until the final bars. It is a typical *bravura* performance which didn't remain in Sinatra's act for any length of time. 'Monique' is identified as being 'brand new'. Absolutely correct. Sinatra had cut the song at his last recording date, just over a fortnight before Monte Carlo. Its relevance is further explained by the singer who reminds his audience that the local premiere of his latest film—'Kings Go Forth'—had taken place immediately prior to the gala performance. Long-time Sinatra lyricist Sammy Cahn had written words to a theme from the film, written by Elmer Bernstein, who was responsible for the complete score. Certainly, Sinatra sings well enough but, frankly, the song is hardly one that lives long in the memory. And, like the afore-mentioned 'Where Or When', its addition to Sinatra's live repertoire was infinitesimally brief, its abandonment even swifter. . . .

One of the most important portions of Sinatra's entire career figured in the year 1962. This was when he undertook a world concert tour, in aid of various charities—involving nine countries and spanning three continents. Bill Miller fronted a sextet which played the framework of big-band arrangements by Riddle, May and the like. As a result of the tour, a total sum, reliably reported to be in excess of $1,000,000 was raised for the respective charities. From a musical standpoint, reports subsequently emanating from the countries indicated that the quality of singing was uniformly of a high standard.

Included in the lengthy itinerary were a brace of concerts at two Paris venues, the Lido and the Olympia. At the Lido, he was obviously feeling in a high-spirited mood—even although there is an unscheduled interruption to proceedings when Sinatra, obviously spotting a member of the audience dozing during his fine reading of 'All the Way', yells out sarcastically: '*Nobody sleeps on this show*!' The Lido programme also includes a fine selection of ballads and swingers, the repertoire encompassing old favourites as well as the more recent additions to Sinatra's discography.

Included in the latter: 'Autumn Leaves', 'In the Still of the Night', and 'The Second Time Around'. 'Autumn Leaves', an obvious inclusion in any French concert programme—the song originates from France and was called originally 'Les Feuilles Mortes'—elicits from Sinatra the same kind of poignant interpretation that had touched the audience at London's Royal Festival Hall five days before. The performance is enhanced by the subtle use of just flute (Harry Klee) and guitar (Al Viola). Flute is also prominent in the accompaniment to 'The Second Time Around', another Cahn-Van Heusen song, written for and performed by Bing Crosby, in a movie titled 'High Time'. The Sinatra reading in Paris is convincing, even though there is a slight strain discernible in places. 'In the Still of the Night' is restyled in a way that Sinatra himself might describe as being 'a romper'. Here, it is the singer who swings the band. He is in irrepressible form, really punching out the lyric, in truly dynamic style. Klee, switching to alto-sax, produces a quite out-of-character solo, in between the vocal choruses, sounding not at all unlike the notorious Herbie Fields.

Amongst the better-known items in his repertoire there are fine versions of 'Too Marvellous For Words' (band and singer meshing superbly, with Sinatra really taking off, rhythmically speaking), 'My Funny Valentine' (shaky vibrato in places but otherwise fine), 'They Can't Take That Away From Me', and 'Chicago' (Sinatra at his most irresistible). 'Night & Day'—a long-established Sinatra favourite—has a fairly new, and rather unusual, setting during the '62 tour. Al Viola's guitar provides typically adroit support as Sinatra, with no other instrumental assistance, provides an object lesson in lyric interpretation. 'I Could Have Danced All Night' finds him in almost mischievous

*Sinatra's recording of 'Where Or When' remained unreleased, inexplicably, until the end of the 1970s. Which could be the reason why it was dropped from his book. He did, however, revive the number in the mid-1960s—but this time it was treated as a swinger.

91

frame of mind—and the singing isn't half-bad. But of all the offerings that night, a pulsating, three-chorus 'You're Nobody Till Somebody Loves You' remains probably the one item above others that must have lifted involuntarily a couple of thousand Parisian *derrières* from their seats in spontaneous approbation. . . .

Arguments will continue to rage—long after the man has finally, and irrevocably, retired—as to whether or not Frank Sinatra should be classified as a jazz singer *per se*. Of course, it really doesn't matter two hoots, yet for some it is apparently of inestimable importance.

Never has a better opportunity presented itself, before or since, to evaluate Sinatra's jazz-worthiness—and in a real live jazz setting—than in 1965, when he was *the* headliner at the Newport Jazz Festival. Held at that time in Newport, Rhode Island, it is still the acknowledged most famous jazz celebration in the world. Sinatra's appearance remains, of course, a slightly sensational scoop by long-time NJF mastermind George Wein, who also booked the Count Basie Orchestra to accompany perhaps the most distinguished vocal personage to grace the festival in many years.

Appropriately, perhaps, Sinatra's NJF debut took place on July 4th—US Independence Day. And his mode of arrival was typically Sinatra in style: by his own helicopter. Not surprising, too, that the festival site was jammed with fans in a manner rarely witnessed before 1965, and not at all again when the NJF moved from the island to New York City.

The music resulting from Sinatra's July 4th appearance? Frankly, it cannot be said he sang at anywhere near to his best. For a seasoned campaigner like Francis Albert, it was, recall those present, something of a nerve-racking experience, even with his beloved Basie band in powerful support. And the band, ironically, might well have inadvertently contributed to the singing being a notch or two below par. For its irremovable enclosure within an unwavering 4/4 rhythm has sometimes had the effect of making Sinatra's rhythmic singing sound stiff and predictable—something apparent also when other non-jazz singers have worked with the band. Certainly, though, he looked fit and sounded in good shape, those in the audience remember, the voice remaining strong throughout a taxing, 18-strong programme.

After being lavishly announced as 'The Chairman of the Board', the concert opens with 'Get Me To the Church On Time'—hardly a jazz festival opener, it could be argued. Certainly, though, the Chairman swings hard, right from the opening bars. 'Fly Me To the Moon'—one of the more successful Sinatra-Basie recordings—also swings powerfully, even although Sonny Payne's over-stressed, four-in-the-beat drumming tends to diminish, rather than accentuate, the jazz pulse. (Payne, who had left the Basie outfit in 1964, was at Newport at Sinatra's personal request. He worked with the singer extensively during 1965). Harry Edison's familiar muted trumpet—another NJF import, especially for the occasion—is present during a rather too solidly-swinging 'I Wish You Love', which has a finale that doesn't lend itself to a jazz festival performance. 'Street of Dreams', likewise, is rather sluggish in places; Sinatra has to fight the majestic might of Basie & Co. during its full-blooded accompaniment to 'Luck Be a Lady'. He triumphs, in the end—but only just. . . .

Numbers such as 'The Gal That Got Away,' 'Call Me Irresponsible' (fine, lightly-swinging FS, with Basie's piano and Edison's trumpet each getting a snatch of solo spotlight), 'My Kind of Town,' 'Please Be Kind' (infinitely better all-round than the LP version by the pair), and 'I Only Have Eyes For You' (apart from some parts of the lyric disappearing in the big-band blast), tend to work more to Sinatra's advantage. 'Where Or When' is swung in an emphatic way this time. His spontaneous-sounding 'Yeah, Base!' salutes a delightful, if disappointingly brief, solo by the Count. More important, however, is that singer and band gell splendidly. The ballads present both Sinatra and Jones with what is, in the event, an insurmountable problem. 'Call Me Irresponsible', as noted, survives its slight transformation to beat-ballad. But 'In the Wee Small Hours of the Morning' and 'It's Easy To Remember' are, sadly, brave failures. (Jones, who also conducts, had the almost impossible task here, of marrying these tunes to a slow-tempo Basie format). And 'All the Way', cast in a similar mould, hovers on the brink of disaster—it works primarily because Jones' score and the band's *pianissimo* playing are both tasteful, unobtrusive. Saddest Sinatra performance comes with 'Too Marvellous For Words'—taken at a much too fast lick, with poor timing and even words omitted on more than one occasion. Not even a particularly strong final note can salvage this, the seventh item on the programme.

Critically, the Sinatra appearance at Newport drew generally favourable comments. *Down Beat*, the bible of jazz-magazine criticism, gave an overall thumbs-up. The always perceptive Dan Morgenstern ranged himself on the side of those who disliked Payne's drumming—although, as he hints, it was most certainly the kind of drumming Sinatra demands. From the moment he stepped onstage, wrote Morgenstern, he took command of his audience—'and he kept it

In an article written specially for the NME just before returning to the States,

FRANK SINATRA
says
Your British Musicians are Wonderful !

AT the outset, let me say that I have thoroughly enjoyed my British tour, as everyone has been so very, very kind. The thousands of people I have played to, the theatre staffs who accorded me royal attention, and all those who have written to me, have made this visit one I shall long remember—one I wish personally to call an encore for.

Show band

I have been particularly pleased with the support I have had from the Billy Ternent Orchestra throughout this extensive itinerary of the British Isles. It's great to play with musicians who know what they are doing, and it made a very pleasant change from the very disappointing backing I had on the Continent.

Disappointing is, in fact putting it most mildly. To be more direct and truthful, some of those guys who were supposed to be musicians couldn't play marbles, never mind an instrument.

Yes, the association between Billy, his boys and myself has been a distinctly happy one.

I was most impressed by the general standard of musicianship in Britain, and your Cyril Stapleton and his BBC Show Band are a really wonderful crew. After that first broadcast I made as the guest on their Thursday night "Show Band Show," I was so enthusiastic that I immediately asked for another airing in July. I was very glad to get it, and very glad to do both dates.

Believe me, those guys—Bill McGuffie, Tommy Whittle, Tommy McQuater, Harry Roche and his trombone sidekicks, Messrs. Chisholm and Armstrong. Louis Stevens and his fiddlemen—in fact the lot—can have anything put down in front of them and they read it on sight—perfectly. That's what I call musicianship.

In the Show Band, Cyril has a crew whom he directs so admirably that it can hold its head high with any group—anywhere. It was a pleasure working with him—it's always a pleasure working with people who know what's happening—and here's another encore I'm yelling for.

NME help

Perhaps my biggest regret is that I didn't get time to play the London Palladium. I tried to fix the two weeks preceding the Coronation, but they were all booked up at the Palladium.

It was my own fault. I left the whole thing too late, owing to the completion of my picture, "From Here to Eternity," in Hollywood.

Incidentally, you may like to know that the NME was the first paper to write up that film. I was in London last year and thought that I had kept my private flat telephone number very secret —but I was wrong. There was the NME asking questions—your newsboys are certainly on the ball. And, in passing, may I say a thank you to the NME publicly for its help?

About "From Here To Eternity." The press notices in the States are being very nicely phrased, thank you. . . but in answer to all the queries I get in the mail, let me emphasise that just because I do not sing in this film I do not intend to forsake musicals for a dramatic career.

Musicals

Musicals are such great fun to make—but they take very much longer to get in the can than a straight dramatic feature. So I reckon to continue to make musicals, and perhaps a straight film once in a while.

Proof? A few hours after I finish this article, I shall be boarding a TWA plane at London Airport with the eventual project of putting that wonderful musical, "Brigadoon," on celluloid.

This is going to be great stuff— and I'm sure I'll enjoy every minute of the time the film is on the floor. How could it be otherwise, working as I shall be with that wonderful person Gene Kelly? Providing some of the glamour will be Cyd Charisse—and that's pretty good, too. . . .

At the moment this film is a little in the formative stage. You see, the exact medium hasn't yet been decided, so Sinatra in 3-D may yet be true !

Och Aye !

One of the most touching incidents of my tour, by the way, happened while I was in Scotland. Two very nice girls knitted my wife and myself a genuine Scottish tam-o'-shanter each. To them another thank you—and I can't wait till Hollywood digs Sandy McSinatra and Wee Bonnie Gardner stepping from the plane !

Next week in New York, I go in front of the cameras again. This time I shall be making the first of a series of TV short films. All I know about them is that they run for 30 minutes, but I'll keep you posted.

Oh, one thing I must tell you— I have turned golf addict ! Last week I dropped in on Bob Halsall, the professional at the famous Birkdale course, for six lessons. How he's improved my golf is beyond mention—so watch out, Crosby ! I'll play you and, what is more, you can have Hope, too . . . as a handicap !

If anyone was to ask me what stood out as the most impelling memory of my tour, I would answer immediately "the manner in which British audiences asked for request numbers."

Taste

You see, you asked me for numbers I had forgotten that I had ever recorded, but they were always GOOD numbers. Which emphasises my point against the rubbish that some publishers put out as "hits." If Joe Q. Public gets a chance to state his preference, it's always for the best tunes—melodies and words that really have something to say.

Well, thanks for everything, England ! I take back with me very pleasant memories of your understanding friendship, and I hope to meet you all again.

FRANK SINATRA

Tuesday evening, August 11

Farewells are never pleasant— and with my flight tonight to America I feel "the sweet sorrow" of partings. I have been accorded a wonderful welcome during my tour of these beautiful Isles, and will carry home a legion of memories.

Tomorrow I shall be in New York, but each day I shall cherish the thought of the very friendly manner in which I was treated by everyone I met up and down your country.

But let this not be Goodbye — just 'so long' for maybe only a few months, and Thank You all.

Very sincerely yours,

Frank

until the last of his 20 songs.* In good voice, he was most impressive on "Street of Dreams", a beautifully phrased second chorus of "Where or When", and a hard-driving "You Make Me Feel So Young". His singing was enhanced by the sensitive obligatos of trumpeter Harry Edison. . . .' Concluded Morgenstern: 'As the Sinatra-Basie package rolls along, it may become more relaxed, but the suspicion remains that the singer is at his best performing for a night-club audience . . .'

By the time Sinatra and the Basie band arrived together in London, to play two midnight charity shows at the Royal Festival Hall, in May, 1970, it was obvious to anyone lucky enough to attend one, let alone both, of the consecutive concerts that the partnership had indeed become more relaxed, as well as a real musical collaboration—and in the best sense of that expression.

This time, however, the accompaniment comprised, the Basie crew apart, Edison, Sinatra regulars Cottler and Viola, together with a fair-size compliment of strings, plus assorted woodwind players, the latter two sections being of the home-grown variety. While some jazz purists might be forgiven for thinking that all this meant a watered-down, studio-type Basie band, with little or no real jazz content, they could well have been pleasantly surprised at just how incandescently it blew on both nights.

After an absolutely triumphant first night, with Sinatra sounding unbelievably good and in his most irrepressible mood, it seemed unlikely that he could repeat this brilliance 24 hours later. Moreover, could there be an equally enthusiastic audience? The answer to both questions: a most profound 'yes'. . . .

When listening to tapes of both these wholly memorable concerts—and making direct comparisons with even the finest other concerts Sinatra has given, in all parts of the world, at *any* time during his career— it is inconceivable that he could have sung so consistently superbly. And it is almost impossible to separate the quality singing of both nights.

Right from a vibrant opener, 'I've Got the World On a String', it is obvious that, as with the previous evening, something special is happening. (Repertoire on both occasions is identical, except that 'My Kind of Town' and 'I Get a Kick Out of You', from the first concert, are absent from the second, but 'April In Paris' is a delightful addition to the latter).

Relaxation is the hallmark of the opening six selection—all impressively swung, with band and vocalist coalescing in a manner hitherto not really apparent to most British fans, whose awareness of the Sinatra-Basie team was restricted at that time to the three albums featuring both talents and released locally during the 1960s. Of the six, 'At Long Last Love' finds Sinatra oozing confidence, playing tantalisingly with rhythm, obviously having a great time. 'Fly Me To the Moon', like 'World On a String', is merely top-class. But it is when the Basie musicians sit back in their seats and the strings and woodwinds really come into their own for the first time, that the concert becomes a major musical event, of unforgettable proportions. In fact, just like the night before.

For the next 20-or-so minutes, the Festival Hall echoes to one of the finest exhibitions of singing ever to grace the auditorium. It isn't just the tecnical skills, with Sinatra seemingly capable of surmounting any technical feats. Just as important—indeed, *more* important—is the marvellous feeling Sinatra imparts into the lyrics of such as 'This Is All I Ask', 'April In Paris', 'Moonlight In Vermont' and 'Try a Little Tenderness'. The last-named is a special treat, with Viola's guitar once again the sole instrument. A marvellously-phrased 'Lady Day'—a suitably emotional tribute to Billie Holiday—an absolutely definitive treatment of the Beatles' 'Yesterday', and a movingly evocative 'Angel Eyes' add further lustre to an incredible display of sustained vocal magic. And it is highly improbable that 'Autumn Leaves' can ever have been performed with such eloquence, such poignancy.

Perhaps, though the *pièce de resistance* of this breath-taking segment of the concert is 'Ol' Man River'. The Kern-Hammerstein II epic has been a Sinatra showcase in live performance since the mid-1940s. Outside of Paul Robeson, it is unlikely any other vocalist, of any musical denomination, can have rendered this larger-than-life pop opus so nobly, so many times. Even so, the versions the Royal Festival Hall audiences hear on two consecutive nights in May, 1970, eclipse any others by Sinatra, before and since. The emotional content of both is deep, the technique awesome. Each night, at the song's conclusion, the Hall erupts. The standing ovations are spontaneous. The reactions are genuine, overwhelmingly warm.

If both concerts had ended with 'Ol' Man River', there cannot have been many present who could have had real cause for complaint. But on May 8th, as with the previous night, there are still more delights to savour. Visibly moved by the reaction to 'Ol' Man River,' one recalls, Sinatra sails unstoppably through a further quintet of popular swingers, best of which are a bubbling 'You Make Me Feel So Young', a joyous 'Lady Is a Tramp', and, perhaps best of all, a palpitating 'Road To Mandalay'—delivered, at long

*In actual fact, Sinatra featured *18* songs at the festival.

Frank caught by the camera at various recent American and British concerts. Top right by Jim McNalis; centre right and bottom left and right by Annette Levine.

last, on Kipling's doorstep. An encore, surely, is scarcely required. But an encore there is . . . and it's surely the most satisfying live 'My Way' of all, with the singer bringing some credence, some dignity and some validity to a pop song that has an abundance of mawkish sentimentality and pompous platitudes . . .

Musicians are notoriously difficult to please when it comes to singers. They demand the very best—as much, of course, because too often they have to accompany the worst, or at very least, the most ordinary. Musicians, of all persuasions, invariably have something positive to say about Sinatra as a live performer. Especially those who have had the opportunity of working *with* the man, as part of his accompanying units, large or small.

Vic Ash is such a musician; a bastion of the British jazz scene for many years, more latterly involved (and comprehensively so) with session work of all kinds. An accomplished musician in every way, Ash dominated the local jazz polls for many years as a much-respected clarinettist. He also plays fine jazz on tenor-sax, and is often called upon to play these and several other blowing instruments of the clarinet and saxophone families, as well as flute. Ash is one of the handful of British instrumentalists, other than the superlative collection of string players, who helped augment the Basie orchestra during the marvellous concerts in May, 1970. It was to be the first of numerous occasions since then that he has appeared in orchestras supporting Sinatra. Indeed, up to and including the singer's London appearances in October, 1980, he has not missed a single Sinatra tour of the UK, plus trips to several European countries, as well as visiting Egypt, Iran and Israel with the singer.

Working with Frank Sinatra is, says Ash, something of a real thrill. For long before May, 1970—indeed, he says, even before Sinatra's first-ever appearances in Britain, in 1950—he had become a firm fan. The reasons for a musician like Vic Ash appreciating Sinatra's singing are, in many ways, similar to those of the devoted, non-musician fans, but they are interesting nevertheless.

'He's such a *musician*—even though he doesn't read or write music. And the individual things—his phrasing, the lovely sound of his voice, his intonation, the feeling . . . everything. It just gets to you. You can't compare it with an instrumental jazz solo, perhaps; not quite to that degree. But it's all there.

'The way he interprets a song is something else. Now, I've never really been one to listen to lyrics: I've always thought the lyricist gets too much credit, it's the composer who should receive more dues. Most people seem to disagree with me on this. But it's since *really* listening to Frank over the many years now I've

worked with him that I've realised how important lyrics are . . .'

Vic Ash lays emphasis, in particular, on how Sinatra projects the lyrical side of a song, the manner in which each phrase or lyric—or maybe just one particular word—is related to the note or notes of the music. 'I think there's hardly a player who doesn't dig Sinatra and the way he sings. That's why all of us who've worked with him are in awe. 'Apart from the unique way he puts over a song, his charisma is extraordinary, right from the moment he walks on stage. And, then, he seems to bring out the best of any arranger that he's used—like Nelson Riddle, May, Jenkins and Don Costa. They all come out with something different for him to their normal thing.' Sinatra has been deeply respectful of musicians at all times. Ash remembers that at no time has Sinatra been less than courteous, always professional to his accompanists. 'For instance, he knows my face. I won't say he'll say: 'Hello, Vic'—he probably would if he knew my name. But after 10–11 years now, he knows my face. And he'll come over and say: "Hi, how y'doing? Nice to see you again . . ."'

Rehearsals with Sinatra are always interesting, says Vic. 'There are quite a few singers who just either come along and hum-sing a little while, maybe one number, then disappear, letting the MD take the orchestra through its paces. But on all his rehearsals, Sinatra will come along and sing *all* the numbers being rehearsed. Actually, it's like having a private concert. It's just him and us. I find they are the best "concerts" for us musicians, really. Because as well there's no hangers-on—just the agent and maybe half-a-dozen people in sight. Yes, in every way he's a real perfectionist.'

Frank Sinatra enjoys playing London. He's said so on numerous occasions. Apart from West Germany, he seems to enjoy his appearances in most of the countries that have played host to his talents over the years—although he must have schizophrenic thoughts, even today, about visiting Australia, where he's experienced a love-hate relationship with the local press. Of course, as an intensely patriotic North American he enjoys performing in front of 'home' audiences. Until more recent times Sinatra's Stateside concerts have tended to be concentrated on the West Coast in general and Las Vegas in particular.

In Vegas, of course, the pickings are handsome, and although internationally-famous night-clubs such as Caesar's Palace and the Sands are themselves hardly conducive to artistic stimulation, regular appearances at such palaces of entertainment are rated as pinnacles of achievement by the all-powerful US music business. And, naturally, for the top-bracket performers themselves such engagements are tremendously lucrative.

One appearance at least at the legendary Carnegie Hall is still rated as a veritable peak of personal and artistic fulfilment by almost every North American musical entertainer of any real worth. Whether it be Vladimir Horowitz or Judy Garland or Benny Goodman, playing the New York auditorium is, for some, the ultimate aspiration. All of which makes it something of a puzzlement that Francis Albert Sinatra didn't tread the hallowed stage for the very first time until he was into his 35th year in the upper strata of the musical section of the entertainment business.

The occasion: yet another Sinatra concert in aid of charity, with the Variety Clubs International benefiting handsomely this time. The date: April 8th, 1974.

When making aural reference, again, to a private tape copy of the concert, it is obvious that Sinatra is in more-than-reasonable voice throughout. Perhaps even more interesting, however, is the fact that on several occasions he forgets parts of certain lyrics. Which would tend to make one imagine that, even after such a long involvement with audiences of all kinds and in all kinds of venues, his apparent nervousness is due, in all probability, to the importance of his first-ever occasion.

There's a kind of false ending to the opening 'Come Fly With Me'—strictly unintentional, one supposes. And even more problems occur in the second number on the bill. There is a longer-than-usual bridge to Neal Hefti's arrangement for 'I Get A Kick Out of You', and Sinatra's re-entry results in an angry piece of self-admonishment ('Where the hell am I?') as, presumably, part of the lyric is temporarily forgotten. Thankfully, he manages to return to the correct place and finishes superbly—in concert, Sinatra often 'corrects' a comparatively rare mistake by bringing forth say, a particularly choice phrase, as compensation. Later on in the programme a line is omitted from 'My Way.' Again, though, the overall performance is excellent.

These aberrations apart, the Carnegie Hall appearance finds Sinatra in top form. As usual, he never omits credit to the songwriters and the arrangers. Appropriately, too, he acknowledges the presence of veteran songwriters Rube Bloom and Harold Arlen. Appropriate also because included in his 13-song programme for the evening are 'Don't Worry 'bout Me' (with music by Bloom) and 'Last Night When We Were Young' (music by Arlen). The latter item was part of a three-ballad medley in the Sinatra book at that period, the Arlen-Ted Koehler song also serving as an opposite link with 'Violets For Your Furs' and 'Here's That Rainy Day'. Once again, the medley of ballads is undoubtedly one of the evening's highlights. So, too, is a beautifully conceived delivery of David Gates'

charming 'If'. A combination of Sinatra 'feel' and tenderness, together with an almost flawless performance, technically speaking, results in one of his finest-ever in-person renditions of this song. And he sounds sincere as he remarks, at the song's conclusion: 'Isn't that a nice song? And a lovely Gordon Jenkins arrangement . . .'

The late Jim Croce's 'Bad, Bad Leroy Brown' has been in Sinatra's book regularly since the mid-1970s. Sometimes singer and song—and a rather awkward-sounding Costa arrangement—have failed to gell too well. Here, with Sinatra sounding supremely relaxed, there are few, if any, problems. Another more contemporary number—'You Will Be My Music'—receives one of its finest Sinatra live performances, following his slightly extravagant introduction to its author: 'This is a song by a young genius from New York City called Joe Raposo . . .' And at the conclusion of another Raposo contribution to the recital—the out-of-the-ordinary 'There Used To Be a Ballpark'— he addresses the composer, who is also in the audience: 'Thank you, Joseph.'

Yet another brace of (more) up-to-date songs receive equally fine renditions—Stephen Sondheim's classic 'Send In the Clowns', and in completely different mood—'That's Life', an R & B-based, extrovert swinger, by the virtually unknown songwriting team of Dean Kay & Kelly Gordon. 'My Kind of Town' is the closer. By which time, any signs of nervousness have long since been well and truly forgotten.

A flawed performance, in part, maybe, but Frank Sinatra's debut at Carnegie Hall had been mostly a memorable experience for those fortunate enough to acquire tickets—the hall was sold out, in double-quick time, and demand for entry could have filled it half-a-dozen times more.

It has been a keen debating point at regular intervals amongst both Sinatra's legion of admirers and also his detractors as to how much longer he can continue to keep the flame lit, to keep on doing what he's done so extraordinarily well, and for such a length of time. Naturally, growing older doesn't mean a singer necessarily gets better and better. (Although there are a small handful of almost freak vocalists—the immensely gifted Sarah Vaughan, whose work today seems every bit as good as in previous years, and sometimes even better, is one—who somehow defy the passage of time). Certainly, it is true that Sinatra's range has decreased considerably during the past five years and more (and his charts have been adjusted accordingly . . . with absolute wisdom). At times, too, his singing voice has tended to show tell-tale strain at more regular intervals.

Yet for all that, he has proved that, with the

The master showman at work—
a portfolio of pictures by
Heather Taylor.

commencement of his fifth decade as a full-time professional vocalist, he can still deliver the goods in prescribed fashion. And, as such, he can still be adjudged overall head and shoulders above his succession of contemporaries, past and present.

Concert-wise, his ultra-loyal British fans might have felt that his appearances in London in September, 1980—one week apiece at both the Royal Festival Hall and the Royal Albert Hall—could possibly offer painful evidence that, at near-65, the end of a more-than-slightly incredible career was nigh. How wrong indeed were all the doubters! One young female fan of Sinatra's, who had been present at his concerts in London in 1975, 1977, 1978 and 1980, is Heather Taylor, a pretty, red-haired illustrative designer and professional photographer who specialises in shooting mostly jazz performers, both at home and abroad. For Heather Taylor, Sinatra is undoubtedly the best singer there is, although it is true she also admires Sarah

Vaughan, Tony Bennett, Peggy Lee, and B. B. King ('. . . and, of course, as a guitarist, too!') Sinatra, though remains the greatest . . .

Even so, she admits, she secretly harboured a slight fear that September '80 might, at long last, prove to be the first time that her favourite singer would really show his musical age. Rightly, though, she kept an open mind about the possibilities of what might or might not happen at the Albert Hall concert for which she had purchased a ticket.

Each time she has seen Sinatra live, she says, there has been something different, whether it be songs, arrangements or musicians. 'Each time I feel: "Wow!" I cannot make comparisons with Sinatra's previous London concerts, simply due to age, or lack of it. When listening to the recollections of the more mature admirers, I realise that no comparisons *should* be made. Every concert is as individual as the man performing.

Heather has vivid memories of Sinatra at the Royal

quieten. He is visibly touched. The orchestra plays 'Auld Lang Syne'. He announces they will be back next September. The applause continues and comes to a height to keep him onstage. But, again, he leaves, is gone.'

Certainly, Heather Taylor's summation of Sinatra's September 20th concert proved to be true for most of the concerts he gave at both renowned London concert halls. Yet, again, he seemed to have pushed away the years; even allowing for the diminished range he sang with power, conviction and impressive musical skill. He had obviously trimmed several pounds from various parts of his anatomy, looked tanned, fit and most happy to be singing before a British audience once again. . . .

For this writer, it had to be admitted that prior to attending the opening concert at the Royal Festival Hall, more than a slight apprehension had crossed the mind: could this occasion signify that, at long last, a distinguished career be drawing to an inevitable conclusion, with that seemingly indestructible artistry showing alarming signs of erosion? Was the London fortnight to prove an extended swansong? The answer was to prove an emphatic 'No'; like Heather Taylor, one other observer had his personal doubts completely shattered less than 15 minutes into that opening concert.

Indeed, his singing overall tended to remind the listener he hadn't sounded as good since probably the Royal Albert Hall in '75. Reviewing the opening concert, this writer opined:

'For those who remain still unmoved by the ineluctable artistry of Frank Sinatra, it must have been a bore as well as a constant source of irritation to have read the reviews that followed his mini-marathon schedule of concert appearances this past September . . . each extolling his uniqueness as a singer who continues to defy the passage of time, and in a manner that defeats any logical explanations. . . .

'Well, I'm merely going to add to the boredom and irritation of the Great Unconverted. For without a shadow of doubt, and for the umpteenth time, the latest Sinatra-in-London celebration has been yet another positive re-affirmation of a long-established talent that stubbornly refuses to become enfeebled and, sadly, die. Furthermore, Sinatra remains very much the kind of performer who transcends any critical re-evaluation which is in any way correlative to your actual Mr Average, even in the wildest sense.'

As usual, the repertoire proved to be varied and, of particular interest to Sinatra buffs of many years, it was gratifying to note the inclusion of no less than seven numbers he had never sung in concert in the U.K. Of these, 'The Best Is Yet to Come' swung lithely,

Albert Hall in 1980, and of experiencing—not for the first time—the familiar electric tension and excitement in the air, even before the concert itself has commenced. 'It's always present at Sinatra concerts. The Sinatra presence, perhaps. Looking around, people seem to go on forever, high into the roof. It's September 20th, second and final house. Frank Sinatra is greeted by a standing ovation. Smiles and gifts all round—especially the Jack Daniels! As the first note is heard, applause stops. Any questions of this man finishing go out of the window. I strain my eyes to follow his every move, peering between people's heads. Each word is perfectly audible, even without a microphone . . .'

And the end? ' . . . applause starts, you don't stop. People rise to their feet, as the lights fill the auditorium; everyone has done the same. Sinatra disappears and, then, unexpectedly, returns—to our delight. Only when he speaks does the applause yet allowed Carolyn Leigh's choice lyric to receive a suitably convincing reading. Of the ballads, 'In the Wee Small Hours of the Morning', 'Guess I'll Hang My Tears Out To Dry' and 'When Your Lover Has Gone' each vied for any Top Ballad of the Concert spot; each projected with depth and with that typical Sinatra skill. Both 'As Time Goes By' and 'I Can't Get Started' were also sung with elegance and freshness. But for most present at the Festival Hall, 'Summer Me, Winter Me' remains *the* highlight. In this glowing rendition of a Legrand-Bergman-Bergman opus that just falls clear of being pretentious, the Sinatra artistry was encapsulated at its veritable peak, including as it did the most sensitive use of the hands. A delightful *pianissimo* treatment of 'I've Got a Crush On You'—with a guitar-only accompaniment provided this time, not by the long-serving Al Viola, but by Tony Mottola, another veteran plectrist—added further lustre to the memorable evening, as well as giving a British audience a chance to hear yet another first-time performance of a song well-established in the Sinatra songbook. And the final, flag-waving 'New York, New York'—positively brand new in terms of Sinatra material—provided an electrifying finale. Delivered with dynamism and power—the final notes sustained true and strong, even when competing with *fortissimo* brass, reeds, *et al*—'New York, New York' must have astonished even his most avid admirers present.

Even in his mid-60s, then, Frank Sinatra, had, once again, confounded his doubters, silenced his critics—and, of course, had scaled the heights of artistic achievement. Even impending old age, at least as a performer, has no real problems for someone who has constantly baffled the gloomy predictions and analyses of both the experts as well as the ill-informed. And there is more than ample evidence to support any claim that, in terms of popularity alone, Sinatra's following during the past 10–20 years has never been as substantial.

It would be foolhardy in the extreme, therefore, even at this late stage in his career, to make any further prognostications concerning either Frank Sinatra's final demise from his position as the most respected pop singer of his age, or indeed as to when his *real* retirement—a final, irrevocable retirement—might be. In the interim, those of us who demand the finest in his field of music should be more than grateful for his sustained artistic excellence: longevity of career isn't necessarily concomitant with continued artistic achievement, yet Sinatra remains a formidable contributor—and nowhere better illustrated than in his involvement with live performance. An area in which, indisputably, he remains The King.

Or to use Heather Taylor's admirable summation of the in-person Sinatra:

'The only way to appreciate just how good Frank Sinatra is—go see him live . . . then go and see the others . . .'

(The author wishes to thank and acknowledge the following for guidance and assistance in the compilation of this chapter: Heather Taylor (who also supplied photographs in respect of Sinatra concerts in London), Charlie Hackett, Editor, 'Perfectly Frank' Magazine (for permission to use part of the author's article 'Sinatra: The Immovable'. Ray Purslow (The Record Centre, Birmingham), Allan Garrick, Phil Napier (The Sinatra Music Society), 'The Sinatrafile', Parts 1–3, John Ridgway (pub. by John Ridgway Books, Alvechurch, Birmingham), for reliable cross-reference.)

Frank Sinatra Film Star

MGA (108)-150

'I never had lessons as an actor. I never went to drama school, although I wish I had had the chance to do so. Most of the people I worked for just could not communicate with me or show me what to do.

'Only Otto Preminger, when I made 'The Man With The Golden Arm' for him, took me on one side and explained what the character of the dopetaker was about and how he could be portrayed.

'Everything else about acting I had to learn for myself, The best lessons I had were by talking to Spencer Tracy and Lee J. Cobb. I confirmed what I suppose I already knew—that the best acting is listening.'

(In conversation with David Lewin on the set of 'Von Ryan's Express' September, 1964.)

* * *

101

'I always try to remember three things as a movie actor.

'First. You must know *why* you are in the movie, understand all the reactions of the man you are playing, figure out *why* he's doing what he is doing.

'Secondly. You must know the script. Some actors are crammers—they cram the night before and just learn their lines for the following day. I don't do it that way. I keep a script in my office, my car, my bedroom, by the telephone, even in the john. And I read the whole script maybe fifty or sixty times before shooting even starts. Then when it comes to shooting a particular scene, you just have to glance at the script to remember the lines, and, more importantly, you know how that scene fits into the picture as a whole.

'Thirdly. You must learn and listen to the lines of others; it's no good just learning your own. With Spencer Tracy, for instance, you don't get time between his lines and yours to think out your next.

'There's only one thing about making movies that really irritates me: this business of miming songs to the vision afterwards. With all the advance in microphone equipment you'd think they could have worked out some way of recording at the same time as filming. I never sing a song exactly the same way twice, so when I come to mime I find it very hard. Somehow miming seems to take away a lot of the spontaneity, and I find myself unconsciously thinking of different ways I might sing the song.'

(Talking to Robin Douglas-Home at the time of making 'Come Blow Your Horn', 1963.)

* * *

'Directing is my favourite medium. It keeps me busier and I like that. I also like the sense of responsibility.

'When I direct other actors I take time with them—I am patient and could sit around for two days discussing with them what I want and how I think they might do it.

'I will do anything to get a good performance from them—scratch their backs or pat their heads or anything. I found out how difficult actors can be and

Frank with the film crew making 'Oceans 11' (1960).

With Director, Robert Aldrich, on location making 'Four for Texas' (1964)

wondered: am I that difficult when I am working for another director?

'I try to communicate to my actors and I have found a new patience while they work it out for themselves. But when they say they are ready they had better be ready. Because then I want to go—and I want to go fast.

'There is too much time wasted in making films—which is why I am always trying to put a hustle on these guys here.'

(From an interview on the set of 'None But The Brave', the first film Sinatra directed.)

* * *

'I don't buy this take and re-take jazz. The key to good acting on the screen is spontaneity—and that's something you lose a little with each take.'

(In conversation with Arnold Shaw, 1968.)

* * *

'I enjoy straight acting and I enjoy musicals. It really depends on the story. I have never decided I would do a musical, or conversely, a dramatic role. If a good script came along and the role was right for me, whatever, I would get into the project with a great deal of enthusiam.'

(Interviewed during filming of 'The Detective', 1968.)

* * *

A moment of relaxation for Frank during the shooting of 'Robin and the Seven Hoods' (1964).

FRANK ON HIS EARLY STARRING
ROLES (1944–1952)

'I was under contract to MGM between 1944 and 1950. Here's what happened. We made ''Anchors Aweigh'' which grossed a whole lot of money, and that was the start of the ''Formula''. You may remember that in ''Anchors'' I was cast as a friendly little sailor with nothing much to say for himself. Then came ''It Happened In Brooklyn'', where I played the part of a friendly little G.I. with nothing much to say for himself.

'By the time we reach ''On The Town'', they'd made me a sailor again, as inarticulate as ever, though in all fairness, let me add that this latter one was a very good movie in other respects. But you see the rut I was in! Even the story was mostly the same. Gene Kelly and Sinatra meet girl, Kelly hates girl, Sinatra loves girl, girl likes Sinatra but loves Kelly, girl rejects Sinatra, Sinatra finds that he loved another girl all the time, Kelly finds out that he loved the first girl all the time—fade out. Sometimes it was someone else instead of Gene, but any other variations were strictly superficial.

'The quickies I made for RKO before signing with MGM were never meant to be anything much, and ''Miracle Of The Bells'', in which I had my first non-musical acting part, turned out less well than we had hoped.

'The first role I could really get my teeth into was when Universal made ''Meet Danny Wilson'' in 1952. It was an unsympathetic character that some people took to be partly biographical, it seems. To that I can only reply that if anyone believes everything he sees in the movies, he must be awfully mixed up, mentally.'
(From 'Sinatra Speaks', 1955)

* * *

ANCHORS AWEIGH (1945)

Frank Sinatra: 'When I arrived at MGM to do ''Anchors Aweigh'' I was a nobody in movies. And because I didn't think I was as talented as some of the people I was working with, I used to go through periods of depression and get terribly embarrassed at myself. After all, what was I then? A crooner who'd been singing for a big band for seven years and whose only claim to fame was that girls swooned whenever I opened my mouth. But after working with Gene, who always saw me through my depressions and encouraged me to do a little better than I thought I was capable of doing, I felt I actually had some talent. I was

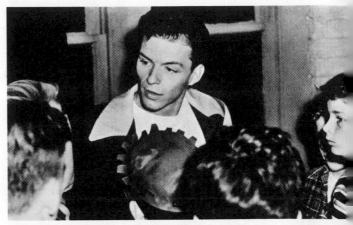

(Above) Frank in his award-winning film 'The House I Live In' (1945). (Below) Frank and Gene Kelly as two sailors painting the town in 'Anchors Aweigh' (1945).

born with a couple of left feet, and it was Gene and only Gene, who got me to dance. Apart from being a great artist, he's a born teacher. I really felt comfortable working for him and enjoyed his company, in spite of his insane insistence on hard work. Gene somehow tricked and cajoled me into working harder than I had ever done in my life before, and I found myself locked into a room rehearsing some of the routine for as long as eight weeks. Eight weeks! You can shoot a whole picture in that time!'

* * *

Gene Kelly, co-star: 'Frank's the hardest worker I've ever known. I think he's a great singer and has what it takes to make a fine actor. He has a native talent that shows up in his singing and an acting talent that makes you believe what he's doing.'

* * *

THE HOUSE I LIVE IN (1945)

Mervyn LeRoy, director: 'One morning in 1945, I had a telephone call from Frank. "Mervyn," he said, "I've got an idea for a short that I want to talk to you about." We got together and he told me his idea. There was a song he did called "The House I Live In". He said that he and Frank Ross (the producer) thought a movie version of that song would be a good thing to do, during those wartime years. He asked me if I'd help them with the project and, since I agreed with him about the worth of the idea, I quickly said I would. After I played the record a few times, I became very excited about it. Ross had a script written, and he and I coproduced it. Axel Stordahl was musical director and Frank was the star. It was a pleasant experience, working with Frank on "The House I Live In." We shot it all in one day. Our little film was well received and then, the next spring, I found myself owning an Oscar. I had been nominated many times, but that was my first and, so far, only Oscar. Winning it was a tremendous thrill, but even more thrilling was to listen to the heartwarming round of applause that came from the audience when my name was mentioned. I must admit that I basked in that sound.'

* * *

FROM HERE TO ETERNITY (1953)

Frank Sinatra: 'I knew that if a picture was ever made, I was the only actor to play Private Maggio, the funny and sour Italo-American. I knew Maggio. I went to high school with him in Hoboken. I was beaten up with him. I might have *been* Maggio . . . When I got on the set I was working with the finest pros. I felt I was playing with the Yankees and I knew it was going well. I learned from all of them. But Montgomery Clift was

particularly helpful. The way he pitched, I couldn't help shining as a catcher.'

Buddy Adler, producer: 'Sinatra dreamt, slept and ate his part. He has the most amazing sense of timing and occasionally he'll drop in a word or two that makes the line actually bounce. It's just right. He never made a fluff. And this from a fellow who really never had any training. I must admit that I kept thinking of him as a singer before the test, and couldn't visualise him in the role. But once the test was made, it was a case of a natural performer up against some great actors. The natural performer was better. I thought to myself, if he's like that in the movie, it's a sure Academy Award.'

Fred Zinnemann, director: 'The test Frank did was unbelievable. Then he played Maggio so spontaneously we almost never had to reshoot a scene.'

* * *

SUDDENLY (1954)

Robert Bassler, producer: 'During the shooting Frank proposed some changes. I steeled myself for there is nothing more disturbing than the cerebration of an actor. But Frank wasn't making demands to exploit himself at the expense of the picture. The suggestions he offered made sense for the picture.'

Frank Sinatra: 'Actors who can't sing can't switch to our side. But there's no reason why a singer can't go dramatic. A singer is essentially an actor.'

* * *

YOUNG AT HEART (1955)

Doris Day, co-star: 'My last picture at Warners was "Young At Heart," a re-make of a previously successful picture called "Four Daughters". There were some lovely new songs, and a first-rate cast that included Gig Young, Ethel Barrymore, Dorothy Malone and Frank Sinatra in the part previously acted by John Garfield. This was the only movie in which I worked with Frank; but years before, just after I made "Romance on the High Seas," I had been on "Your Hit Parade" radio show with him. Frank was the star of the show. I can't say that I got to know Frank then, even though we were together at rehearsals. Our reunion on "Young At Heart" was the first time I had seen him since those "Hit Parade" days. In "Four Daughters," John Garfield had died at the end, giving his performance and the film a sharp poignancy, but Sinatra refused to die. I thought it was a mistake, because there was an inevitability about that character's death that would have given more dimension to Sinatra's performance. . . . Frank didn't like to rehearse. He didn't like doing a scene over and over. He liked to come on, do one take, and have it printed.

That was all right with me. I think that repeating a scene makes a performance mechanical. There is something more alive and creative when you do a scene for the first time with all your juices flowing . . . I always felt there was a sad vulnerability about Frank. Perhaps that's why I always had understanding and compassion for what he did. I liked him. We had a fine relationship. There were many things about him that I admired.'

* * *

NOT AS A STRANGER (1955)

Robert Mitchum, co-star: 'Frank made the film with his own special acting touches . . . He's a tiger—afraid of nothing, ready for anything. He'll fight anybody about anything. He's really an amazing guy—frail, undersized, with a scarred-up face—who's ready to take on the whole world. It's easier when you've got as much talent as he has.'

* * *

GUYS AND DOLLS (1955)

Vivian Blaine, co-star: 'Although we had respect for Marlon Brando, I was more in awe of Sinatra. Frank and I got to be known as the "One-Take Kids". We always did a scene fast. Brando, on the other hand, was slow. He once took 135 takes. Nobody could believe it.'
Frank Sinatra: 'I think Brando, who is a dedicated actor, felt a little strange sharing a movie with a singer. I understood that, but in the musical numbers Brando suddenly discovered that he was working with a dedicated singer.'

* * *

THE MAN WITH THE GOLDEN ARM (1955)

Otto Preminger, director: 'I told Frank he could have extensive rehearsals and as many retakes as he liked of the drug withdrawal scene. But he said he knew exactly how he wanted to play it—"Just keep those cameras grinding" he said. We shot the scene in one take. When he was working with beautiful blonde Kim, Sinatra didn't seem to be so eager to get away from the set. He was very patient. Sometimes he would do twenty-five or thirty takes with Kim. Later he told me he considered it his best picture.'
Kim Novak, co-star: 'I respect him more than any actor I've met. He's real. He's honest. That's why he gets into trouble constantly.'
Frank Sinatra: 'It was a part I'd had my eye on for a

long time. John Garfield first wanted to do it, and after he died, I tried to buy the book. It doesn't matter that I didn't get it. It only mattered that, after all those years of waiting, I got to play the part. At first it looked as if we wouldn't get a seal of approval for it, but the movie people were just being stupid. Every manner of thing has been seen on the screen—drunks in "Lost Weekend," insane persons in "The Snake Pit"—but about narcotics, everbody's supposed to stick his head in the ground. I wanted to play this part so that they could feel what a terrible thing it does to a human being. I remember back when I was a kid in Hoboken. There were a couple of older guys on the block who acted funny, and later I found out they were on the junk. In poor, tough neighbourhoods like that, one peddler can ruin a lot of kid's lives. That's why it is such a good part. It says something.'

* * *

HIGH SOCIETY (1956)
Celeste Holm, co-star: 'I sang "Who Wants To Be A Millionaire" with Frank and loved every minute of it. A woman doesn't have to be in love with Sinatra to enjoy his company. I wasn't and I did. He's a stimulating talker on any subject: books, music, cooking, his children, whom he quotes oftener than most fathers, and sports.'
Grace Kelly, co-star: 'I'd always longed to do a musical and, of course, working with Bing Crosby and Frank Sinatra was simply marvellous. They create a certain excitement and are two very strong personalities. So it was fascinating for me to be in the middle—watching the tennis match go back and forth from one to another with tremendous wit and humour—each one trying to outdo the other . . . Frank and I did two numbers, "You're Sensational" and "Mind If I Make Love To You". He has an endearing sweetness and charm as a person and an actor.'

* * *

THE PRIDE AND THE PASSION (1957)

Stanley Kramer, producer: 'Sinatra didn't appear to be happy, but he worked hard and insisted on doing a lot of things you'd normally expect a star to leave to a double. He ran through explosions and fires. I had him trudging up and down mountains, wading in rivers, crawling in mud from one end of Spain to the other, and he never complained once . . . Occasionally, he would start a scene as if he didn't know what was going on. It looked like a palpable case of unpreparedness. But after a couple of minutes he was going like

'From Here to Eternity' (1953)

'Suddenly' (1954)

'Young at Heart'
(1955)

'Not as a Stranger' (1955)

'Guys and Dolls' (1955)

some high-precision machine. Frank is a tremendously talented man, intuitive and fast . . .'

Sophia Loren, co-star: 'Before he came to Spain, I heard all sorts of things. He is moody, he is difficult, he is a tiger, he fights. Here he is kindly, friendly. He has even helped me with my English, and taught me how people really speak in Hollywood. He is a regular gasser. I dig him.'

* * *

PAL JOEY (1957)

Rita Hayworth, co-star: 'There had been a plan for me to play in "Pal Joey" back in 1944 with Gene Kelly. I was to be the young girl Joey ditches for the older woman. But it got shelved. Then when it was revived I was cast as Vera Simpson the older woman! Working with Frank was electric, he really got into that part.'

Frank Sinatra: 'To me, Rita Hayworth *is* Columbia. They may have made her a star, but she gave them class.'

* * *

KINGS GO FORTH (1958)

Frank Sinatra: 'I took this part as a performer, not as a lecturer on racial problems. When it comes to bigotry, though, I think that the intellectual can be twice as dangerous as the person with no education. The uneducated man can be taught he is wrong. But the intellectual will rationalise . . . I think most people who have any kind of common sense and think fairly will not go out of the theatre and start race riots. As for the bigots, they'll scream at anything.'

* * *

SOME CAME RUNNING (1958)

Vincente Minelli, director: 'If you can get the company into Frank's fast tempo and enthusiasm and pace, there are fewer shooting days and you spend less money. We were virtual prisoners in Madison (where the film was made). People came from all over the State. Autograph seekers, curiosity seekers. We couldn't go to a restaurant. It was a terrible way to live.'

Shirley Maclaine, co-star: 'One night Dean (Martin), Frank and I were sitting in a house watching television when there was a terrible crash and a woman dashed into the hallway, knocking over two lamps. She raced into the living room, saw Frank and dived on top of him, pinning him to the sofa. Then she began kissing him . . . Women always seem to behave like that around Sinatra. They positively drool. It's true of all sex symbols, of course, but it's particularly true of

him. To be fair to the woman it was very late and there was a full moon and Sinatra brings out the worst in women . . .'

* * *

A HOLE IN THE HEAD (1959)

Edward G. Robinson, co-star: 'The original play, "Hole in the Head" by Arnold Schulman, had been about a Jewish family, but with Frank as the star they became Italians. I told them I reckoned the real reason for this was because the Jews were out of fashion—the world was sick to death of their suffering at the hands of Hitler! Still, Frank and I became good friends on the set, especially when we discovered we shared the same birthday. It was a friendly film to work on. Later I did another picture with Frank in 1964, "Robin and the Seven Hoods." '

* * *

NEVER SO FEW (1959)

Richard Johnson, co-star: 'The thing I realised about Frank was that he doesn't work for money, he works for respect. He wanted to be respected and accepted as an actor. When I first came to the set he admitted he was impressed with me because of my reputation as a Shakespearian actor. This meant something to him, you see, because he had never been in a play by Shakespeare. He valued my opinion and, in a funny sort of way, was in awe of me. Not as much as I was in awe of him, mind you, but nevertheless, in awe. But we became good friends pretty soon.'

* * *

CAN-CAN (1960)

Shirley Maclaine, co-star: 'I find it hard to get enough words to say about Frank. He is about as naturally talented as anybody I've ever known in my life. His potential is fantastic. The thing is, I wish he would work harder at what he's doing. I don't think when you polish something you can help but improve it. He won't polish. He feels polishing might make him stagnant. He doesn't even like to rehearse. Now I don't mind that because he and I have such a rapport . . . we look at each other, and we kind of sense what we're going to do. We don't really need to rehearse. But other actors and actresses can't always react to him that way. This is a very complicated man. I don't really know about him. Sometimes just when I've got him all

'High Society' (1956)

'The Pride and the Passion' (1957).

'The Man with the Golden Arm' (1955)

'A Hole in the Head' (1959)

'Pal Joey' (1957).

figured out, he does something that makes everything all different—and then he does something that makes me think, "Oh, yeah, that fits in! Maybe I do know him." '

Juliet Prowse, co-star: ' "Can-Can" was my first big break. I was nothing and Frank was one of the biggest names in the business. Yet he was always kind and I found him a very vibrant person.'

* * *

THE CLAN MOVIES (1960–1964)

'Oceans Eleven' (1960), 'Sergeants 3' (1962), '4 For Texas' (1964), 'Robin and the Seven Hoods' (1964).

Frank Sinatra: 'We're not setting out to make "Hamlet" or "Gone With The Wind". The idea is to hang out together, find fun with the broads and have a great time. We gotta makes pictures that people enjoy. Entertainment, period. We gotta have laughs . . . Of course, they're not *great* movies. No one could claim that. But every movie I've made through my own company has made money, and it's not so easy to say that. "Oceans Eleven" has grossed millions of dollars, and "Sergeants 3" is already well on the way to doing the same.'

Sammy Davis Jr: 'The whole thing was madly chaotic because we were doing two shows a night in Las Vegas and then, in the early hours, they would set up the cameras and lighting for shooting the next day. All the time the casino was running more or less as usual, twenty-four hours a day, and there were thousands of people trying to get in to see the action. Frank was very easy to work with. He was always at the helm of things and we kept it that way. He made the actual filming as painless as possible because he got bored easily and couldn't bear hanging around the set. When we worked together there was a feeling of close camarad- erie and we seemed to move as one force. We managed to carry that onto the screen. "Oceans Eleven" was a lot of fun, but I think "Sergeants 3" was the best film we ever did together. It was a good story with a lot of fine points and we packed it with action.'

Peter Lawford: 'How the first film, "Oceans Eleven", came about was like this. I was sitting on the beach at Santa Monica one day when a fellow told me this story. It was dreamed up by another fellow who worked at a gas station nearby. The plot sounded terrific to me, and I asked him to put it down on paper. The idea of these eleven veterans robbing the Las Vegas casinos of millions grabbed me, and in turn Frank and Jack Warner who actually said, "Let's not make the picture, let's pull the job!" '

110

Dean Martin: 'They say this is hard work, this acting. What bullshit! It's a gasser, the whole thing, the whole bit. It's fun. Anybody who says it's work doesn't know his—doesn't know what he's talking about. You go to the studio, everybody's nice to you, they bring you things, you work a few hours, you sleep while you're waiting, you get paid, you have a ball. Work? Work, my ass! I'm having the time of my life. Why, just appearing with Frank, Sam, Joe, Pete— at the Summit Meeting—why that's more fun than I ever had in my whole life!'

Joey Bishop: 'Frank has such consideration for the guys he works with. When we were doing "Oceans Eleven" he gave all of us a leather script holder. And it goes far beyond that. We were shooting at Warner's. Every day, everybody who worked that day got invited to his dressing room for lunch, not a commissary lunch, one he sent out for. One day there was a fellow who had maybe one, maybe two, lines to say. He didn't come to the lunch. Maybe he thought Frank wouldn't want him, his part was so small. Frank sent a car to pick him up and bring him there. Another thing, there was one day when there was a scene where Buddy Lester just had to stand there. No lines. Frank called the director and said, 'Take two of my lines away from me and give them to Buddy, it doesn't look right he should stand there with nothing to say.' He took *his own* lines

'4 for Texas' (1964).

'The Devil at Four o'Clock' (1961) 'Robin and the Seven Hoods' (1964)　　　　　　(Below) 'None But the Brave' (1965)

(Above) 'Can-Can' (1960) (Below) 'Never So Few' (1959) 'The Manchurian Candidate' (1962)

and gave them to Buddy, and he's *the star*! These are the things Frank does that nobody ever hears about.'
Bing Crosby, co-star in 'Robin and the Seven Hoods': 'I just took the part for a lark. I thought, gee, this will be fun working with these guys—we'll have a lot of laughs. It was a good part with some good songs, but I don't think they got involved enough. It was right at the time of Jack Kennedy's assassination and there were a lot of delays. We didn't feel like working for a few days and for some reason the co-ordination fell apart.'

*   *   *

THE DEVIL AT FOUR O'CLOCK (1961)

Spencer Tracy, co-star: 'Nobody at Metro ever had the financial power Frank Sinatra has today. "The Devil at Four o'Clock" was a Sinatra Picture. Sinatra was the star. Although we worked very differently, he knew what he wanted and there were no fireworks though some people said there would be.'
Frank Sinatra: 'I called Tracy the 'Grey Fox'. He's clever and he gets it together. I learned a lot from him, everybody did.'

*   *   *

THE MANCHURIAN CANDIDATE (1962)

Frank Sinatra: 'I'm more excited about this part than any other part I've played. I'm saying kinds of things in this script that I've never had to speak on the screen before. Never had to speak at all, for that matter. Long, wild speeches. Sometimes before I've even ad-libbed for three whole pages of script, just been myself talking as I would do normally. But this is different. Very, very different.'
George Axelrod, Script-writer and co-producer: 'I thought it would be terrific to have that marvellous, beat-up Sinatra face giving forth long incongruous speeches.'

*   *   *

NONE BUT THE BRAVE (1965)

Frank Sinatra, producer, director and star: 'It is an anti-war story and deals with a group of Americans and a group of Japanese stranded together on a Pacific island during the war. I have tried to show that when men do not *have* to fight there is a community of interests. I found out that directing was in some ways tougher than I had thought. The director has so many things to worry about—pace, wardrobe, the performance. Next time I won't try to perform when I direct.'

MARRIAGE ON THE ROCKS (1965)

Deborah Kerr, co-star: 'We had a ball. It was so much fun—a joke, and all quite ludicrous. Frank would come in one morning and say, "We don't need this scene!" and just tear it out of the script and throw it away. Then Dino, perfectly happy and absolutely relaxed, would murmur, "What a great way to earn a living; what other business is there where you can come in every morning and meet lots of people whom you absolutely adore, do something you like doing—and get paid for it?" And then there was this green chiffon evening dress I wore which gave them both absolute hysterics. I'm very tall, you see, and both Frank and Dino very short. When they saw me in this dress they called me the "Jolly Green Giant", after the popular brand of peas. Whenever I came on the set it was, "Ah—here comes the Jolly Green Giant!"'
Frank Sinatra: 'I love Deborah. She's a marvellous lady, a good friend and an absolutely brilliant actress.'

*   *   *

THE TONY ROME FILMS (1967–1968)

Humphrey Bogart (whom Frank credited with giving him the inspiration for these films): 'Frank's a hell of a guy. He tries to live his own life. If he could only stay away from the broads and devote some time to developing himself as an actor, he'd be one of the best in the business.'
Jill St. John, co-star in 'Tony Rome': 'He's a charmer, a real ladies' man.'
Raquel Welch, co-star in 'Lady In Cement': 'I think Frank is suspicious of most women. He thinks they only go for him because of who he is. That's why he likes Nancy, his first wife. She knew him when he was nothing, and he trusts her absolutely.'

*   *   *

CONTRACT ON CHERRY STREET (1977)

Frank Sinatra: 'I've been absent from films because of a lack of good scripts. We seem to have used up all the plots. We filmed "Cherry Street" entirely on location during two-and-a-half months of very hot weather in New York. In the old days we would have done it all on a Hollywood studio lot but you can't get away with that today. You just can't build a New York street that looks authentic enough . . . I'm 62 years old and I want to continue what I'm doing for a few years more. After that I'll quit before I become a bore. I'm dying to do a good comedy right now. But try and find one. I'd also like to do a musical movie but who's making those big musicals any more? I'll find something, though. I'll just keep reading things and talking to people.'

Filmography

1935

MAJOR BOWES' AMATEUR THEATRE OF THE AIR (Biograph Productions)
Produced & Directed by John H. Auer.
A short film featuring several of Major Bowes' acts—Frank appeared with an instrumental group 'blacked up' as a negro minstrel!

1941

LAS VEGAS NIGHTS (Paramount Pictures)
Produced by William LeBaron. Directed by Ralph Murphy. Screenplay by Ernest Pagano and Harry Clork.
With: Constance Moore, Bert Wheeler, Phil Regan, Lillian Cornell, Virginia Dale, Hank Ladd, Betty Brewer, Henry Kolker, Francetta Malloy and Tommy Dorsey and his Orchestra.
Frank appears briefly as the male soloist with the Dorsey Orchestra in this musical story of girls and gambling in Las Vegas. He sings one song, 'I'll Never Smile Again.'

1942

SHIP AHOY (MGM)
Produced by Jack Cummings. Directed by Edward Buzzell. Screenplay by Harry Clork.
With: Eleanor Powell, Red Skelton, Bert Lahr, Virginia O'Brien, William Post Jr., and Tommy Dorsey and his Orchestra.
A deadly plot by foreign agents is thwarted on board a floating nightclub in Puerto Rico. Frank is featured prominently as Dorsey's singer in the nightclub and he sings, 'The Last Call for Love', 'Poor You' and 'Moonlight Bay'.

1943

REVEILLE WITH BEVERLEY (Columbia Pictures)
Produced by Sam White. Directed by Charles Barton. Screenplay by Howard J. Green, Jack Henley and Albert Duffy.
With: Ann Miller, Dick Purcell, William Wright, Franklin Pangborn, Tim Ryan and Frank Sinatra.
Frank's first starring role as one of the featured acts which turns an early morning radio record show into a huge success when it switches from classical to popular songs. He sings 'Night and Day', the Cole Porter standard.

HIGHER AND HIGHER (RKO Radio Pictures)
Produced and Directed by Tim Whelan. Screenplay by Jay Dratler and Ralph Spence.
With: Michele Morgan, Jack Haley, Frank Sinatra, Leon Errol, Victor Borge, Barbara Hale, Mel Tormé, Dooley Wilson and Marcy McGuire.
Adapted from a Broadway musical about a group of servants plotting to restore their employer's fortune by marrying off the scullery maid to a wealthy husband. Frank, who is nearly lured into this plot, but finds true love in the end, sings 'You're On Your Own', 'I Couldn't Sleep a Wink Last Night', 'A Lovely Way to Spend an Evening', 'The Music Stopped' and 'I Saw You First'.

Frank in one of his earliest screen appearances in 'Ship Ahoy' (1942)

MUSIC AT WAR (The March of Time)
Produced by March of Time Inc in conjunction with US Navy.
During 1943 Frank was filmed singing 'The Song Is You' at Hunter College, New York, before an audience of WAVES to form a segment of this film. RKO Pictures objected ot his appearance in the picture, however, and the sequence was deleted before release.

1944
STEP LIVELY (RKO Radio Pictures)
Produced by Robert Fellows. Directed by Tim Whelan. Screenplay by Warren Duff and Peter Milne.
With: Frank Sinatra, Gloria Haven, George Murphy, Adolphe Menjou, Walter Slezak and Eugene Pallette.
Frank is a would-be playwright whose dreams of a Broadway hit are ruined by an unscrupulous producer—but instead he becomes an over-night success as a singer. Another prize is the lovely Gloria Haven to whom he gives his first screen kiss. With her he sings, 'Come Out, Come Out, Wherever You Are' and 'Some Other Time', as well as 'Where Does Love Begin' and 'As Long As There's Music' on his own.

THE ROAD TO VICTORY (Warner Bros.)
Produced by Jack L. Warner. Directed by LeRoy Prinz. Screenplay by James Bloodworth.
With: Frank Sinatra, Jack Carson, Bing Crosby, Cary Grant, James Lydon and Irene Manning.
A musical entertainment produced by Warner Bros for the U.S. Treasury Department War Activities Committee, in which Frank sings 'There'll Be A Hot Time In The Town Of Berlin' written by Joe Bushkin and John De Vries.

1945
ANCHORS AWEIGH (MGM)
Produced by Joe Pasternak. Directed by George Sidney. Screenplay by Isobel Lennart.
With: Frank Sinatra, Gene Kelly, Kathryn Grayson, Pamela Britton, Jose Iturbi, Rags Ragland and Edgar Kennedy.
The first pairing of Sinatra and Kelly on screen in a song and dance story about two sailors on leave in Hollywood who fall in love and, after the inevitable problems, live happily ever after. Frank sings with Gene 'We Hate To Leave', 'I Begged Her' and 'If You Knew Suzy', and on his own, 'Brahms' Lullaby', 'What Makes the Sunet?', 'The Charm of You', 'I Fall in Love Too Easily' and 'Tonight We Love'.

THE HOUSE I LIVE IN (RKO Radio Pictures)
Produced by Frank Ross. Directed by Mervyn LeRoy. Screenplay by Albert Maltz.
With: Frank Sinatra and a group of youngsters.
Frank's short film about racial intolerance in which he sings 'If You Are But A Dream' in a recording studio and then, while taking a break, lectures a group of boys persecuting another for his religion. He finishes by singing to them 'The House I Live In'.

THE ALL STAR BOND RALLY (Twentieth Century Fox)
Produced by Tony Fanchon. Directed by Michael Audley. Screenplay by Don Quinn.
With: Frank Sinatra, Harry James and his Orchestra, Bing Crosby, Vivian Blaine, Jeanne Crain, Linda Darnell, Betty Grable, Bob Hope, Harpo Marx and Carmen Miranda.
Another Treasury Department War Activities Committee film in which a host of stars convey the message to 'Buy, Buy, Buy a War Bond'. Frank sings 'Saturday Night' accompanied by Harry James.

SPECIAL CHRISTMAS TRAILER (MGM)
Produced by MGM Directed by Harry Loud.
With: Frank Sinatra.
A three minute trailer distributed by MGM during December 1945 in which Frank sings 'Silent Night, Holy Night'.

1946
TILL THE CLOUDS ROLL BY (MGM)
Produced by Arthur Freed. Directed by Richard Whorf. Screenplay by Myles Connolly and Jean Holloway.
With: June Allyson, Lucille Bremer, Judy Garland, Kathryn Grayson, Van Heflin, Lena Horne, Van Johnson, Angela Lansbury, Tony Martin, Virginia O'Brien, Dinah Shore, Robert Walker and Frank Sinatra.
Frank appears as a guest star in this retelling of the life and music of Jerome Kern set against the various backgrounds of his songs. He sings the Kern classic, 'Ol' Man River'.

1947
IT HAPPENED IN BROOKLYN (MGM)
Produced by Jack Cummings. Directed by Richard Whorf. Screenplay by Isobel Lennart.
With: Frank Sinatra, Kathryn Grayson, Peter Lawford, Jimmy Durante and Gloria Grahame.
The pairing of Frank and Peter Lawford as aspiring singer and songwriter in a story of New Yorkers readjusting after the war. Jimmy Durante provides the humour, Kathryn Grayson the love interest, and Frank sings 'I Believe' and 'The Song's Gotta Come From The Heart' (with Durante), 'La Ci Darem La Mano' (with Grayson) as well as 'The Brooklyn Bridge', 'Whose Baby Are You?', 'Time After Time' and 'It's The Same Old Dream'.

1948
THE MIRACLE OF THE BELLS (RKO Radio Pictures)
Produced by Jesse L. Lasky and Walter MacEwen. Directed by Irving Pichel. Screenplay by Ben Hecht

'It Happened In Brooklyn' (1947)

and Quentin Reynolds.
With: Frank Sinatra, Fred MacMurray, Alida Valli, Lee J. Cobb and Charles Meredith.
A straight dramatic role for Frank as the home town priest involved in the dilemma of whether or not to release a film in which a local girl, dying from tuberculosis, has a star part. He sings one song unaccompanied, 'Ever Homeward'.

THE KISSING BANDIT (MGM)
Produced by Joe Pasternak. Directed by Laslo Benedek. Screenplay by Isobel Lennart and John Briard Harding.
With: Frank Sinatra, Kathryn Grayson, J. Carrol Naish, Mildred Natwick, Billy Gilbert, Ricardo Montalban, Ann Miller and Cyd Charisse.
A colourful musical about a young man drawn into the dashing role of a romantic bandit in California in the 1830s. Frank sings 'Senorita' with Kathryn Grayson, and 'What's Wrong With Me?', 'If I Steal A Kiss' and 'Siesta'.

LUCKY STRIKE SALESMAN'S MOVIE (American Tobacco Co)
Produced by The American Tobacco Co.
A ten-minute promotional film showing tobacco in transition from the growing stage to going on sale. Frank sings 'Embraceable You' with the Hit Parade Orchestra conducted by Axel Stordahl.

1949
TAKE ME OUT TO THE BALL GAME (MGM)
Produced by Arthur Freed. Directed by Busby Berkeley. Screenplay by Harry Tugent and George Wells.
With: Frank Sinatra, Gene Kelly, Esther Williams, Betty Garrett, Edward Arnold, Jules Munshin and Richard Lane.
Sinatra and Kelly feature as a song-and-dance partnership who double as baseball players during the season and help the beautiful new female owner of the team to thwart attempts to wreck it. The two men sing 'Take Me Out To The Ball Game', 'Yes, Indeedy', 'O'Brien To Ryan To

Goldberg' and 'Strictly U.S.A.' as well as 'She's The Right Girl For Me' and 'It's Fate, Baby, It's Fate' with Betty Garrett. Another tune, 'Boys and Girls Like You and Me' was deleted from the finished film.*

ON THE TOWN (MGM)
Produced by Arthur Freed. Directed by Gene Kelly and Stanley Donen. Screenplay by Adolph Green and Betty Comden.
With: Frank Sinatra, Gene Kelly, Betty Garrett, Ann Miller, Jules Munshin and Vera-Ellen.
Three sailors on the loose for 24 hours in New York see the sights and meet three girls with whom they fall in love. Frank sings with Gene Kelly in 'New York, New York', 'Prehistoric Man' and 'On The Town', and with Betty Garrett in 'Come Up To My Place', 'You're Awful' and 'Count On Me'.

1951
DOUBLE DYNAMITE (RKO Radio Pictures)
Produced by Irving Cummings Jr. Directed by Irving Cummings Sr. Screenplay by Melville Shavelson.
With: Frank Sinatra, Jane Russell, Groucho Marx, Don McGuire and Howard Freeman.
A lucky win on the horses seems likely to give Frank and Jane Russell, as a couple of bank employees, the finance to get married. Then Jane is accused of embezzlement—but with the help of their friend, Groucho Marx, they are able to set matters straight and finally marry. Frank sings 'Kisses and Tears' with Jane Russell and 'It's Only Money' with Groucho Marx.

MEET DANNY WILSON (Universal-International)
Produced by Leonard Goldstein. Directed by Joseph Pevney. Screenplay by Don McGuire.
With: Frank Sinatra, Shelley Winters, Alex Nicol, Raymond Burr, Tommy Farrell and Tony Curtis.
Frank plays a struggling young singer who suddenly makes it big on the night club circuit, only to find he is in the clutches of a racketeer. Helped by the love of Shelley Winters he finally breaks free, but at the cost of a close friend's life. Frank sings 'A Good Man Is Hard To Find' with Shelley Winters, along with 'You're A Sweetheart', 'Lonesome Man Blues', 'She's Funny That Way', 'That Old Black Magic', 'When You're Smiling', 'All Of Me', 'I've Got A Crush On You' and 'How Deep Is The Ocean?'.

1953
FROM HERE TO ETERNITY (Columbia Pictures)
Produced by Buddy Adler. Directed by Fred Zinnemann. Screenplay by Daniel Taradash.
With: Burt Lancaster, Montgomery Clift, Deborah Kerr, Donna Reed, Ernest Borgnine, Frank Sinatra, Merle Travis and Philip Ober.
Frank's magnificent portrayal of Private Angelo Maggio in this story of Army life on Honolulu just prior to the Japanese attack on Pearl Harbour in 1941, won him an

Oscar and established him as a dramatic actor of great range. The film itself won eight Oscars in the 1953 Academy Awards.

1954

SUDDENLY (United Artists)
Produced by Robert Bassler. Directed by Lewis Allen. Screenplay by Richard Sale.
With: Frank Sinatra, Sterling Hayden, James Gleason, Nancy Gates and Willis Bouchey.
John Baron—played by Sinatra—is a nobody who wants to find a place in history by killing the President of the United States. Holding a family hostage to further his plan, he is at the centre of a whirlpool of human emotions and taut drama as the police remorselessly close in.

FINIAN'S RAINBOW (Distributors Corporation)
Produced and Directed by John Hubley.
With: Frank Sinatra, Ella Logan, Barry Fitzgerald, Ella Fitzgerald, Louis Armstrong and Jim Backus.
This was to be a full-length animated cartoon film of the famous Irish story, featuring the voices of various stars including Frank. Although the songs for the film were recorded, it had to be abandoned before the animation work commenced. Frank sang 'If This Isn't Love' and 'Old Devil Moon' with Ella Logan, 'Ad Lib Blues' with Louis Armstrong, 'Necessity' with Ella Fitzgerald and as a solo, and 'Great Come And Get It Day' as a solo.

1955

YOUNG AT HEART (Warner Bros.)
Produced by Henry Blanke. Directed by Gordon Douglas. Screenplay by Liam O'Brien.
With: Frank Sinatra, Doris Day, Gig Young, Ethel Barrymore, Dorothy Malone and Robert Keith.
Frank plays a moody and frustrated pianist involved in the staging of a musical comedy, who slowly comes to realise that love is the answer to his problems—in the delightful form of Doris Day. Frank duets with her on 'You My Love' and also sings solo, 'Young At Heart', 'Someone To Watch Over Me', 'Just One Of Those Things' and 'One For My Baby'.

NOT AS A STRANGER (United Artists)
Produced and directed by Stanley Kramer. Screenplay by Edna and Edward Anhalt.
With: Robert Mitchum, Olivia De Havilland, Frank Sinatra, Gloria Grahame, Broderick Crawford, Charles Bickford, Lon Chaney, Lee Marvin and Virginia Christine.
A drama of hospital life in which Frank plays a cynical young doctor observing the problems suffered by Robert Mitchum as a surgeon torn between his wife, a younger woman and the demands of his profession.

THE TENDER TRAP (MGM)
Produced by Lawrence Weingarten. Directed by Charles Walters. Screenplay by Julius J. Epstein.
With: Frank Sinatra, Debbie Reynolds, David Wayne,

Celeste Holm, Jarma Lewis, Lola Albright, Carolyn Jones and Howard St. John.
Frank stars as Charlie Reader, a theatrical agent with an eye for the girls, whose views on love and marriage are rudely shattered when he finds himself falling in love with the young and winsome Debbie Reynolds. He confesses to his dilemma in the James Van Heusen and Sammy Cahn song '(Love Is) The Tender Trap'.

GUYS AND DOLLS (MGM)
Produced by Samuel Goldwyn. Directed by Joseph L. Mankiewicz. Screenplay by Joseph L. Mankiewicz.
With: Marlon Brando, Jean Simmons, Frank Sinatra, Vivian Blaine, Stubby Kaye, Johnny Silver, Robert Keith and B. S. Pully.
Frank is Nathan Detroit, organiser of crap games, trying to find a safe place for his gamblers to play and win a bet with big-time gambler, Marlon Brando, that he can't seduce the demure Jean Simmons. This lavish and colourful musical has Frank singing 'Adelaide', 'Sue Me' with Vivian Blaine, and 'The Oldest Established Permanent Floating Crap Game In New York' and 'Guys And Dolls', both with Stubby Kaye and Johnny Silver.

THE MAN WITH THE GOLDEN ARM (United Artists)
Produced and directed by Otto Preminger. Screenplay by Walter Newman and Lewis Meltzer.
With: Frank Sinatra, Eleanor Parker, Kim Novak, Arnold Stang, Darren McGavin and Shelly Manne.
Frankie Machine, card-sharper, would-be drummer and drug addict, tries to build himself a new life against the background of underworld Chicago with drug pushers on one side and the developing love of Kim Novak on the other. Frank gives a powerful performance which received an Academy Award nomination. His song, 'The Man With The Golden Arm' was deleted from the film when it was released.

1956

MEET ME IN LAS VEGAS (MGM)
Produced by Joe Pasternak. Directed by Roy Rowland. Screenplay by Isobel Lennart.
With: Dan Dailey, Cyd Charisse, Jerry Colonna and Paul Henreid, with guest star, Frank Sinatra.
Frank appears briefly in one scene in this story of gambling in Las Vegas. He is seen playing a fruit machine in the Sands Hotel.

JOHNNY CONCHO (United Artists)
Produced by Frank Sinatra. Directed by Don McGuire. Screenplay by David P. Harmon and Don McGuire.
With: Frank Sinatra, Keenan Wynn, William Conrad, Phyllis Kirk and Wallace Ford.
Frank made his debut as a producer on this film in which he starred as a Western gunman forced almost against his will to step into the shoes of his murdered brother and rid an Arizona town of the two gunslingers who are terrorising the community.

HIGH SOCIETY (MGM)
Produced by Sol C. Siegel. Directed by Charles Walters. Screenplay by John Patrick.
With: Bing Crosby, Grace Kelly, Frank Sinatra, Celeste Holm, John Lund, Louis Calhern, Sidney Blackmeir and Louis Armstrong.
Frank plays a charming but pushy young reporter covering a society wedding in this lush, musical extravaganza. Grace Kelly is the bride-to-be, and Bing Crosby her former husband, who attends the gathering with thoughts of winning her back. Frank's songs, all by Cole Porter, are 'Who Wants To Be A Millionaire?', 'You're Sensational', Well, Did You Evah?' and 'Mind If I Make Love To You?'.

AROUND THE WORLD IN EIGHTY DAYS (United Artists)
Produced by Michael Todd. Directed by Michael Anderson. Screenplay by James Poe, John Farrow and S. J. Perelman.
With: David Niven, Cantinflas, Shirley McLaine, Robert Newton, and a host of guest stars including Frank Sinatra.
Based on Jules Verne's classic novel of global adventure, Frank only has a cameo part as a piano player in a Barbary Coast saloon—nonetheless making one of the most impressive entrances when he swivels round on his stool to face the camera.
1957

THE PRIDE AND THE PASSION (United Artists)
Produced and directed by Stanley Kramer. Screenplay by Edna and Edward Anhalt.
With: Cary Grant, Frank Sinatra, Sophia Loren and Theodore Bikel.
A blood and guts drama with Frank starring as a Spanish guerrillero leading a group of men who haul a massive gun across Spain during the Peninsular Wars. This piece of weaponry enables them to raise a siege around a French-occupied fort and ultimately achieve a famous victory.

THE JOKER IS WILD (Paramount Pictures)
Produced by Samuel J. Briskin. Directed by Charles Vidor. Screenplay by Oscar Saul.
With: Frank Sinatra, Mitzi Gaynor, Jeanne Crain, Eddie Albert, Beverly Garland, Jackie Coogan and Sophie Tucker.

The real-life story of Joe E. Lewis, a night club singer whose career is ruined by gangsters, but then climbs back to success as one of America's great comics, beating a drink problem along the way. Frank sings 'At Sundown', 'I Cried For You', 'If I Could Be With You', 'All The Way', as well as 'Chicago' which was deleted from the film before release, and parodies of 'Out Of Nowhere', 'Swingin' On A Star', 'All The Way' and 'Martha, Martha'.

PAL JOEY (Columbia Pictures)
Produced by Fred Kohlmar, Directed by George Sidney. Screenplay by Dorothy Kingsley.
With: Frank Sinatra, Rita Hayworth, Kim Novak, Barbara Nichols and Hank Henry.
One of Frank's most famous screen roles as Joey Evans, the 'gilt-edged heel' who messes up his own life and those around him—women in particular. The film is vibrant and colourful and has the outstanding Rodgers and Hart tunes which Frank sings: 'I Didn't Know What Time It Was', 'There's A Small Hotel', 'The Lady Is A Tramp', 'Bewitched, Bothered and Bewildered', 'What Do I Care For A Dame?' and his duet with Kim Novak whose voice was dubbed by Trudy Erwin, 'I Could Write A Book'.
1958

KINGS GO FORTH (United Artists)
Produced by Frank Ross. Directed by Delmer Daves. Screenplay by Merle Miller.
With: Frank Sinatra, Tony Curtis, Natalie Wood, Leora Dana and Karl Swenson.
A complex role for Frank in a taboo-breaking picture about the love of an American soldier and a girl of mixed blood. Tony Curtis as the catalyst of the story heightens the drama which is only resolved by his death.

SOME CAME RUNNING (MGM)
Produced by Sol C. Siegel. Directed by Vincent Minelli. Screenplay by John Patrick and Arthur Sheekman.
With: Frank Sinatra, Dean Martin, Shirley MacLaine, Martha Hyer, Arthur Kennedy, Nancy Gates and Leora Dana.
Fresh out of the Army and struggling to establish himself as a writer, Frank has to try and adjust to life in his home town. His love life is also complicated by the coldness of Martha Hyer and the adoration of Shirley MacLaine—

Frank with Groucho Marx in 'Double Dynamite' (1951).

As a piano player in 'Around the World in Eighty Days' (1956).

Frank and chorus line in 'Pal Joey' (1957).

With Peter Lawford and Dean Martin in '4 for Texas' (1964).

Frank with Sammy Davis Jr., in 'Robin and the Seven Hoods' (1964).

A bearded Frank in 'Never So Few' (1959).

and all the time tragedy stalks him to the end of the picture.

1959

A HOLE IN THE HEAD (United Artists)

Produced and directed by Frank Capra. Screenplay by Arnold Schulman.

With: Frank Sinatra, Edward G. Robinson, Eleanor Parker, Carolyn Jones, Thelma Ritter and Keenan Wynn.

A film about the machinations of a Florida hotel owner, played by Frank, to raise enough money to stay in business. Edward G. Robinson is his wealthy older brother who promises him assistance, but with strings attached. Ultimately he relents, falling prey to the lotus life of Miami and provides all the cash that is needed. Frank sings two songs, 'All My Tomorrows' and 'High Hopes'.

NEVER SO FEW (MGM)

Produced by Edmund Grainger. Directed by John Sturges. Screenplay by Millard Kaufman.

With: Frank Sinatra, Gina Lollobrigida, Peter Lawford, Steve McQueen, Richard Johnson, Paul Henreid, Brian Donlevy, Dean Jones and Charles Bronson.

Another war film, set in Burma, Frank plays the leader of a mixed band of G.I.'s and guerrillas fighting the Japanese. He experiences corruption among the local people, division among the American commanders, and a forlorn love affair with Gina Lollobrigida.

INVITATION TO MONTE CARLO (Valiant Films)

Produced, directed and written by Euan Lloyd.

With: Germaine Damar, Gilda Emmanueli, Prince Rainier of Monaco, Princess Grace of Monaco, Frank Sinatra.

A travel film to promote Monaco in which Frank makes a brief appearance in a sequence which takes place on the French Riviera.

1960

CAN-CAN (Twentieth Century Fox)

Produced by Jack Cummings. Directed by Walter Lang. Screenplay by Dorothy Kingsley and Charles Lederer.

With: Frank Sinatra, Shirley MacLaine, Maurice Chevalier, Louis Jourdan, Juliet Prowse and Marcel Dalio.

Lively and colourful movie about old Paris and the efforts of lawyer François Durnais (Sinatra) to prevent a group of dancers being imprisoned for dancing the Can-Can which has been declared illegal. Frank's excellent songs, all by Cole Porter, are 'Montmartre' and 'I Love Paris' with Maurice Chevalier, 'C'est Magnifique', 'Let's Do It' both with Shirley MacLaine, and 'It's All Right With Me' with Louis Jourdan.

OCEANS ELEVEN (Warner Bros.)
Produced and directed by Lewis Milestone. Screenplay by Harry Brown and Charles Lederer.
With: Frank Sinatra, Dean Martin, Sammy Davis Jr., Peter Lawford, Angie Dickinson, Richard Conte, Cesar Romero, Patrice Wymore, Joey Bishop, Akim Tamiroff and Henry Silva.
First of the so-called 'Clan Movies' in which Frank and friends play a group of ex-Army veterans who get together to rob five gambling casinos in Las Vegas of millions of dollars. Despite a masterfully successful operation, the money all goes up in flames in the end! The Van Heusen and Cahn team wrote the two songs, 'Ain't That A Kick In The Head' and 'Eee-O Eleven'.

PEPE (Columbia Pictures)
Produced and directed by George Sidney. Screenplay by Dorothy Kingsley and Claude Binyon.
With: Cantinflas, Dan Dailey, Shirley Jones and numerous guest stars including Frank Sinatra.
Frank has a small cameo role in Las Vegas where he teaches the star, Cantinflas, how to gamble in order to win enough money to buy the white horse he has set his heart upon and which he is pursuing with its owner across America.

1961
THE DEVIL AT FOUR O'CLOCK (Columbia Pictures)
Produced by Fred Kohlmar. Directed by Mervyn LeRoy. Screenplay by Liam O'Brien.
With: Spencer Tracy, Frank Sinatra, Kerwin Mathews, Jean Pierre Aumont and Barbara Luna.
Frank is one of three convicts who help Father Doonan (Spencer Tracy) when a volcano erupts and threatens to destroy a tiny island. Responding in what seems like a contrary way to their characters, the men rescue a party of children, and see them safely off the island before the final cataclysm.

1962
SERGEANTS 3 (United Artists)
Produced by Frank Sinatra. Directed by John Sturges. Screenplay by W. R. Burnett.
With: Frank Sinatra, Dean Martin, Sammy Davis Jr., Peter Lawford, Joey Bishop, Henry Silva, Ruta Lee, Buddy Lester and Hank Henry.
Frank, Dean and Peter as the three Cavalry men of the title who track down a fanatical tribe of Sioux Indians and then by a mixture of bravery and luck manage to prevent a massacre.

THE ROAD TO HONG KONG (United Artists)
Produced by Melvin Frank. Directed by Norman Panama. Screenplay by Norman Panama and Melvin Frank.
With: Bing Crosby, Bob Hope, Joan Collins, Dorothy Lamour, Robert Morley and guest stars Frank Sinatra and Dean Martin.
Crosby and Hope's 'Interplanetary Fly-It-Yourself Space Kit' transports them from the Far East to a planet called Plutonius where they come across two spacemen played by Frank and Dean.

THE MANCHURIAN CANDIDATE (United Artists)
Produced by George Axelrod and John Frankenheimer. Directed by John Frankenheimer. Screenplay by George Axelrod.
With: Frank Sinatra, Laurence Harvey, Janet Leigh, Angela Lansbury, Henry Silva, James Gregory and Leslie Parrish.
A tense drama in which Frank plays a major in American Army Intelligence on the track of a Communist 'sleeper' agent who has been programmed to kill a presidential nominee. Again the picture demonstrated Frank's skill in a dramatic role playing opposite the accomplished actor Laurence Harvey.

SINATRA IN ISRAEL (Israeli Federation of Histadruth)
Produced by the Israeli Federation of Histadruth.
A short film made during Frank's visit to Israel, which he narrates, and in which he also sings two songs, 'In The Still Of The Night' and 'Without A Song'.

1963
COME BLOW YOUR HORN (Paramount Pictures)
Produced by Norman Lear and Bud Yorkin. Directed by Bud Yorkin. Screenplay by Norman Lear.
With: Frank Sinatra, Lee J. Cobb, Molly Picon, Barbara Rush, Jill St. John, Tony Bill, Dan Blocker and Dean Martin.
Playing a New York man-about-town, Frank introduces his young brother to the delights of big city life, only to have the younger man take his girls, upset his peace of mind and generally ruin his normal style of life. Frank finds a solution by marrying, settling down and bequeathing his bachelor pad to his delighted brother! The title song, which Frank sings, is another Van Heusen and Cahn tune.

THE LIST OF ADRIAN MESSENGER (Universal Pictures)
Produced by Edward Lewis. Directed by John Huston. Screenplay by Anthony Veiller.
With: George C. Scott, Dana Wynter, Clive Brook, Gladys Cooper, Herbert Marshall, and various guest stars including Frank Sinatra.
Frank appears as a Gypsy stableman in this murder mystery concerning the strange deaths of a group of people

on a list. He and the five other well-known guest stars all unmask to reveal their identities at the end of the film.

1964

4 FOR TEXAS (Warner Bros.)
Produced and directed by Robert Aldrich. Screenplay by Teddi Sherman and Robert Aldrich.
With: Frank Sinatra, Dean Martin, Anita Ekberg, Ursula Andress, Charles Bronson, Victor Buono and The Three Stooges.
Another Western romp in 'The Clan' series with Frank and Dean initially falling out after having survived a bandit attack, but ultimately coming together to outwit the mastermind behind local crime.

ROBIN AND THE SEVEN HOODS (Warner Bros.)
Produced by Frank Sinatra. Directed by Gordon Douglas. Screenplay by David R. Schwartz.
With: Frank Sinatra, Dean Martin, Sammy Davis Jr., Peter Falk, Barbara Rush, Victor Buona, Hank Henry and Bing Crosby.
The Robin Hood story transposed into the Chicago underworld of 1928 with Frank as Robbo, the leader of one gang, opposing the intrusion of another, Guy Gisborne. The only winners, however, are Barbara Rush as Marian and Bing Crosby as Allen A. Dale who organise a women's reform movement and put the gangsters to flight. Frank sings 'My Kind Of Town' and three songs with Bing Crosby and Dean Martin, 'Style', 'Mister Booze' and 'Don't Be A Do-Badder'. Another tune by Frank, 'I Like To Lead When I Dance' was deleted from the finished film.

1965

NONE BUT THE BRAVE (Warner Bros.)
Produced and directed by Frank Sinatra. Screenplay by John Twist and Katsuya Susaki.
With: Frank Sinatra, Clint Walker, Tommy Sands, Brad Dexter, Tony Bill and Tasuya Mihashi.
Frank took on the task of producing and directing as well as starring in this picture about American and Japanese soldiers on a small Pacific island far away from the main action of the war. An uneasy truce between the two groups seems to be on the verge of becoming something more concrete until the appearance of an American destroyer re-opens hostilities with devastating effects on both sides.

VON RYAN'S EXPRESS (Twentieth Century Fox)
Produced by Saul David. Directed by Mark Robson. Screenplay by Wendell Mayes and Joseph Landon.
With: Frank Sinatra, Trevor Howard, Raffaella Carra, Brad Dexter, Sergio Fantoni, John Leyland, Edward Mulhare and Wolfgang Preiss.
An unusual war story of an American Colonel, played by Frank, who leads the escape of a group of prisoners from an Italian P.O.W. Camp, hi-jacking a German train to reach Switzerland. Von Ryan himself meets a spectacular death within an ace of success.

MARRIAGE ON THE ROCKS (Warner Bros.)
Produced by William H. Daniels. Directed by Jack Donohue. Screenplay by Cy Howard.
With: Frank Sinatra, Deborah Kerr, Dean Martin, Cesar Romero, Hermione Baddeley, Tony Bill, John McGiver and Nancy Sinatra.
Frank plays an advertising executive whose comfortable existence is suddenly turned upside-down when his wife of 19 years (Deborah Kerr) tells him she wants a divorce. The situation is further complicated when they are inadvertently but actually divorced while trying to repair their marriage on holiday in Mexico! But all ends happily after a helter-skelter of comic incidents.

WILL ROGERS HOSPITAL TRAILER (Will Rogers Teaching Institute)
Produced by Will Rogers Hospital.
In this short film, Frank narrates an appeal on behalf of the Will Rogers Memorial Fund, conducting the cameras through the hospital, research laboratories and the teaching institute at Saranac Lake, New York.

1966

CAST A GIANT SHADOW (United Artists)
Produced and directed by Melville Shavelson. Screenplay by Melville Shavelson.
With: Kirk Douglas, Senta Berger, Angie Dickinson, James Donald, Garry Merrill, Haym Topol and guest stars, Yul Brynner, John Wayne and Frank Sinatra.
A dramatic story about the formation of the State of Israel in 1949, with the British on the verge of withdrawing from Palestine and the Arabs hostile to the new nation. Frank plays a pilot of fortune who aids in the struggle by dropping seltzer bottles on Arab strongholds when the bombs run out!

THE OSCAR (Embassy Pictures)
Produced by Clarence Greene. Directed by Russell Rouse. Screenplay by Harlan Ellison, Russell Rouse and Clarence Greene.
With: Stephen Boyd, Elke Sommer, Milton Berle, Eleanor Parker, Joseph Cotton, Jill St. John, Tony Bennett, Edie Adams, Ernest Borgnine, Peter Lawford, Nancy Sinatra and Frank Sinatra.
Frank appears as himself at the climax of this film accepting an Oscar Award in Hollywood. The movie deals with the ruthless career of an actor named Frank Fane (Stephen Boyd) who is convinced he is on the verge of winning the coveted Oscar—only to see it snatched away at the crucial moment by . . . Frank Sinatra.

ASSAULT ON A QUEEN (Paramount Pictures)
Produced by William Goetz. Directed by Jack Donohue. Screenplay by Rod Serling.
With: Frank Sinatra, Virna Lisi, Tony Franciosa, Richard Conte, Alf Kjellin and Errol John.
An audacious plan to hi-jack the 'Queen Mary' using a former U-Boat submarine seems on the verge of success

until the raiders are spotted by a Coast Guard cutter. In a dramatic climax only Frank, as the leader of the raiders, and the beautiful Virna Lisi escape to dream of what might have been. . . .

1967

THE NAKED RUNNER (Warner Bros.)
Produced by Brad Dexter. Directed by Sidney J. Furie. Screenplay by Stanley Mann.
With: Frank Sinatra, Peter Vaughan, Derren Nesbitt, Nadia Gray and Toby Robins.
Frank, an American businessman, is lured into a plot to kill a defecting British spy by a former wartime colleague. But like so many espionage stories, there is twist and turn in the plot, and however unwilling Frank is to perform his mission, events conspire to give him no option but to carry out the shooting.

TONY ROME (Twentieth Century Fox)
Produced by Aaron Rosenberg. Directed by Gordon Douglas. Screenplay by Richard L. Breen.
With: Frank Sinatra, Jill St. John, Richard Conte, Gena Rowlands, Simon Oakland, Rocky Graziano and Sue Lyon.
Playing a smooth Miami private detective called Tony Rome, Frank becomes involved in diamonds, death and beautiful women in a struggle for a vast family fortune. Daughter Nancy sings the title song.

1968

THE DETECTIVE (Twentieth Century Fox)
Produced by Aaron Rosenberg. Directed by Gordon Douglas. Screenplay by Abby Mann.
With: Frank Sinatra, Lee Remick, Ralph Meeker, Jack Klugman, Horace McMahon, Tony Musante and Robert Duvall.
Superior performance by Frank as a dedicated New York detective on the track of a brutal murderer. Events begin to overwhelm him both at home—where his wife, Lee Remick, has become a nymphomaniac—and on the case where events lead him to have the wrong man executed for the crime. He is compelled to leave the Force to which he has given his life, and is at a loss as to how to rebuild his shattered world.

LADY IN CEMENT (Twentieth Century Fox)
Produced by Aaron Rosenberg. Directed by Gordon Douglas. Screenplay by Marvin H. Albert and Jack Guss.
With: Frank Sinatra, Raquel Welch, Dan Blocker, Richard Conte, Martin Gabel and Pat Henry.
The second Tony Rome movie, which sees Frank looking for buried treasure off the coast of Florida and instead finding the dead body of a naked girl—the 'lady in cement'. The solution to the mystery makes for a fast-paced and exciting picture.

1970

DIRTY DINGUS MAGEE (MGM)
Produced and directed by Burt Kennedy. Screenplay by Tom and Frank Waldman and Joseph Heller.
With: Frank Sinatra, George Kennedy, Anne Jackson, Lois Nettleton and Jack Elam.
Frank goes West as a shifty and unscrupulous robber. His yen for money and beautiful girls is matched only by his ability to keep one step ahead of law and retribution.

1974

THAT'S ENTERTAINMENT (MGM)
Produced by MGM. Directed by Jack Haley Jr. Screenplay by Bud Friedgen and David E. Blewitt.
In this montage film, Frank is represented by extracts from five of his films, 'Take Me Out To The Ball Game', 'On The Town', 'Anchors Aweigh', 'High Society' and 'It Happened In Brooklyn'. In the last sequence he appears singing a duet with Jimmy Durante, 'The Song's Gotta Come From The Heart'.

1976

THAT'S ENTERTAINMENT PART 2 (MGM)
Produced by MGM. Directed by Gene Kelly. Screenplay by Bud Friedgen and David E. Blewitt.
A follow-up to the earlier successful montage film. In this picture Frank is represented by extracts from 'The Tender Trap', 'Till The Clouds Roll By', 'Anchors Aweigh', 'It Happened In Brooklyn' and 'High Society'.

1977

CONTRACT ON CHERRY STREET (Artanis/Columbia Pictures)
Produced and Directed by William A. Graham. Screenplay by Edward Anhalt.
With: Frank Sinatra, Martin Balsam, Jay Black, Verna Bloom, Martin Gabel, Harry Guardino, Henry Silva.
Another film of police life (this one made specially for television) in which Frank stars as Detective Frank Hovannes, a tough New York cop involved in crime and brutality in the city's Little Italy district.

1980

THE FIRST DEADLY SIN (Filmways Pictures)
Produced by George Pappas and Mark Shanker. Directed by Brian Hutton. Screenplay by Lawrence Sanders.
With: Frank Sinatra, Faye Dunaway, David Duckes, Brenda Vaccaro, Martin Gabel, Anthony Zerbe and James Whitmore.
Frank acted as executive producer on this his latest film and once more starred as a veteran police officer, Sergeant Edward Delaney. Delaney embroils himself in cracking a series of seemingly meaningless psychotic killings, while at home his wife is slowly dying from a mysterious illness.

The Sinatra Sessions

A Complete Listing of All his Recording Sessions,
1939–1982

By Ed O'Brien & Scott P. Sayers Jr.
(The Sinatra Society of America)

FOREWORD

Frank Sinatra holds the record for the longest span between Top 40 hits on the Billboard charts, first appearing with the Tommy Dorsey Orchestra in 1940 with 'I'll Never Smile Again' and recently appearing 40 years later with 'Theme from New York, New York.' The longevity and productivity of the Sinatra career in both the concert arena and in the recording studio are unmatched.

We believe this listing to be the most accurate and complete account of the Sinatra recording career. It is not intended to be a discography, but simply a chronological listing of all Sinatra recording sessions with a listing of the best source(s) available for each song.

We have not included listings of underground records. By their very nature they tend to be ephemeral. Therefore, if a recording is available only in pirate form, we have listed it as never released. We have, as often as possible, listed each recording as follows; initial release/45/album. We have listed a foreign album as a source only when it is the only album available with the song.

Not one, two or even ten Sinatra collectors have all of the information on the Sinatra recording career. The data seems to be unlimited. For example, Reprise has recorded Sinatra in concert many times with plans to release the material on albums: at the Kennedy Inauguration in 1961, several times at the Sands in the early 60s, and in April, 1974 at Carnegie Hall. Unfortunately, none of these tapes was ever numbered, mastered, or pressed for release, and therefore we have not included them in our listing. On occasion, Frank Sinatra has planned and rehearsed songs in the studio only to decide against recording them. During the recent 'Trilogy' sessions Mr Sinatra rehearsed and taped one run-through of 'Surrey With The Fringe On Top' with Billy May, but they decided against mastering the song. Our point is that no book can list every achievement in his entire career. We have simply listed the songs that Frank Sinatra is known to have recorded between 1939 and 1982.

Our research tools have included studio worksheets, recording session material, interviews with musicians, and the invaluable help of Sinatra archivists Ric Ross, John Brady, Stan Cooper, and Richard Warrick. We sincerely hope that our effort will accurately document the outstanding career of the performer who has dominated popular music for over 40 years.

Scott Sayers Jr.
Ed O'Brien

GUIDE TO ABBREVIATIONS

Col . . . . Columbia album	N/R . . . . never released
Cap . . . . Capitol album	P2M . . . . Columbia House, special order LP
E.P. . . . . extended play	Rep . . . . Reprise album
HL . . . . Harmomy album	S/D . . . . Sinatra/Dorsey
HS . . . . Harmony stereo album	WB . . . . Warner Brothers

In our listings we have indicated the arranger for a session or group of sessions only once. When there is a change in arrangers, we then note that change. Also, unless indicated otherwise, the arranger also does the conducting.

In the Dorsey section we have not indicated the arranger when it was a basic band arrangement done 'in-house' or by Dorsey. There is no arranger for certain 1943 sessions because of the musicians' strike.

We have not listed sessions where there was not a Sinatra vocal, but only orchestral tracks put down.

THE BEGINNING 1939–1942

New York City   **February 3, 1939**
Demo Disc   Our Love   Time 2:05 N/R

FRANK SINATRA AND HARRY JAMES

New York City   **July 13, 1939**
             Arrangements by Andy Gibson
B25057-1   From The Bottom Of My   Brunswick 8443
             Heart   Col. 2739 alt. take
B25059-1   Melancholy Mood   Brunswick 8443
                                        Col. 2739

New York City   **August 17, 1939**
             Arrangements by Andy Gibson
B25212-2   My Buddy   Columbia 35242,
                                        37520 Col. 2739
B25215-1   It's Funny To Everyone   Columbia 35209,
             But Me   36738 HL 7159

New York City   **August 31, 1939**
             Arrangements by Andy Gibson
B25285-1   Here Comes The Night   Columbia 35227
                                        Col. 2739
B25288-1   All Or Nothing At All   Columbia 35587
                                        Col. 1130

Chicago   **October 13, 1939**
             Arrangements by Andy Gibson
WC2798-1   On A Little Street In   Columbia 35261,
             Singapore   36700 HL 7159
WC2799-1   Who Told You I Cared   Columbia 35261
                                        P2M 5267

Hollywood   **November 8, 1939**
             Arrangements by Andy Gibson
LA2046-1   Ciribiribin   Columbia 35316,
                                        37141 Col. 1130
LA2047-1   Every Day Of My Life   Columbia 35531,
                                        36700

FRANK SINATRA AND TOMMY
DORSEY

Chicago   **February 1, 1940**
BS044780-1   The Sky Fell Down   Victor 26518
             Arranged by   SD 1000
             Axel Stordahl
BS044682-1   Too Romantic   Victor 26500
                                        SD 1000

New York City   **February 26, 1940**
BS047706-1   Shake Down The Stars   Victor 26525
                                        SD 1000
BS047707-1   Moments In The Moonlight   Victor 26525
                                        SD 1000
BS047708-1   I'll Be Seeing You   Victor 26539
                                        SD 1000

New York City   **March 4, 1940**
BS047746-1   Say It   Victor 26535
                                        SD 1000

BS047747-1   Polka Dots And   Victor 26539
             Moonbeams   SD 1000
             Arranged by Axel
             Stordahl

New York City   **March 12, 1940**
BS048129-1   The Fable Of The Rose   Victor 26555
             Arranged by Axel   SD 1000
             Stordahl
BS048130-1   This Is The Beginning Of   Victor 26555
             The End   SD 1000

New York City   **March 25, 1940**
BS048430-2   Imagination   N/R
BS048431-2   Yours Is My Heart Alone   N/R

New York City   **March 29, 1940**
BS048479-1   Hear My Song Violetta   Victor 26616
                                        SD 1000 alt. take
BS048480-1   Fools Rush In   Victor 26593
                                        SD 1000
BS048481-1   Devil May Care   Victor 26593
                                        SD 1000

New York City   **April 10, 1940**
BS048758-1   April Played The Fiddle   Victor 26606
                                        SD 1000
BS048766-1   I Haven't Time To Be   Victor 26606
             A Millionaire   SD 1000
BS048430-3   Imagination   Victor 26581
                                        SD 1000
BS048431-3   Yours Is My Heart Alone   Victor 26616
                                        SD 1000

New York City   **April 23, 1940**
BS048938-1   You're Lonely And I'm   Victor 26596
             Lonely   SD 1000
             (The Dorsey
             Sentimentalists)
BS048939-1   East Of The Sun   Bluebird 10726
             Arranged by Sy Oliver   SD 1000
             W/Band Chorus
BS048940-1   Head On My Pillow   Bluebird 10726
                                        SD 1000
BS048941-1   It's A Lovely Day   Victor 26596
             Tomorrow   SD 1000
BS048942-3   I'll Never Smile Again   N/R
             Arranged by Fred Stulce
             W/The Pied Pipers

New York City   **May 23, 1940**
BS048942-4   I'll Never Smile Again   Victor 26628,
             Arranged by Fred Stulce   27521
             W/The Pied Pipers   SD 1000
BS050852-1   All This And Heaven Too   Victor 26653
                                        SD 1000
BS050853-1   Where Do You Keep Your   Victor 26653
             Heart?   SD 1000

New York City   **June 13, 1940**
BS051279-1   Whispering   Bluebird 10771
             W/The Pied Pipers   Victor 20-1597
                                        SD 1000

New York City   **June 27, 1940**
BS051579-1   Trade Winds   Victor 26660
                                        SD 1000
BS051581-1   The One I Love   Victor 26660
             Arranged by Sy Oliver   SD 1000
             W/The Pied Pipers

New York City   **July 17, 1940**

BS051874-1	The Call Of The Canyon	Victor 26678 SD 1000
BS051875-1	Love Lies	Victor 26678 SD 1000
BS051876-1	I Could Make You Care	Victor 26717 SD 1000
BS051877-1	The World Is In My Arms	Victor 26717 SD 1000

New York City   **August 29, 1940**

BS055543-1	Our Love Affair	Victor 26736 SD 1000
BS055563-1	Looking For Yesterday	Victor 26738 SD 1000
BS055564-1	Tell Me At Midnight	Victor 26747 SD 1000
BS055565-1	We Three Arranged by Sy Oliver	Victor 26747 SD 1000

New York City   **September 9, 1940**

| BS055960-1 | When You Awake | Victor 26764
SD 1000 |
| BS055961-1 | Anything | Victor 27208
SD 1000 |

New York City   **September 17, 1940**

BS056131-1	Shadows On The Sand	Victor 26761 SD 1000
BS056133-2	You're Breaking My Heart All Over Again	Victor 26761 SD 1000
BS056135-1	I'd Know You Anywhere	Victor 26770 SD 1000

Hollywood   **October 16, 1940**

| PBS055110-1 | Do You Know Why? | Victor 26798
SD 1000 |

Hollywood   **November 11, 1940**

| PBS055157-1 | Not So Long Ago | Victor 27219
SD 1000 alt. take |
| PBS055158-1 | Stardust
Arranged by Paul Weston
W/The Pied Pipers | Victor 27233
27520
SD 1000 |

New York City   **January 6, 1941**
W/The Pied Pipers & Connie Haines

| BS058760-1 | Oh Look At Me Now
Arranged by Sy Oliver | Victor 27274,
20-1578
SD 1000 |
| BS058761-1 | You Might Have Belonged
To Another | Victor 27274
SD 1000 |

New York City   **January 15, 1941**

| BS058877-1 | You Lucky People You
Arranged by Sy Oliver | Victor 27350
SD 1000 |
| BS058879-1 | It's Always You | Victor, 27345,
20-1530
SD 1000 |

New York City   **January 20, 1941**

BS060346-1	I Tried	Victor 27317 SD 1000
BS060347-1	Dolores Arranged by Sy Oliver W/The Pied Pipers	Victor 27317 SD 1000
BS060349-2	Without A Song Arranged by Sy Oliver	Victor 36396 (12 inch) SD 1000

New York City   **February 7, 1941**

| BS060626-1 | Do I Worry?
W/The Pied Pipers | Victor 27338
SD 1000 |
| BS060628-1 | Everything Happens To Me | Victor 27359,
20-1577
SD 1000 |

New York City   **February 17, 1941**

| BS060902-1 | Let's Get Away From It All
Arranged by Sy Oliver
W/The Pied Pipers &
Connie Haines & Jo
Stafford | Victor 27377
SD 1000 |

New York City   **May 28, 1941**

BS065913-1	I'll Never Let A Day Pass By	Victor 27461 SD 1000
BS065915-1	Love Me As I Am	Victor 27483 SD 1000
BS065916-1	Free For All W/The Pied Pipers	N/R
BS065917-1	This Love Of Mine Arranged by Axel Stordahl	Victor 27508 SD 1000

New York City   **June 27, 1941**

BS066430-1	I Guess I'll Have To Dream The Rest Arranged by Axel Stordahl W/The Pied Pipers	Victor 27526 SD 1000
BS066431-1	You And I Arranged by Sy Oliver	Victor 27532 SD 1000
BS066432-2	Neiani Arranged by Axel Stordahl W/The Pied Pipers	Victor 27508 SD 1000
BS065916-2	Free For All W/The Pied Pipers	Victor 27532 SD 1000

New York City   **July 15, 1941**

| BS066923-1 | Blue Skies
Arranged by Sy Oliver
W/Band Chorus | Victor 27566
SD 1000 |

New York City   **August 19, 1941**

BS067651-1	Two In Love	Victor 27611, 20-1597 SD 1000
BS067652-2	Violets For Your Furs Arranged by Heinie Beau	N/R
BS067653-1	The Sunshine Of Your Smile	N/R
BS067654-1	Pale Moon	Victor 27591 SD 1000

New York City   **September 18, 1941**

BS067913-1	I Think Of You	Victor 27701 SD 1000
BS067914-1	How Do You Do Without Me?	Victor 27710 SD 1000
BS067915-1	A Sinner Kissed An Angel	Victor 27611 SD 1000

New York City   **September 26, 1941**

| BS067652-3 | Violets For Your Furs
Arranged by Heinie Beau | Victor 27690
SD 1000 |
| BS067653-2 | The Sunshine Of Your
Smile | Victor 27638
SD 1000 |

Hollywood		December 22, 1941
PBS061991-1	How About You?	Victor 27749
		SD 1000

Hollywood   **January 19, 1942**

Four Sides Without Dorsey
Arranged and Conducted by Axel Stordahl

PBS072042-1	The Night We Called It A Day	Bluebird 11463
		R.C.A. LPM 1632
PBS072043-1	The Lamplighter's Serenade	Bluebird 15515
		Victor 20-1589
		R.C.A. LPM 1632
PBS072044-1	The Song Is You	Bluebird 11515
		R.C.A. LPM 1632
PBS072045-1	Night And Day	Bluebird 11463
		Victor 20-1589
		R.C.A. LPM 1632

Hollywood   **February 19, 1942**

PBS072107-1*a	Snooty Little Cutie	Victor 27876,
	Arranged by Sy Oliver	20-2116
	W/The Pied Pipers	SD 1000
PBS072108-1	Poor You	Victor 27849
	Arranged by Axel Stordahl	SD 1000
PBS072109-1*b	I'll Take Tallulah	Victor 27869
	Arranged by Sy Oliver	SD 1000
	W/The Pied Pipers	
PBS072110-1	The Last Call For Love	Victor 27849
	Arranged by Axel Stordahl	SD 1000
	W/The Pied Pipers	

Hollywood   **March 9, 1942**

PBS072171-1	Somewhere A Voice Is Calling	Victor 27887,
		20-2006
	Arranged by Sy Oliver	SD 1000

New York City   **May 18, 1942**

Arrangements by Axel Stordahl
W/The Pied Pipers

BS075204-1	Just As Though You Were Here	Victor 27903
		SD 1000
BS075205-1	Street of Dreams	Victor 27903
		SD 1000

New York City   **June 9, 1942**

Arrangements by Axel Stordahl

BS075264-1	Take Me	Victor 27923
		SD 1000
BS075265-1	Be Careful It's My Heart	Victor 27923
	W/The Pied Pipers	SD 1000

New York City   **June 17, 1942**

BS075282-1	In The Blue Of Evening	Victor 27947,
	Arranged by Axel Stordahl	20-1530
		SD 1000
BS075285-1	Dig Down Deep	Victor 20-1539
	W/The Pied Pipers	SD 1000

New York City   **July 1, 1942**

Arrangements by Axel Stordahl

BS075400-1	There Are Such Things	Victor 27974
	W/The Pied Pipers	SD 1000
BS075402-1	Daybreak	Victor 27974
		SD 1000
BS075403-1	It Started All Over Again	Victor 20-1522
	W/The Pied Pipers	SD 1000

*a—Also with Connie Haines
*b—Also Jo Stafford and Tommy Dorsey

New York City   **July 2, 1942**

| BS075407-1 | Light A Candle In The Chapel | Victor 27941 |
| | Arrangement by Axel Stordahl | SD 1000 |

Unreleased Alternates Which May Exist in R.C.A. Archives:

February 1, 1940	The Sky Fell Down (Take 2)
	Too Romantic (Take 2)
February 26, 1940	Shake Down The Stars (Take 2)
March 12, 1940	This Is The Beginning Of The End (Take 2)
June 27, 1940	Trade Winds (Take 2)
	The One I Love (Take 2)
September 17, 1940	You're Breaking My Heart
	All Over Again (Take 1)
January 20, 1941	Without A Song (Take 1)
June 27, 1941	Neiani (Take 1)
September 18, 1941	I Think Of You (Take 2)

THE COLUMBIA YEARS 1943–1952

New York City   **June 7, 1943**

Arrangements by Axel Stordahl
The Bobby Tucker Singers

CO33249-3	Close To You	Columbia 36678
		Col. 2739
CO33250	People Will Say We're In Love	N/R
	Arranged by Alec Wilder	
CO33251-3	You'll Never Know	Columbia 36678
		Col. 2L 6

New York City   **June 22, 1943**

The Bobby Tucker Singers

CO33268-2	Sunday, Monday Or Always	Columbia 36679
	Arranged by Alec Wilder	Col. 2474
CO33269-1	If You Please	Columbia 36679
CO33250	People Will Say We're In Love	N/R
	Arranged by Alec Wilder	

New York City   **August 5, 1943**

The Bobby Tucker Singers

CO33250-6	People Will Say We're In Love	Columbia 36682
	Arranged by Alec Wilder	Col. 2572
CO33283-1	Oh What A Beautiful Mornin'	Columbia 36682
	Arranged by Alec Wilder	Col. B2515 (45 EP)

New York City   **November 3, 1943**

The Bobby Tucker Singers

CO33368-1	I Couldn't Sleep A Wink Last Night	Columbia 36687
		Col. 2572, 2913
CO33369-PB	The Music Stopped	Col. 2913

New York City   **November 10, 1943**

The Bobby Tucker Singers

CO33373-3	A Lovely Way To Spend An Evening	Columbia 36687
		Col. B2515 (45 EP)
		alt. take
		Col. 2913
CO33374-3	The Music Stopped	HL 7405

New York City		**November 13, 1944**
	Arrangements by Axel Stordahl	
CO33810-1	There's No You	Columbia 36797
		Col. 2739
CO33811-1	White Christmas	Columbia 36756,
	W/The Bobby Tucker	36860, 37152,
	Singers	38257
		Col. 1032 - HL
		7400
New York City		**November 14, 1944**
	Arrangements by Axel Stordahl	
CO33808-2	If You Are But A Dream	Columbia 36756,
		36814
		Col. 2L 6
		Col. 2474 alt. take
CO33809-1	Saturday Night	Columbia 36762,
		50069
		Col. 2474
New York City		**December 1, 1944**
	Arrangements by Axel Stordahl	
CO33928-1	I Dream Of You	Columbia 36762
		Col. 1136
CO33929-1	I Begged Her	Columbia 36774
	W/The Ken Lane Singers	Col. 2913
CO33930-2	What Makes The Sunset	Columbia 36774
		Col. 2913 alt. take
CO33931-1	I Fall In Love Too Easily	Columbia 36830
	W/Piano Solo by Dave	Col. 2913
	Mann	
New York City		**December 3, 1944**
	Arrangements by Axel Stordahl	
CO33932-1	Nancy	N/R
CO33933-1	The Cradle Song	Columbia 36868
		Col. 1448
XCO33934-1	Ol' Man River	Columbia 55037
		(12 inch)
		Col. 2L 6, 2572
XCO33935-1	Stormy Weather	Columbia 55037
	W/The Ken Lane Singers	(12 inch)
		Col. 2L 6
CO33936-1	The Charm Of You	Columbia 36830
		Col. 2739, 2913
Hollywood		**December 19, 1944**
	Arrangements by Axel Stordahl	
HCO1183-1	Embraceable You	Columbia 37259
		Col. 1359
HCO1184-1	When Your Lover Has	Columbia 36791
	Gone	Col. 2739
HCO1185-1	Kiss Me Again	Columbia 38287
HCO1186-1	She's Funny That Way	Columbia 37259
		Col. 743
Hollywood		**January 29, 1945**
	Arrangements by Axel Stordahl	
HCO1257-1	My Melancholy Baby	Columbia 38287
		Col. 1359
HCO1258-1	Where Or When	Columbia 38685
	W/The Ken Lane Singers	Col. 1448
HCO1259-1	All The Things You Are	Columbia 37258
	W/The Ken Lane Singers	Col. 1448
HCO1260-1	Mighty Lak' A Rose	Columbia 36860
Hollywood		**March 6, 1945**
	Arrangements by Axel Stordahl	
HCO1286-1	I Should Care	Columbia 36791
		Col. 2739

HCO1287-1	Homesick That's All	Columbia 36820
	W/The Ken Lane Singers	
HCO1288-1	Dream	Columbia 36797,
	W/The Ken Lane Singers	40522
		Col. 2474
HCO1289-1	A Friend Of Yours	Columbia 36820
	W/The Ken Lane Singers	Col. 2739
Hollywood		**May 1, 1945**
	Arrangements by Axel Stordahl	
HCO1377-1	Put Your Dreams Away	Columbia 36814
		Col. 2L 6, 2474
HCO1378-1	Over The Rainbow	Columbia 37258
	W/The Ken Lane Singers	Col. 743
HCO1379-1	You'll Never Walk Alone	Columbia 36825,
	W/The Ken Lane Singers	50066
		Col. 2L 6
HCO1380-1	If I Loved You	Columbia 36825,
		50066
		Col. 2L 6
Hollywood		**May 16, 1945**
	Arrangements by Axel Stordahl	
	With the Chariotteers	
HCO1395-2	Lily Belle	Columbia 36854
HCO1396-1	Don't Forget Tonight	Columbia 36854
	Tomorrow	
HCO1397-1	I've Got A Home In That	Columbia 37853
	Rock	
HCO1398-1	Jesus Is A Rock	Columbia 37853
	(In A Weary Land)	
New York City		**May 24, 1945**
	Arrangements by Xavier Cugat	
CO34817-1	Stars In Your Eyes	Columbia 36842
CO34818-1	My Shawl	Columbia 36842
		Col. 2739
Hollywood		**July 30, 1945**
	Arrangements by Axel Stordahl	
HCO1499-1	Someone To Watch Over	Columbia 36921,
	Me	38220
		HS 11277
HCO1500-1	You Go To My Head	Columbia 36918
		Col. 2L 6
HCO1501-1	These Foolish Things	Columbia 36919
		Col. 743
HCO1502-1	I Don't Know Why	Columbia 36918
		Col. 743
Hollywood		**August 22, 1945**
	Arrangements by Axel Stordahl	
HCO1519-1	The House I Live In	Columbia 36886
		Col. 2L 6, 2474,
		2913
HCO1520-1	Day By Day	Columbia 36905,
		40565
		Col. 2572
HCO1521-1	Nancy	Columbia 36868,
		50053
		Col. 606 (first
		pressing)
		Col. 2474 alt. take
HCO1522-1	You Are Too Beautiful	Columbia 36947
		Col. 2739
Hollywood		**August 27, 1945**
	Arrangements by Axel Stordahl	
	With The Ken Lane Singers	

HCO1525-1	America The Beautiful	Columbia 36886
HCO1526-1	Silent Night	Columbia 37145, 38256, 50079 Col. 1032 - HL 7400
HCO1527-1	The Moon Was Yellow	Columbia 38683 Col. 2572
HCO1528-1	I Only Have Eyes For You	Columbia 38550 HS 11390

New York City   **November 15, 1945**
Arrangements by Mitch Miller

| CO35426-1 | Old School Teacher | N/R |
| CO35427-1 | Just An Old Stone House | Columbia 38809 |

New York City   **November 19, 1945**
Arrangements by Axel Stordahl

| CO35441-2 | Full Moon And Empty Arms | Columbia 36947 Col. 2572 |
| CO35442-2 | Oh What It Seemed To Be | Columbia 36905 HS 11390 |

New York City   **November 30, 1945**
Arrangement by Axel Stordahl

| CO35484-1 | I Have But One Heart | Columbia 37554 HS 11277 Col. 2572 |

New York City   **December 7, 1945**
Arrangements by Axel Stordahl

CO35496-1	A Ghost Of A Chance	Columbia 36919 Col. 743 Phil. BBR8038 (10 inch) alt. take (England)
CO35497-1	Why Shouldn't I?	Columbia 36920 Col. 2739
CO35498-1	Try A Little Tenderness	Columbia 36920, 39498 HL 7504 alt. take
CO35499-1	Paradise	Columbia 36921 HL 7405

Hollywood   **February 3, 1946**
Arrangements by Axel Stordahl

HCO1674-3	All Through The Day	Columbia 36962
HCO1675-1	One Love	Columbia 37054 Col. 2739
HCO1676-2	Two Hearts Are Better Than One	Columbia 36962
HCO1677-1	How Cute Can You Be?	Columbia 37048 Col. 606

Hollywood   **February 24, 1946**
Arrangements by Axel Stordahl

HCO1733-1	From This Day Forward	Columbia 36987
HCO1734-1	Where Is My Bess?	Columbia 37064 Col. 1297
HCO1735-1	Begin The Beguine	Columbia 37064 Col. 2L 6
HCO1736-1	Something Old, Something New	Columbia 36987 Col. 2739

Hollywood   **March 10, 1946**
Arrangements by Axel Stordahl

HCO1748-1	They Say It's Wonderful	Columbia 36975 Col. 1297 alt. take
HCO1749-1	That Old Black Magic	Columbia 37257 Col. 743
HCO1750-1	The Girl That I Marry	Columbia 36975, 50053 Col. 2474

HCO1751-1	I Fall In Love With You Everyday	Columbia 39493
HCO1752-1	How Deep Is The Ocean?	Columbia 37257 Col. 2L 6
HCO1753-1	Home On The Range	Columbia DC385 (England)

New York City   **April 7, 1946**
Arrangement by Axel Stordahl

| XCO36056-1 | Soliloquy-Part 1 | Col. 2L 6 |
| XCO36057-1 | Soliloquy-Part 2 | Col. 2L 6 |

Hollywood   **May 28, 1946**
Arrangements by Axel Stordahl

XHCO1849-1	Soliloquy-Part 2	Columbia 7492M (12 inch) Col. B1620 (45 EP)
XHCO1850-1	Soliloquy-Part 1	Columbia 7492M (12 inch) Col. B1620 (45 EP)
HCO1851-1	Somewhere In The Night	Columbia 37054
HCO1852-1	Could 'ja W/The Pied Pipers	Columbia 38608
HCO1853-1	Five Minutes More	Columbia 37048, 50069 Col. 2474

Hollywood   **July 24, 1946**
Arrangements by Axel Stordahl

HCO1922-1	The Things We Did Last Summer	Columbia 37089 Col. 1136
HCO1923-1	You'll Know When It Happens	Columbia DO 3041 (Australia)
HCO1924-1	This Is The Night	Columbia 37193, 38853
HCO1925-1	The Coffee Song	Columbia 37089 Col. 2474 alt. take

Hollywood   **July 30, 1946**
Arrangements by Axel Stordahl

HCO1930-1	Among My Souvenirs	Columbia 37161, 50003 HS 11390
HCO1931-1	I Love You	Columbia 38684 HS 11277
HCO1932-1	September Song	Columbia 37161, 50003 Col. 2572
HCO1933-1	Blue Skies	Col. 2740
HCO1934-1	Guess I'll Hang My Tears Out To Dry	Columbia 38474 Col. 2740

Hollywood   **August 8, 1946**
Arrangements by Axel Stordahl

HCO1945-1	Adeste Fideles	Columbia 37145, 38256, 50079 Col. 1032 - HL 7400
HC01946-1	Lost In The Stars	Columbia 38650 Col. 1136, 1297
HCO1947-1	Jingle Bells W/The Ken Lane Singers	Columbia 37152, 38257 Col. 1032 - HL 7400
HCO1948-1	Falling In Love With Love	Col. 606

Hollywood   **August 22, 1946**
Arrangements by Axel Stordahl

| HCO1969-1 | Hush-A-Bye Island | Columbia 37193 |
| HCO1970-1 | So They Tell Me | N/R |

Matrix	Title	Release
HCO1971-1	There's No Business Like Show Business W/Chorus	Columbia 38829 Col. 1297
HCO1972-1	(Once Upon A) Moonlight Night	Columbia 38316

Hollywood October 15, 1946
Arrangements by Axel Stordahl

Matrix	Title	Release
HCO2090-1	Strange Music	N/R
HCO2091-1	Poinciana	Columbia DB2357 (England)
HCO2092-1	The Music Stopped	N/R
HCO2093-1	Why Shouldn't It Happen To Us	Columbia 37251 Col. 2740
HC02094-1	None But The Lonely Heart	N/R

Hollywood October 24, 1946
Arrangements by Axel Stordahl

Matrix	Title	Release
HCO2116-1	Time After Time	Columbia 37300 Col. 2572, 2913
HCO2117-1	It's The Same Old Dream W/Four Hits & A Miss	Columbia 37288 Col. 2740, 2913
HCO2118-1	I'm Sorry I Made You Cry	Columbia 37256

Hollywood October 31, 1946
Arrangements by Axel Stordahl

Matrix	Title	Release
HCO2094-2	None But The Lonely Heart	N/R
HCO2121-1	The Brooklyn Bridge	Columbia 37288 Col. 2913
HCO2122-1	I Believe	Columbia 37300 Col. 2913
HCO2123-1	I Got A Gal I Love	Columbia 37231

Hollywood November 7, 1946
Arrangements by Axel Stordahl

Matrix	Title	Release
HCO2134-1	The Dum Dot Song W/The Pied Pipers	Columbia 37966
HCO2135-1	All Of Me Arranged by George Siravo	Columbia DB2330 (England)
HCO2136-1	It's All Up To You W/Dinah Shore	Columbia DO3104 (Australia)
HCO2137-1	My Romance W/Dinah Shore	N/R

New York City December 15, 1946

Matrix	Title	Release
CO37161-1	Always Arranged by Axel Stordahl	Columbia DO3009 (Australia)
CO37162-1	I Want To Thank Your Folks Arranged by Axel Stordahl	Columbia 37251
CO37163-1	That's How Much I Love You Arranged by Page Cavanaugh W/The Page Cavanaugh Trio	Columbia 37231
CO37164-1	You Can Take My Word For It Baby Arranged by Page Cavanaugh W/The Page Cavanaugh Trio	Columbia 40229 Col. 2740
CO37177	Sweet Lorraine Arranged by Sy Oliver W/The Metronome All Stars	Columbia 37293 Col. 2740 alt. take

Hollywood January 9, 1947
Arrangements by Axel Stordahl

Matrix	Title	Release
HCO2181-1	Always	Columbia 38686 Col. 1359
HCO2182-1	I Concentrate On You	Columbia 37256 Col. 2L 6
HCO2183-1	My Love For You	Columbia DB2388 (England)

Hollywood March 11, 1947
Arrangements by Axel Stordahl

Matrix	Title	Release
HCO2256-1	Mam'selle	Columbia 37343 HL 7405
HCO2257-1	Ain'tch Ever Comin' Back? W/The Pied Pipers	Columbia 37554 Col. 1136
HCO2258-1	Stella By Starlight	Columbia 37343 HS 11277

Hollywood March 31, 1947
Arrangements by Axel Stordahl

Matrix	Title	Release
HCO2280-1	There But For You Go I	Columbia 37382 Col. 1297
HCO2281-2	Almost Like Being In Love	Columbia 37382 Col. 606 (2nd pressing) Col. 606 alt. take 1st pressing

Hollywood April 25, 1947
Arrangements by Axel Stordahl

Matrix	Title	Release
HCO2310-1	Tea For Two W/Dinah Shore	Columbia 37528
HCO2311-1	My Romance W/Dinah Shore & Chorus	Columbia 37528 Col. 2740 alt. take

Hollywood June 26, 1947
Arrangements by Axel Stordahl

Matrix	Title	Release
HCO2419-1	Have Yourself A Merry Little Christmas	Col. 1032 HL 7400
HCO2420-1	Christmas Dreaming	Col. 1032 HL 7400
HCO2421-1	The Stars Will Remember	N/R

Hollywood July 3, 1947
Arrangements by Axel Stordahl

Matrix	Title	Release
HCO2419-3	Have Yourself A Merry Little Christmas	Columbia 38259 Col. 6019 (10 inch)
HCO2420-2	Christmas Dreaming	Columbia 37809
HCO2421-2	The Stars Will Remember	Columbia 37809

Hollywood July 23, 1947
Arrangement by Axel Stordahl

Matrix	Title	Release
HCO2433-1	It All Came True	Columbia DB2381 (England)

Hollywood August 11, 1947
Arrangements by Axel Stordahl

Matrix	Title	Release
HCO2519-1	That Old Feeling	Col. 902, HL 7405
HCO2520-1	If I Had You	HL 7405 alt. take
HCO2521-1	The Nearness Of You	Col. 902, HS 11277
HCO2522-1	One For My Baby	Columbia 38474 Col. 2L 6, 2740

Hollywood August 17, 1947
Arrangements by Axel Stordahl

Matrix	Title	Release
HCO2538-1	But Beautiful	Columbia 38053 Col. 1448
HCO2539-1	A Fellow Needs A Girl	Columbia 37883 Col. 902
HCO2540-1	So Far	Columbia 37883

Hollywood			**September 23, 1947**
	Arrangement by Alvy West		
	W/Alvy West And The Little Band		
HCO2642-1	It All Came True		Columbia 37966
			Col. 2740

New York City			**October 19, 1947**
CO38269-1	Can't You Just See Yourself		Columbia 37978
	Arrangement by Dick		Col. 1297
	Jones		
CO38270-1	You're My Girl		Columbia 37978
	Arrangement by Axel		Col. 1297
	Stordahl		
CO38271-1	All Of Me		Columbia 38163
	Arrangement by George		Col. 606-HS 11277
	Siravo		

New York City			**October 22, 1947**
	Arrangements by Axel Stordahl		
CO38272-1	I'll Make Up For Everything		Columbia 38089
CO38273-1	Strange Music		Columbia 38684
			Col. 1448 alt. take
CO38274-1	Laura		Columbia 38472
			Col. 2L 6-HL 7405
CO38275-1	Just For Now		N/R

New York City			**October 24, 1947**
	Arrangements by Tony Mottola		
CO38284-1	My Cousin Louella		Columbia 38045
CO38285-1	We Just Couldn't Say Goodbye		Columbia 38129
CO38286-1	S'posin'		Columbia 38210
			Col. 606

New York City			**October 26, 1947**
	Arrangements by Axel Stordahl		
CO38287-1	None But The Lonely Heart		Columbia 38685
			Col. 1359
CO38288-1	The Song Is You		Col. 1136
CO38275-1	Just For Now		Columbia 38225

New York City			**October 29, 1947**
	Arrangements by Axel Stordahl		
CO39293-1	What'll I Do		Columbia 38045
CO38294-2	Poinciana		Columbia 38829
			Col. 2740
CO38295-1	Senorita		Columbia 38334
			Col. 2913
CO38296-2	The Music Stopped		Columbia 38683

New York City			**October 31, 1947**
	Arrangements by Axel Stordahl		
CO38301-1	Mean To Me		Col. 902, 2572
CO38302-1	Spring Is Here		Columbia 38473
			HL 7405
CO38303-1	Fools Rush In		Columbia 38473
			Col. 743

New York City			**November 5, 1947**
	Arrangements by Axel Stordahl		
CO38331-1	When You Awake		Columbia 38475
			Col. 6059 (10 inch)
CO38332-1	It Never Entered My Mind		Columbia 38475, 39498
			Col. 1136
CO38333-1	I've Got A Crush On You		Columbia 38151, 50028
	Trumpet solo/Bobby		Col. 2L 6, 2474
	Hackett		

New York City			**November 9, 1947**
	Arrangements by Axel Stordahl		
CO38369-1	Body And Soul		Columbia 38472
	Trumpet solo/Bobby		Col. 6059 (10 inch)
	Hackett		Col. 1448 alt. take
			Col. 2740-2nd alt. take
CO38370-1	I'm Glad There Is You		Columbia 40229
			Col. 2L 6-alt take

New York City			**November 25, 1947**
	Arrangements by Axel Stordahl		
CO38408-1	I Went Down To Virginia		Columbia 38163
			Col. 2740
CO38409-1	If I Only Had A Match		Columbia 38053
			Col. 2740

New York City			**December 4, 1947**
	Arrangements by Axel Stordahl		
CO38482-1	If I Steal A Kiss		Columbia 38334
			Col. 2913
CO38483-1	Autumn In New York		Columbia 38316
			HS 11390
CO38484-1	Everybody Loves Somebody		Columbia 38225
			Col. 2740

New York City			**December 8, 1947**
	Arrangements by Axel Stordahl		
CO38496-1	A Little Learnin' Is A Dangerous Thing—Part 1 W/Pearl Bailey		Columbia 38362
			Col. B2542 (45 EP)
CO38497-1	A Little Learnin' Is A Dangerous Thing—Part 2 W/Pearl Bailey		Columbia 38362
			Col. B2542 (45 EP)
CO38498-1	Ever Homeward		Columbia 38151
			Col. 2913-alt. take

Hollywood			**December 26, 1947**
	Arrangements by Axel Stordahl		
HCO3052-1	But None Like You		Columbia 38129
HCO3053-1	Catana		N/R
HCO3054-1	Why Was I Born?		N/R

Hollywood			**December 28, 1947**
	Arrangements by Axel Stordahl		
HCO3067-1	O Little Town Of Bethlehem W/The Ken Lane Singers		Columbia 38258
			Col. 1032-HL 7400
HCO3068-1	It Came Upon The Midnight Clear W/The Ken Lane Singers		Columbia 38258
			Col. 1032-HL 7400
HCO3069-1	White Christmas		Columbia DO3745 (Australia)
HCO3070-1	For Every Man There's A Woman		Columbia 38089
			Col. 902
HCO3071-1	Help Yourself To My Heart		N/R
HCO3072-1	Santa Claus Is Comin' To Town		Columbia 38259
			Col. 1032-HL 7400
HCO3054-2	Why Was I Born?		Columbia 38686
			Col. 2L 6 alt. take

Hollywood			**December 30, 1947**
	Arrangements by Axel Stordahl		
HCO3089-1	If I Forget You		Columbia 41133
			Col. 1136
HCO3090-1	Where Is The One?		Columbia 38421
HCO3091-1	When Is Sometime?		Columbia 38417

Hollywood   March 16, 1948
Arrangements by Axel Stordahl
(Pre-recorded in Hollywood, December 9, 1947)

| HCO3224-1 | It Only Happens When I Dance With You | Columbia 38192 |
| HCO3225-1 | A Fella With An Umbrella | Columbia 38192 |

Hollywood   April 10, 1948
Arrangement by Jeff Alexander
W/The Jeff Alexander Choir

| HCO3250-1 | Nature Boy | Columbia 38210 |
| | | Col. 1448 |

New York City   December 15, 1948
Arrangement by Mitchell Ayres

| CO40254-1 | Once In Love With Amy | Columbia 38391 |
| | | Col. 902 |

Hollywood   December 15, 1948 (Evening)
Arrangements by Phil Moore
W/The Phil Moore Four

HCO3475-1	Why Can't You Behave?	Columbia 38393
		Col. 1297
HCO3476-1	Bop Goes My Heart	Columbia 38421

Hollywood   December 16, 1948
Arrangements by Axel Stordahl

| HCO3467-1 | Sunflower | Columbia 38391 |

Hollywood   December 19, 1948
Arrangements by Axel Stordahl

HCO3479-1	Comme Ci Comme Ça	Columbia 38407
		Col. 2740
HCO3480-1	No Orchids For My Lady	Columbia 38393
HCO3481-1	While The Angelus Was Ringing	Columbia 38407

Hollywood   January 4, 1949
Arrangements by Phil Moore
W/The Phil Moore Four

HCO3511-1	If You Stub Your Toe On The Moon	Columbia 38417
		Col. 2740
HCO3512-1	Kisses And Tears	N/R

Hollywood   February 28, 1949
Arrangements by Axel Stordahl

HCO3617-1	Some Enchanted Evening	Columbia 38446
		Col. 1297
HCO3618-1	Bali Ha'i W/Chorus	Columbia 38446
		Col. 1297

Hollywood   March 3, 1949
Arrangements by Axel Stordahl

HCO3635-1	The Right Girl For Me	Columbia 38456
		Col. 2741, 2913
HCO3636-1	Night After Night	Columbia 38456

Hollywood   April 10, 1949
Arrangements by Axel Stordahl

HCO3692-1	The Hucklebuck W/The Ken Lane Quintet	Columbia 38486
		Col. 2741
HCO3693-1	It Happens Every Spring	Columbia 38486

Hollywood   May 6, 1949
Arrangements by Axel Stordahl

| HCO3748-1 | Let's Take An Old Fashioned Walk W/Doris Day & The Ken Lane Singers | Columbia 38513 |
| HCO3749-1 | Just One Way To Say I Love You | Columbia 38513 |

New York City   July 10, 1949
Arrangements by Hugo Winterhalter

CO40951-1	It All Depends On You	Columbia 38550
		Col. 606
CO40952-1	Bye Bye Baby W/The Pastels	Columbia 38556
		Col. 1241-alt. take
CO40953-1	Don't Cry Joe W/The Pastels	Columbia 38555
		Col. 902-alt. take

New York City   July 15, 1949
Arrangements by Hugo Winterhalter

CO40970-1	Every Man Should Marry	N/R
CO40971-1	If I Ever Love Again W/The Double Daters	Columbia 38572
		Col. 2741
CO40972-1	Just A Kiss Apart	N/R

Hollywood   July 21, 1949
Arrangements by Morris Stoloff

HCO3853-1	Just A Kiss Apart	Columbia 38556
HCO3854-1	Every Man Should Marry	Columbia 38572
HCO3855-1	The Wedding Of Lili Marlene	Columbia 38555

Hollywood   September 15, 1949
Arrangements by Jeff Alexander

HCO3903-1	That Lucky Old Sun W/Chorus	Columbia 38608
		Col. 902
HCO3904-1	Mad About You	Columbia 38613
		Col. 953
HCO3905-1	Stromboli	Columbia 38613
		Col. 953

Hollywood   October 30, 1949
Arrangements by Axel Stordahl
W/The Modernaires

RHCO3937-1	The Old Master Painter	Columbia 38650
RHCO3938-1	Why Remind Me?	Columbia 38662
		Col. 2741

Hollywood   November 8, 1949
Arrangements by Axel Stordahl

RHCO3939-1	Sorry W/The Modernaires	Columbia 38662
		Col. 953
RHCO3940-1	Sunshine Cake W/Paula Kelly	Columbia 38705
		Col. 2741
RHCO3941-1	Sure Thing W/The Modernaires	Columbia 38705
		Col. 2741

Hollywood   January 12, 1950
Arrangements by Axel Stordahl
W/The Jeff Alexander Choir

RHCO3999-1	God's Country	Columbia 38708
RHCO4000-2	Sheila	Columbia 40565
RHCO4001-1	Chattanoogie Shoe Shine Boy	Columbia 38708

Hollywood   February 23, 1950
Arrangements by Axel Stordahl
W/The Modernaires

RHCO4020-1	Kisses And Tears W/Jane Russell	Columbia 38790
		Col. 2530 (10 inch)
RHCO4021-1	When The Sun Goes Down	Columbia 38790
		Col. 1359

New York City   March 10, 1950
Arrangement by Mitch Miller

| CO42967-1 | American Beauty Rose | Columbia 38809, 40522 |
| | | Col. 1241 |

New York City		April 8, 1950
	Arrangements by George Siravo	
CO43100-1	Peach Tree Street	Columbia 38853
	W/Rosemary Clooney	
CO43101-1	There's Something Missing	N/R

New York City		April 14, 1950
	Arrangements by George Siravo	
CO43126-1	Should I?	Columbia 38998
		Col. 1241
CO43127-1	You Do Something To Me	Columbia 38998
		Col. 1241
CO43128-1	Lover	Columbia 38996
		Col. 743

New York City		April 24, 1950
	Arrangements by George Siravo	
CO43180-1	When You're Smiling	Columbia 38996
		Col. 1241
CO43181-1	It's Only A Paper Moon	Columbia 38997
		Col. 2741
CO43182-1	My Blue Heaven	Columbia 38892
		Col. 2741
CO43183-2	The Continental	Columbia 38997
		Col. 1241

New York City		June 28, 1950
	Arrangements by Mitch Miller	
	W/The Mitch Miller Singers	
CO44015-1	Goodnight Irene	Columbia 38892
		Col. 1448
CO44016-1	Dear Little Boy Of Mine	Columbia 38960
		Col. 1448

New York City		August 2, 1950
	Arrangement by Percy Faith	
CO44185-1	Life Is So Peculiar	Columbia 38960
	W/Helen Carroll &	
	The Swantones	

New York City		September 18, 1950
	Arrangements by Axel Stordahl	
CO44366-1	Accidents Will Happen	Columbia 39014
CO44367-1	One Finger Melody	Columbia 39014

New York City		September 21, 1950
	Arrangements by Axel Stordahl	
CO44376-1	Remember Me In Your	Columbia 39069
	Dreams	
	W/The Whipoorwills	
CO44377-1	If Only She'd Look My	
	Way	Col. 953
CO44378-1	London By Night	Columbia 39592
CO44379-1	Meet Me At The Copa	N/R

New York City		October 9, 1950
	Arrangements by Axel Stordahl	
CO44427-1	Come Back To Sorrento	Columbia 39118
		Col. 1359
CO44428-1	April In Paris	Columbia 39592
		Col. 2L 6
CO44429-1	I Guess I'll Have To	Columbia 39044
	Dream The Rest	Col. 953
	W/The Whipoorwills	
CO44430-1	Nevertheless	Columbia 39044
	Arrangement by George	Col. 2741
	Siravo	
	W/Trumpet solo by	
	Billy Butterfield	

New York City		November 5, 1950
	Arrangement by Axel Stordahl	
CO44615-1	Let It Snow, Let It Snow,	Columbia 39069
	Let It Snow	Col. 1032
	W/Vocal Quartet	

New York City		November 16, 1950
	Arrangements by Axel Stordahl	
CO44634-1	Take My Love	Columbia 39118
		Col. 953
CO44635-1	I Am Loved	Columbia 39079
		Col. 953
CO44636-1	You Don't Remind Me	Columbia 39079
CO44637-1	You're The One	N/R

New York City		December 11, 1950
	Arrangements by Axel Stordahl	
CO44714-1	Love Means Love	Columbia 39141
	W/Rosemary Clooney	
CO44715-1	Cherry Pies Ought To Be	Columbia 39141
	You	
	W/Rosemary Clooney	

New York City		January 16, 1951
	Arrangements by Axel Stordahl	
CO45111-1	Faithful	Columbia 39213
	W/Vocal Chorus	
CO45112-1	You're The One	Columbia 39213
	W/Piano solo by	Col. 2741
	Stan Freeman	
CO45113-1	There's Something Missing	N/R
	Arrangement by George	
	Siravo	
	W/Vocal Chorus	

New York City		March 2, 1951
	Arrangements by Axel Stordahl	
CO45156-1	Hello Young Lovers	Columbia 39294
		Col. 606
CO45157-1	We Kiss In A Shadow	Columbia 39294
		Col. 953

New York City		March 27, 1951
	Arrangements by Axel Stordahl	
CO45184-1	I Whistle A Happy Tune	Columbia 39346
		Col. 1297
CO45185-1	I'm A Fool To Want You	Columbia 39425,
		41133
		Col. 2572, 2741
CO45186-1	Love Me	Columbia 39346
		Col. 2741

New York City		May 10, 1951
	Arrangements by Axel Stordahl	
CO45819-1	Mama Will Bark	Columbia 39425
	W/Dagmar	
	Imitations by Donald Bain	
CO45820-1	It's A Long Way From	Columbia 39493
	Your House To My	
	House	

Hollywood		July 9, 1951
	Arrangements by Ray Conniff	
	W/The Harry James Orchestra	
RHCO4561-1	Castle Rock	Columbia 39527
		Col. 2L 6
RHCO4562-1	Farewell, Farewell To Love	Columbia B2542
		(45 EP)
		Col. 1241

RHCO4563-1	Deep Night	Columbia 39527 Col. 1241	

Hollywood   **October 16, 1951**
Arrangement by Joseph Gershenson

RHCO10022-2	A Good Man Is Hard To Find W/Shelley Winters	N/R

Hollywood   **January 7, 1952**
Arrangements by Axel Stordahl

RHCO10081-1	I Could Write A Book W/The Jeff Alexander Choir	Columbia 39652 Col. 953
RHCO10082-1	I Hear A Rhapsody W/The Jeff Alexander Choir	Columbia 39652 Col. 1359
RHCO10083-1	Walkin' In The Sunshine	Columbia 39726 Col. 2741

Hollywood   **February 6, 1952**
Arrangements by Axel Stordahl

RHCO10110-1	My Girl	Columbia 39726
RHCO10114-1	Feet Of Clay	Columbia 39687
RHCO10115-1	Don't Ever Be Afraid To Go Home	Columbia 39687

Hollywood   **June 3, 1952**
Arrangements by Axel Stordahl

RHCO10178-1	Luna Rossa W/The Norman Luboff Choir	Columbia 39787 Col. 1359
RHCO10179-1	The Birth Of The Blues Arrangement by Heinie Beau	Columbia 39882, 50028 Col. 2L 6, 2741
RHCO10180-1	Azure-Te (Paris Blues)	Columbia 39819 Col. 2741
RHCO10181-1	Tennessee Newsboy	Columbia 39787
RHCO10190-1	Bim Bam Baby	Columbia 39819 Col. 1241

New York City   **September 17, 1952**
Arrangement by Percy Faith

CO48181-1	Why Try To Change Me Now	Columbia 39882 Col. 2741

THE CAPITOL YEARS
1953–1962

Los Angeles   **April 2, 1953**
Arrangements by Axel Stordahl

11394	Lean Baby Arrangement by Heinie Beau	Capitol 2450 Cap. 1429
11395	I'm Walking Behind You	Capitol 2450 Cap. SYS 5637
11396	Don't Make A Beggar Of Me	Cap. T2602 Cap. E-ST24311 (England)

Los Angeles   **April 30, 1953**
Arrangements by Nelson Riddle

11504	I've Got The World On A String	Capitol 2505 Cap. T768
11511	Don't Worry 'Bout Me	Capitol 2787 Cap. T768
11512	I Love You	Capitol 2638 Cap. W1429

11513	South Of The Border	Capitol 2638 Cap. T768

Los Angeles   **May 2, 1953**
Arrangements by Nelson Riddle

11524	Anytime, Anywhere	Capitol 2560 Cap. W1164
11525	My One And Only Love	Capitol 2505 Cap. T768
11526	From Here To Eternity	Capitol 2560 Cap. T768
11527	I Can Read Between The Lines	Cap. W1432

Los Angeles   **November 5, 1953**
Arrangements by Nelson Riddle

11846	A Foggy Day	Cap. W1432
11847	My Funny Valentine	Cap. W1432
11852	They Can't Take That Away From Me	Cap. W1432
11853	Violets For Your Furs	Cap. W1432

Los Angeles   **November 6, 1953**
Arrangements by Nelson Riddle

11858	Like Someone In Love	Cap. W1432
11859	I Get A Kick Out Of You	Cap. W1432
12033	Little Girl Blue	Cap. W1432
12034	The Girl Next Door	Cap. W1432

Los Angeles   **December 8, 1953**
Arrangements by Nelson Riddle

12051	Take A Chance	Capitol 2703 Cap. E-ST24311 (England)
12052	Ya Better Stop	Cap. E-ST24311 (England)
12053	Why Should I Cry Over You?	Capitol 3050 Cap. W1429

Los Angeles   **December 9, 1953**
Arrangements by Nelson Riddle

11991	Rain (Falling From The Skies)	Capitol 2816 Cap. T768
11992	Young At Heart	Capitol 2703 Cap. T768
11993	I Could Have Told You	Capitol 2787 Cap. W1164

Los Angeles   **March 1, 1954**
Arrangements by Nelson Riddle

12365	Day In, Day Out	Capitol EAP-590 (45 EP) Cap. E-ST24311 (England) Cap. W581
12366	Last Night When We Were Young	
12367	Three Coins In The Fountain	Capitol 2816 Cap. T768

Los Angeles   **April 2, 1954**
Arrangement by Nelson Riddle

12400	The Sea Song W/Chorus	N/R

Los Angeles   **April 7, 1954**
Arrangements by Nelson Riddle

12430	Sunday	Cap. W1429
12431	Just One Of Those Things	Cap. W1429
12432	I'm Gonna Sit Right Down And Write Myself A Letter	Cap. W1429

12433	Wrap Your Troubles In Dreams	Cap. W1429

Los Angeles   **April 19, 1954**

Arrangements by Nelson Riddle

12564	All Of Me	Cap. W1429
12565	Jeepers Creepers	Cap. W1429
12566	Get Happy	Cap. W1429
12567	Take A Chance On Love	Cap. W1429

Los Angeles   **May 13, 1954**

Arrangements by Nelson Riddle

12642	The Gal That Got Away	Capitol 2864
		Cap. T768
12643	Half As Lovely (Twice As True)	Capitol 2864
		Cap. W982
12644	It Worries Me	Capitol 2922
		Cap. W1432

Los Angeles   **August 23, 1954**

Arrangements by Nelson Riddle
W/Vocal Chorus

12937	When I Stop Loving You	Capitol 2922
		Cap. W1164
12938	White Christmas	Capitol 2954
		Cap. TP81 (England)
12939	The Christmas Waltz	Capitol 2954
		Cap. TP81 (England)

Los Angeles   **September 23, 1954**

Arrangements by Nelson Riddle

12702	Don't Change Your Mind About Me W/Chorus	Capitol 3050
		Cap. SYS 5637
12703	Someone To Watch Over Me	Capitol 2993
		Cap. W1432
12704	You My Love	Capitol 2993
		Cap. W1164

Los Angeles   **December 13, 1954**

Arrangements by Dick Reynolds
Ray Anthony & His Orchestra

13141	Melody Of Love	Capitol 3018
		Cap. T2602
13302	I'm Gonna Live Till I Die	Capitol 3018
		Cap. W1164

Los Angeles   **February 8, 1955**

Arrangements by Nelson Riddle

13556	Dancing On The Ceiling	Cap. W581
13557	Can't We Be Friends	Cap. W581
13558	Glad To Be Unhappy	Cap. W581
13559	I'll Be Around	Cap. W581

Los Angeles   **February 16, 1955**

Arrangements by Nelson Riddle

13457	What Is This Thing Called Love?	Cap. W581
13458	Ill Wind	Cap. W581
13459	I See Your Face Before Me	Cap. W581
13523	Mood Indigo	Cap. W581

Los Angeles   **February 17, 1955**

Arrangements by Nelson Riddle

13460	I Get Along Without You Very Well	Cap. W581
13461	In The Wee Small Hours Of The Morning	Cap. W581
13573	When Your Lover Has Gone	Cap. W581

13574	This Love Of Mine	Cap. W581

Los Angeles   **February 23, 1955**

Arrangement by Nelson Riddle

13575	Soliloquy-no completed master	N/R

Los Angeles   **March 4, 1955**

Arrangements by Nelson Riddle

13486	It Never Entered My Mind	Cap. W581
13487	Not As A Stranger	Capitol 3130
		Cap. W1164
13585	Deep In A Dream	Cap. W581
13586	I'll Never Be The Same	Cap. W581

Los Angeles   **March 7, 1955**

Arrangements by Nelson Riddle

13594	If I Had Three Wishes	Capitol 3102
		Cap. W1164
13595	How Could You Do A Thing Like That To Me	Capitol 3130
		Cap. W1429
13596	Two Hearts, Two Kisses Arrangement by Dave Cavanaugh W/The Nuggets	Capitol 3084
		Cap. T2602
13597	From The Bottom To The Top Arrangement by Dave Cavanaugh W/The Nuggets	Capitol 3084
		Cap. T2602

Los Angeles   **March 23, 1955**

Arrangement by Nelson Riddle

13628	Learnin' The Blues	Capitol 3102
		Cap. T768

Los Angeles   **July 29, 1955**

Arrangements by Nelson Riddle

14286	Same Old Saturday Night	Capitol 3218
		Cap. W1164
14288	Fairy Tale	Capitol 3218
		Cap. W1164

Los Angeles   **August 15, 1955**

Arrangements by Nelson Riddle

14118	Look To Your Heart W/Chorus	Capitol EAP-673 (45 EP)
		Cap. W1164
14119	Love And Marriage	Capitol 3260
		Cap. T768
14120	The Impatient Years	Capitol 3260
		Cap. W1164
14121	Our Town	Capitol EAP-673 (45 EP)
		Cap. W1164

Los Angeles   **September 13, 1955**

Arrangements by Nelson Riddle

14429	(Love Is) The Tender Trap	Capitol 3290
		Cap. T768
14430	You'll Get Yours	Capitol 3350
		Cap. T2602

Los Angeles   **October 17, 1955**

Arrangements by Nelson Riddle

14287	You Forgot All The Words	Capitol 3552
		Cap. 982
14633	Love Is Here To Stay	Cap. W653
14634	Weep They Will	Capitol 3290
		Cap. T1919

Los Angeles		January 9, 1956
Arrangements by Nelson Riddle		
14605	You Brought A New Kind Of Love To Me	Cap. W653
14606	I Thought About You	Cap. W653
14607	You Make Me Feel So Young	Cap. W653
14608	Memories Of You	Cap. E-ST24311 (England)

Los Angeles		January 10, 1956
Arrangements by Nelson Riddle		
14613	Pennies From Heaven	Cap. W653
14614	How About You	Cap. W653
14616	You're Getting To Be A Habit With Me	Cap. W653

Los Angeles		January 12, 1956
Arrangements by Nelson Riddle		
14940	It Happened In Monterey	Cap. W653
14941	Swingin' Down The Lane	Cap. W653
14942	Flowers Mean Forgiveness W/Chorus	Capitol 3350 Cap. T2602
14943	I've Got You Under My Skin	Cap. W653

Los Angeles		January 16, 1956
Arrangements by Nelson Riddle		
14956	Makin' Whoopee	Cap. W653
14957	Old Devil Moon	Cap. W653
14958	Anything Goes	Cap. W653
14959	Too Marvellous For Words	Cap. W653
14960	We'll Be Together Again	Cap. W653

Los Angeles		March 8, 1956
Arrangements by Nelson Riddle W/The Hollywood String Quartet		
E15186	Don't Like Goodbyes	Cap. W789
E15187	P.S. I Love You	Cap. W789
E15188	Love Locked Out	Cap. W789
E15189	If It's The Last Thing I Do	Cap. T2602 Cap. E-ST24311 (England)

Los Angeles		April 4, 1956
Arrangements by Nelson Riddle W/The Hollywood String Quartet		
E15310	I've Had My Moments	Cap. W789
E15311	Blame It On My Youth	Cap. W789
E15312	Everything Happens To Me	Cap. W789
E15313	Wait Till You See Her	Cap. W1825

Los Angeles		April 5, 1956
Arrangements by Nelson Riddle		
E15278	The End Of A Love Affair W/The Hollywood String Quartet	Cap. W789
E15296	It Could Happen To You W/The Hollywood String Quartet	Cap. W789
E15318	There's A Flaw In My Flue W/The Hollywood String Quartet	Cap. E-ST24311 (England)
E15360	With Every Breath I Take W/The Hollywood String Quartet	Cap. W789

E15315	How Little We Know	Capitol 3423 Cap. W982
E15316	Wait For Me	Capitol 3469 Cap. W982
E15317	You're Sensational	Capitol 3469 Cap. SMAS-94408 (Capitol Record Club)

Los Angeles		April 9, 1956
Arrangements by Nelson Riddle		
E15330	Something Wonderful Happens In Summer	N/R
E15331	Five Hundred Guys	Capitol 3423 Cap. SYS5637
E15332	Hey Jealous Lover W/Chorus	Capitol 3552 Cap. W982
E15333	No One Ever Tells You	Capitol 4103 Cap. W803

Los Angeles		April 20, 1956
MGM Studio Orchestra—Directed by Johnny Green		
E15405	You're Sensational Arrangement by Nelson Riddle	Cap. SW750
E15406	Who Wants To Be A Millionaire W/Celeste Holm Arrangement by Conrad Salinger	Capitol 3508 Cap. SW750
E15407	Mind If I Make Love To You Arrangement by Nelson Riddle	Capitol 3508 Cap. SW750

Los Angeles		May 7, 1956
MGM Studio Orchestra—Directed by Johnny Green		
E15721	Well Did You Evah W/Bing Crosby Arrangement by Skip Martin	Capitol 3507 Cap. SW750

Los Angeles		October 1, 1956
Arrangements by Nelson Riddle W/The Hollywood String Quartet		
E16159	I Couldn't Sleep A Wink Last Night	Cap. W789
E16160	It's Easy To Remember	Cap. W789
E16161	Close To You	Cap. W789

Los Angeles		November 15, 1956
Arrangements by Nelson Riddle		
E16192	I Got Plenty O' Nuttin'	Cap. W803
E16193	I Won't Dance	Cap. W803
E16194	Stars Fell On Alabama	Cap. W803

Los Angeles		November 20, 1956
Arrangements by Nelson Riddle		
E16196	At Long Last Love	Cap. W803
E16197	I Guess I'll Have To Change My Plan	Cap. W803
E16198	I Wish I Were In Love Again	Cap. W803
E16199	Nice Work If You Can Get It	Cap. W803

Los Angeles		November 26, 1956
Arrangements by Nelson Riddle		
E16205	The Lady Is A Tramp	Cap. W1825 Cap. W912-alt. take

E16206	Night And Day	Cap. W803
E16207	The Lonesome Road	Cap. W803
E16208	If I Had You	Cap. W803

Los Angeles   **November 28, 1956**
Arrangements by Nelson Riddle

E16209	I Got It Bad And That Ain't Good	Cap. W803
E16210	From This Moment On	Cap. W803
E16211	Oh Look At Me Now	Cap. W803
E16212	You'd Be So Nice To Come Home To	Cap. W803

Los Angeles   **December 3, 1956**
Arrangements by Nelson Riddle

| E16217 | Your Love For Me | Capitol 3608
Cap. T2602 |
| E16218 | Can I Steal a Little Love | Capitol 3608
Cap. T2602 |

Los Angeles   **March 14, 1957**
Arrangements by Nelson Riddle

| E16731 | So Long My Love | Capitol 3703
Cap. W982 |
| E16732 | Crazy Love | Capitol 3703
Cap. W982 |

Los Angeles   **April 10, 1957**
Arrangements by Gordon Jenkins

E16820	Where Is The One	Cap. SW855
E16821	There's No You	Cap. SW855
E16822	The Night We Called It A Day	Cap. SW855
E16823	Autumn Leaves	Cap. SW855

Los Angeles   **April 29, 1957**
Arrangements by Gordon Jenkins

E17008	I Cover The Waterfront	Cap. SW855
E17009	Lonely Town	Cap. SW855
E17010	Laura	Cap. SW855
E17011	Baby Won't You Please Come Home	Cap. SW855

Los Angeles   **May 1, 1957**
Arrangements by Gordon Jenkins

E16863	Where Are You	Cap. SW855
E16869	I Think Of You	Cap. SW855
E17040	I'm A Fool To Want You	Cap. SW855
E17041	Maybe You'll Be There	Cap. SW855

Los Angeles   **May 20, 1957**
Arrangements by Nelson Riddle

E17069	Witchcraft	Capitol 3859 Cap. SW1538
E17070	Something Wonderful Happens In Summer	Capitol 3744 Cap. W982
E17071	Tell Her You Love Her	Capitol 3859 Cap. T1919
E17072	You're Cheatin' Yourself (If You're Cheatin' On Me)	Capitol 3744 Cap. W982

Los Angeles   **July 10, 1957**
Arrangements by Gordon Jenkins
W/The Ralph Brewster Singers

E17289	It Came Upon A Midnight Clear	Cap. W894
E17290	O Little Town Of Bethlehem	Cap. W894
E17291	Hark The Herald Angels Sing	Cap. W894

| E17292 | Adeste Fideles (O Come All Ye Faithful) | Cap. W894 |

Los Angeles   **July 16, 1957**
Arrangements by Gordon Jenkins
W/The Ralph Brewster Singers

E17331	Jingle Bells	Cap. W894
E17332	The First Noel	Cap. W894
E17333	Have Yourself A Merry Little Christmas	Cap. W894
E17334	The Christmas Waltz	Capitol 3900 Cap. W894

Los Angeles   **July 17, 1957**
Arrangements by Gordon Jenkins
W/The Ralph Brewster Singers

E17339	Mistletoe and Holly	Capitol 3900 Cap. W894
E17340	The Christmas Song	Cap. W894
E17341	Silent Night	Cap. W894
E17342	I'll Be Home For Christmas	Cap. W894

Los Angeles   **August 13, 1957**
Arrangements by Nelson Riddle
Orchestra directed by Morris Stoloff

E17468	I Could Write A Book	Cap. SM912
E17469	Bewitched	Cap. SM912
E17470	All The Way Orchestra directed by Nelson Riddle	Capitol 3793 Cap. SW1538
E17471	There's A Small Hotel	Cap. SM912
E17472	Chicago Orchestra directed by Nelson Riddle	Capitol 3793 Cap. SW1729

Los Angeles   **September 25, 1957**
Arrangements by Nelson Riddle
Orchestra directed by Morris Stoloff

| E17553 | I Didn't Know What Time It Was | Cap. SM912 |
| E17561 | What Do I Care For A Dame | Cap. SM912 |

Los Angeles   **October 1, 1957**
Arrangements by Billy May

E17639	On The Road To Mandalay	Cap. SW920
E17640	Let's Get Away From It all	Cap. SW920
E17641	Isle of Capri	Cap. SW920

Los Angeles   **October 3, 1957**
Arrangements by Billy May

E17647	Autumn In New York	Cap. SW920
E17648	London By Night	Cap. SW920
E17649	April in Paris	Cap. SW920
E17650	Moonlight In Vermont	Cap. SW920

Los Angeles   **October 8, 1957**
Arrangements by Billy May

E17696	Blue Hawaii	Cap. SW920
E17697	Come Fly With Me	Cap. SW920
E17698	Around The World	Cap. SW920
E17699	It's Nice To Go Trav'ling	Cap. SW920
E17700	Brazil	Cap. SW920

Los Angeles   **November 25, 1957**
Arrangements by Nelson Riddle

E17974	I Believe	Cap. W982
E17975	Everybody Loves Somebody	Cap. W982
E17976	It's The Same Old Dream	Cap. W982

E17977	Time After Time	Capitol 4155
		Cap. W982

Los Angeles　　　　　　　　　　　　December 11, 1957

Arrangements by Nelson Riddle

E18052	You'll Always Be The One I Love	Capitol 4466
		Cap. W982
E18053	If You Are But A Dream	Cap. W982
E18054	Put Your Dreams Away	Cap. W982

Los Angeles　　　　　　　　　　　　March 3, 1958

Arrangements by Billy May

E18522	Nothing In Common W/Keely Smith	Capitol 3952
E18523	How Are Ya Fixed For Love W/Keely Smith	Capitol 3952
E18524	Same Old Song And Dance	Capitol 4003
		Cap. T2602

Los Angeles　　　　　　　　　　　　May 29, 1958

Arrangements by Nelson Riddle
Orchestra directed by Felix Slatkin

E19239	Monique (Song From Kings Go Forth) Arrangement by Felix Slatkin	Capitol 4003 Cap. SW1729
E19240	Ebb Tide	Cap. SW1053
E19241	Angel Eyes	Cap. SW1053
E19242	Spring Is Here	Cap. W1053
E19255	Guess I'll Hang My Tears Out To Dry	Cap. SW1053
E19256	Only The Lonely	Cap. SW1053
E19257	Lush Life—no completed master	N/R
E19258	Willow Weep For Me	Cap. SW1053

Los Angeles　　　　　　　　　　　　June 24, 1958

Arrangements by Nelson Riddle

E19478	Blues In The Night	Cap. SW1053
E19479	What's New	Cap. SW1053
E19480	Gone With The Wind	Cap. SW1053

Los Angeles　　　　　　　　　　　　June 25, 1958

Arrangements by Nelson Riddle

E19420	Goodbye	Cap. SW1053
E19421	It's A Lonesome Old Town	Cap. W1053
E19422	One For My Baby W/Piano solo by Bill Miller	Cap. SW1053

Los Angeles　　　　　　　　　　　　September 11, 1958

Arrangements by Nelson Riddle

E30096	Mr. Success	Capitol 4070 Cap. SW1729
E30097	Sleep Warm	Capitol 4070 Cap. SW1538
E30100	Where Or When	Cap. E-ST24311 (England)

Los Angeles　　　　　　　　　　　　September 30, 1958

Arrangement by Billy May

E30213	It All Depends On You	Cap. E-ST24311 (England)

Los Angeles　　　　　　　　　　　　October 1, 1958

Arrangement by Nelson Riddle

E30104	I Couldn't Care Less	Cap. SYS5637 Cap. E-ST24311 (England)

Los Angeles　　　　　　　　　　　　October 28, 1958

Arrangement by Nelson Riddle

E30380-a	To Love And Be Loved	Capitol 4103

Los Angeles　　　　　　　　　　　　December 5, 1958

Arrangement by Nelson Riddle

E30380-b	To Love And Be Loved	Cap. SW1538

Los Angeles　　　　　　　　　　　　December 9, 1958

Arrangements by Billy May

E30771	The Song Is You	Cap. SW1069 Cap. E-ST24311-alt. take (England)
E30772	Something's Gotta Give	Cap. SW1069
E30773	Just In Time	Cap. SW1069

Los Angeles　　　　　　　　　　　　December 22, 1958

Arrangements by Billy May

E30876	Day In, Day Out	Cap. SW1069
E30877	Baubles, Bangles And Beads	Cap. SW1069
E30878	Dancing In The Dark	Cap. SW1069
E30879	Saturday Night Arrangement by Heinie Beau	Cap. SW1069
E30880	Cheek To Cheek	Cap. SW1069

Los Angeles　　　　　　　　　　　　December 23, 1958

Orchestra directed by Billy May

E30887	Too Close For Comfort Arrangement by Heinie Beau	Cap. SW1069
E30888	I Could Have Danced All Night Arrangement by Billy May	Cap. SW1069
E30889	Come Dance With Me Arrangement by Billy May	Cap. SW1069
E30890	The Last Dance Arrangement by Heinie Beau	Cap. SW1069

Los Angeles　　　　　　　　　　　　December 29, 1958

Arrangements by Nelson Riddle

E30893	The Moon Was Yellow	Capitol 4677 Cap. SW1729
E30894	They Came To Cordura	Capitol 4284 Cap. SW1729
E30895	All My Tomorrows	Capitol 4214 Cap. SW1538
E30896	French Foreign Legion	Capitol 4155 Cap. SW1538

Los Angeles　　　　　　　　　　　　March 24, 1959

Arrangements by Gordon Jenkins

E31391	A Ghost Of A Chance	Cap. SW1221
E31392	Why Try To Change Me Now	Cap. SW1221
E31393	None But The Lonely Heart	Cap. SW1221
E31394	Stormy Weather	Cap. SW1221

Los Angeles　　　　　　　　　　　　March 25, 1959

Arrangements by Gordon Jenkins

E31421	Here's That Rainy Day	Cap. SW1221
E31422	The One I Love Belongs To Someone Else	Cap. SYS5637 Cap. E-ST24311 (England)

Los Angeles		March 26, 1959
Arrangements by Gordon Jenkins		
E31424	I Can't Get Started	Cap. SW1221
E31425	Where Do You Go	Cap. SW1221
E31426	A Cottage For Sale	Cap. SW1221
E31427	Just Friends	Cap. SW1221

Los Angeles		May 8, 1959
Arrangements by Nelson Riddle		
E31632	High Hopes	Capitol 4214
	W/Eddie Hodges &	Cap. SW1538
	'A Bunch Of Kids	
E31633	Love Looks So Well	Cap. SW1729
	On You	

Los Angeles		May 14, 1959
E31679	This Was My Love	Capitol 4408
		Cap. SW1538
E31682	Talk To Me	Capitol 4284
	Arrangement by	Cap. SW1538
	Nelson Riddle	
E31680	When No One Cares	Cap. SW1221
	Arrangement by Gordon	
	Jenkins	
E31681	I'll Never Smile Again	Cap. SW1221
	Arrangement by Gordon	
	Jenkins	

Los Angeles		February 19, 1960
Arrangements by Nelson Riddle		
E33339	It's All Right With Me	Cap. SW1301
E33340	C'est Magnifique	Cap. SW1301
E33341	I Love Paris	Cap. SW1301
	W/Maurice Chevalier	

Los Angeles		February 20, 1960
Arrangements by Nelson Riddle		
E33348	Let's Do It	Cap. SW1301
	W/Shirley MacLaine	
E33349	Montmart'	Cap. SW1301
	W/Maurice Chevalier &	
	Chorus	

Los Angeles		March 1, 1960
Arrangements by Nelson Riddle		
E33350	You Go To My Head	Cap. SW1417
E33351	Fools Rush In	Cap. SW1417
E33352	That Old Feeling	Cap. SW1417
E33353	Try A Little Tenderness	Cap. SW1417

Los Angeles		March 2, 1960
Arrangements by Nelson Riddle		
E33364	She's Funny That Way	Cap. SW1417
E33365	The Nearness Of You	Cap. SW1729
E33366	Nevertheless	Cap. SW1417

Los Angeles		March 3, 1960
Arrangements by Nelson Riddle		
E33363	Dream	Cap. SW1417
E33386	I've Got A Crush On You	Cap. SW1417
E33387	Embraceable You	Cap. SW1417
E33388	Mam'selle	Cap. SW1417
E33390	How Deep Is The Ocean	Cap. SW1417

Los Angeles		April 12, 1960
Arrangements by Nelson Riddle		
E33650	Nice 'N' Easy	Capitol 4408
		Cap. SW1417
E33651	River Stay 'Way From	Capitol 4376
	My Door	Cap. SW1538

E33652	I Love Paris	Capitol 4815
		Cap. SW1729
E33653	It's Over, It's Over,	Capitol 4376
	It's Over	Cap. SW1538
	W/Chorus	

Los Angeles		August 22, 1960
Arrangements by Nelson Riddle		
E34373	When You're Smiling	Cap. SW1491
E34374	I Concentrate On You	Cap. SW1491
E34375	You Do Something To Me	Cap. SW1491
E34376	S'posin'	Cap. SW1491
E34381	Should I	Cap. SW1491

Los Angeles		August 23, 1960
Arrangements by Nelson Riddle		
E34386	My Blue Heaven	Capitol 4546
		Cap. SW1491
E34387	I Can't Believe That You're	Cap. SW1491
	In Love With Me	
E34388	Always	Cap. SW1491
E34389	It All Depends On You	Cap. SW1491

Los Angeles		August 31, 1960
Arrangements by Nelson Riddle		
E34409	It's Only A Paper Moon	Cap. SW1491
E34410	September In The Rain	Cap. SW1491
E34411	Hidden Persuasion	Capitol 4815
		Cap. SW1729

Los Angeles		September 1, 1960
Arrangements by Nelson Riddle		
E34413	Sentimental Baby	Capitol 4546
		Cap. SW1729
E34414	Ol' MacDonald	Capitol 4466
		Cap. SW1538
E34415	Blue Moon	Cap. SW1491

Los Angeles		March 20, 1961
Orchestra directed by Billy May		
E35576	On The Sunny Side Of The	Cap. SW1594
	Street	
	Arrangement by Heinie	
	Beau	
E35577	Day By Day	Cap. SW1594
	Arrangement by Billy	
	May	
E35578	Sentimental Journey	Capitol 4615
	Arrangement by Heinie	Cap. SW1594
	Beau	
E35579	Don't Take Your Love	Cap. SW1594
	From Me	
	Arrangement by Heinie	
	Beau	

Los Angeles		March 21, 1961
Orchestra directed by Billy May		
E35592	Yes Indeed	Cap. SW1594
	Arrangement by Billy	
	May	
E35593	American Beauty Rose	Capitol 4615
	Arrangement by Heinie	Cap. SW1594
	Beau	
E35594	I've Heard That Song	Capitol 4677
	Before	Cap. SW1594
	Arrangement by Billy	
	May	

| E35595 | That Old Black Magic | Cap. SW1594 |
| | Arrangement by Heinie Beau | |

Los Angeles   **March 22, 1961**
Arrangements by Billy May

E35616	Five Minutes More	Capitol 4729
		Cap. SW1594
E35617	Almost Like Being In Love	Cap. SW1594
E35618	Lover	Cap. SW1594
	Arrangement by Heinie Beau	
E35619	Paper Doll	Cap. SW1594

Los Angeles   **September 11, 1961**
Arrangements by Axel Stordahl

E36463	I'll Be Seeing You	Cap. SW1676
E36464	I'll See You Again	Cap. SW1676
E36465	September Song	Cap. SW1676
E36466	Memories Of You	Cap. SW1676
E36471	There Will Never Be Another You	Cap. SW1676
		Cap. SW1676
E36472	When The World Was Young	Cap. SW1676

Los Angeles   **September 12, 1961**
Arrangements by Axel Stordahl

E36481	Somewhere Along The Way	Cap. SW1676
E36482	A Million Dreams Ago	Cap. SW1676
E36483	These Foolish Things	Cap. SW1676
E36484	As Time Goes By	Cap. SW1676
E36485	It's A Blue World	Cap. SW1676
	Arrangement by Heinie Beau	
E36486	I'll Remember April	Capitol 4729
	Arrangement by Heinie Beau	Cap. SW1676

Los Angeles   **March 6, 1962**
Arrangement by Skip Martin

| E37303 | I Gotta Right To Sing The Blues | Capitol 4677 |
| | | Cap. SW1729 |

THE REPRISE YEARS
1960–1983

Los Angeles   **December 19, 1960**
Arrangements by Johnny Mandel

100	Ring-A-Ding-Ding	Rep. FS1001
101	Let's Fall In Love	Rep. FS1001
102	In The Still Of The Night	Rep. FS1001
103	A Foggy Day	Rep. FS1001
104	Let's Face The Music And Dance	Rep. FS1001
105	You'd Be So Easy To Love	Rep. FS1001
106	A Fine Romance	Rep. FS1001

Los Angeles   **December 20, 1960**
Arrangements by Johnny Mandel

107	The Coffee Song	Rep. FS1001
108	Be Careful It's My Heart	Rep. FS1001
109	Have You Met Miss Jones	N/R
110	I've Got My Love To Keep Me Warm	Rep. FS1001
111	Zing Went The Strings Of My Heart	N/R

| 112 | You And The Night And The Music | Rep. FS1001 |
| 113 | When I Take My Sugar To Tea | Rep. FS1001 |

Los Angeles   **December 21, 1960**
Arrangements by Felix Slatkin

114	The Last Dance	N/R
115	The Second Time Around	Reprise 20,001
		Rep. FS5238 (Italy)
116	Tina	Reprise 20,001-20, 151
		Rep. FS5239 (Italy)

Los Angeles   **March 20, 1961**
Arrangements by Sy Oliver

197	Take Me	N/R
198	Without A Song	N/R
199	Polka Dots And Moonbeams	N/R

Los Angeles   **March 21, 1961**
Arrangements by Sy Oliver

200	There Are Such Things	N/R
201	In The Blue Of Evening	N/R
202	I'll Be Seeing You	N/R
203	I'm Getting Sentimental Over You	N/R
204	Imagination	N/R

Los Angeles   **May 1, 1961**
Arrangements by Sy Oliver

233	I'll Be Seeing You	Reprise 20,023
		Rep. FS1003
234	I'm Getting Sentimental Over You	Reprise 20,025
		Rep. FS1003
235	Imagination	Reprise 20,024
		Rep. FS1003
236	Take Me	Reprise 20,028
		Rep. FS1003

Los Angeles   **May 2, 1961**
Arrangements by Sy Oliver

237	Without A Song	Reprise 20,027
		Rep. FS1003
238	Polka Dots And Moonbeams	Reprise 20,026
		Rep. FS1003
239	Daybreak	Reprise 20,028
		Rep. FS1003

Los Angeles   **May 3, 1961**
Arrangements by Sy Oliver

240	The One I Love Belongs To Somebody Else W/Sy Oliver	Reprise 20,023
		Rep. FS1003
241	There Are Such Things	Reprise 20,026
		Rep. FS1003
242	It's Always You	Reprise 20,024
		Rep. FS1003
243	It Started All Over Again	Reprise 20,027
		Rep. FS1003
244	East Of The Sun	Reprise 20,025
		Rep. FS1003

Los Angeles   **May 17, 1961**
Arrangements by Billy May

275	You're Nobody Till Somebody Loves You	N/R
276	Don't Cry Joe	N/R
277	Moonlight On The Ganges	N/R
278	Granada	N/R

Los Angeles		May 18, 1961
Arrangements by Billy May		
279	The Curse Of An Aching Heart	Reprise 20,010 Rep. FS1002
280	Love Walked In	Rep. FS1002
281	Please Don't Talk About Me When I'm Gone	Rep. FS1002
282	Have You Met Miss Jones	Rep. FS1002

Los Angeles		May 19, 1961
Arrangements by Billy May		
283	Don't Be That Way	Rep. FS1002
284	I Never Knew	Rep. FS1002
285	Falling In Love With Love	Rep. FS1002
286	It's A Wonderful World	Rep. FS1002

Los Angeles		May 23, 1961
Arrangements by Billy May		
287	Don't Cry Joe	Rep. FS1002
288	You're Nobody Till Somebody Loves You	Rep. FS1002
289	Moonlight On The Ganges	Rep. FS1002
290	Granada	Reprise 20,010 (edited) Rep. FS1002 (edited) Rep. F1002-mono (unedited)

Hollywood		November 20, 1961
Arrangements by Don Costa		
591	As You Desire Me	N/R
592	Stardust	Reprise 20,059 Rep. FS1004
593	Yesterdays	Rep. FS1004
594	I Hadn't Anyone Till You	Rep. FS1004

Hollywood		November 21, 1961
Arrangements by Don Costa		
595	It Might As Well Be Spring	Rep. FS1004
596	Prisoner Of Love	Rep. FS1004
597	That's All	Rep. FS1004
598	Don't Take Your Love From Me	N/R
599	Misty	Rep. FS1004

Hollywood		November 22, 1961
Arrangements by Don Costa		
600	Come Rain Or Come Shine	Reprise 20,059 Rep. FS1004
601	Night And Day	Rep. FS1006
602	All Or Nothing At All	Rep. FS1004
634	Pocketful Of Miracles Arrangement by Nelson Riddle	Reprise 20,040 Rep. FS1010 F1010-mono-alt. take
635	Name It And It's Yours Arrangement by Nelson Riddle	Reprise 20,040 Rep. FS5238 (Italy)

Los Angeles		January 15, 1962
Arrangements by Gordon Jenkins		
819	The Song Is Ended	Rep. FS1007
820	All Alone	Rep. FS1007
821	Charmaine	Rep. FS1007
822	When I Lost You	Rep. FS1007

Los Angeles		January 16, 1962
Arrangements by Gordon Jenkins		
823	Remember	Rep. FS1007
824	Together	Rep. FS1007
825	The Girl Next Door	Rep. FS1007
826	Indiscreet	Reprise 20,107 Rep. FS1007

Los Angeles		January 17, 1962
Arrangements by Gordon Jenkins		
827	What'll I Do	Rep. FS1007
828	Oh How I Miss You Tonight	Rep. FS1007
829	Are You Lonesome Tonight	Rep. FS1007
830	Come Waltz With Me	N/R

Los Angeles		February 27, 1962
Arrangements by Neal Hefti		
924	Everybody's Twistin'	Reprise 20,063 Rep. FS5238 (Italy)
925	Nothing But The Best	Reprise 20,063 Rep. FS5238 (Italy)

Hollywood		April 10, 1962
Arrangements by Neal Hefti		
1007	I'm Beginning To See The Light	Rep. FS1005
1008	I Get A Kick Out Of You	Rep. FS1005
1009	Ain't She Sweet	Rep. FS1005
1010	I Love You	Rep. FS1005
1011	They Can't Take That Away From Me	Rep. FS1005
1012	Love Is Just Around The Corner	Reprise 20,092 Rep. FS1005

Hollywood		April 11, 1962
Arrangements by Neal Hefti		
1013	At Long Last Love	Rep. FS1005
1014	Serenade In Blue	Rep. FS1005
1015	Goody, Goody	Reprise 20,092 Rep. FS1005
1016	Don'cha Go 'Way Mad	Rep. FS1005
1017	Tangerine	Rep. FS1005
1018	Pick Yourself Up	Rep. FS1005

London		June 12, 1961
Arrangements by Robert Farnon		
1023	If I Had You	Rep. FS1006
1024	The Very Thought Of You	Rep. FS1006
1025	I'll Follow My Secret Heart	Rep. FS1006
1026	A Garden In The Rain	Rep. FS1006

London		June 13, 1962
Arrangements by Robert Farnon		
1027	London By Night	Rep. FS1006
1028	The Gypsy	Rep. FS1006
1029	Roses of Picardy	N/R
1030	A Nightingale Sang In Berkeley Square	Rep. FS1006

London		June 14, 1962
Arrangements by Robert Farnon		
1031	We'll Meet Again	Rep. FS1006
1032	Now Is The Hour	Rep. FS1006
1033	We'll Gather Lilacs	Rep. FS1006

Los Angeles		August 27, 1962
Arrangements by Nelson Riddle Orchestra directed by Neal Hefti		
1426	The Look Of Love	Reprise 20,107 Rep. FS1013

1427	I Left My Heart In San Francisco	Reprise 20,107-withdrawn two weeks after release Rep. FS5238 (Italy)

Los Angeles — **October 2, 1962**
Arrangements by Neal Hefti
W/Count Basie And His Orchestra

1492	Nice Work If You Can Get It	Rep. FS1008
1493	Please Be Kind	Rep. FS1008
1494	I Won't Dance	Rep. FS1008
1495	Learnin' The Blues	Rep. FS1008

Los Angeles — **October 3, 1962**
Arrangements by Neal Hefti
W/Count Basie And His Orchestra

1496	I'm Gonna Sit Right Down And Write Myself A Letter	Rep. FS1008
1497	I Only Have Eyes For You	Rep. FS1008
1498	My Kind Of Girl	Rep. FS1008
1499	Pennies From Heaven	Rep. FS1008
1500	The Tender Trap	Rep. FS1008
1501	Looking At The World Through Rose Coloured Glasses	Rep. FS1008

Los Angeles — **October 22, 1962**
Arrangement by Billy May

1509	Me And My Shadow W/Sammy Davis Jr.	Reprise 20,128 Rep. FS5238 (Italy)

Los Angeles — **January 21, 1963**
Arrangements by Nelson Riddle

1671	Come Blow Your Horn	Reprise 20,184 Rep. FS1013
1672	Call Me Irresponsible	Reprise 20,151 Rep. FS1010

Hollywood — **February 18, 1963**
Arrangements by Nelson Riddle

1820	Lost In The Stars	Rep. FS1009
1821	My Heart Stood Still	Rep. FS1009
1822	Ol' Man River	Rep. FS1009

Hollywood — **February 19, 1963**
Arrangements by Nelson Riddle

1823	This Nearly Was Mine	Rep. FS1009
1824	You'll Never Walk Alone	Rep. FS1009
1825	I Have Dreamed	Reprise 20,184 Rep. FS1009

Hollywood — **February 20, 1963**
Arrangements by Nelson Riddle

1826	California W/Chorus	N/R
1827	Bewitched	Rep. FS1009
1828	America The Beautiful W/Chorus	N/R

Hollywood — **February 21, 1963**
Arrangements by Nelson Riddle

1829	Soliloquy	Rep. FS1009
1830	You Brought A New Kind Of Love To Me	Reprise 20,209 Rep. FS6167

Los Angeles — **April 29, 1963**
Arrangements by Nelson Riddle

2023	In The Wee Small Hours Of The Morning	Rep. FS1010
2024	Nancy	Rep. FS1010
2025	Young At Heart	Rep. FS1010

2026	The Second Time Around	Rep. FS1010
2027	All The Way	Rep. FS1010

Los Angeles — **April 30, 1963**
Arrangements by Nelson Riddle

2028	Witchcraft	Rep. FS1010
2029	How Little We Know	Rep. FS1010
2030	Put Your Dreams Away	Rep. FS1010
2031	I've Got You Under My Skin	Rep. FS1010
2032	Oh What It Seemed To Be	Rep. FS1010

Los Angeles — **July 10, 1963**
Orchestra directed by Morris Stoloff

2149	We Open In Venice Arrangement by Billy May W/Dean Martin & Sammy Davis Jr.	Rep. FS2017 Rep. W54100 (Italy)
2188	Guys And Dolls Arrangement by Bill Loose W/Dean Martin	Rep. FS2016 Rep. W54100 (Italy)

Los Angeles — **July 18, 1963**
Arrangements by Nelson Riddle
Orchestra directed by Morris Stoloff

2161	Old Devil Moon	Rep. FS2015 Rep. W54100 (Italy)
2166	When I'm Not Near The Girl I Love	Reprise 0398 Rep. FS2015 Rep. FS6167 Rep. W54100 (Italy)
2190	I've Never Been In Love Before	Rep. FS2016 Rep. FS6167 Rep. W54100 (Italy)

Los Angeles — **July 24, 1963**
Arrangements by Nelson Riddle
Orchestra directed by Morris Stoloff

2156	So In Love W/Keely Smith	Rep. FS2017 Rep. W54100 (Italy)
2180	Some Enchanted Evening W/Rosemary Clooney	Rep. FS2018 Rep. W54100 (Italy)
2193	Luck Be A Lady Arrangement by Billy May	Rep. FS2016 Rep. FS1015
2177-A	Guys And Dolls (Reprise) Arrangement by Bill Loose W/Dean Martin	Rep. FS2016 Rep. W54100 (Italy)

Los Angeles — **July 29, 1963**
Orchestra directed by Morris Stoloff

2184	Fugue For Tinhorns Arrangement by Bill Loose W/Bing Crosby & Dean Martin	Reprise 20,217 Rep. FS2016 Rep. W54100 (Italy)
2185	The Oldest Established (Permanent Floating Crap Game In New York) Arrangement by Billy May W/Bing Crosby & Dean Martin	Reprise 20, 217 Rep. FS2016,1016

Los Angeles		**July 31, 1963**
2171-B	Some Enchanted Evening	Rep. FS2018
	Arrangement by Nelson	Rep. W54100
	Riddle	(Italy)
	Orchestra directed by	
	Morris Stoloff	
2172	Twin Soliloquies	Rep. FS2018
	(Wonder How It Feels)	Rep. W54100
	Arrangement by Nelson	(Italy)
	Riddle	
	Orchestra directed by	
	Morris Stoloff	
	W/Keely Smith	
2103	Here's To Losers	Reprise 0373
	Arrangement by Marty	Rep. FS1013
	Paich	
	Orchestra directed by	
	Marty Paich	
2104	Love Isn't Just For The	Reprise 20,209
	Young	Rep. FS1013
	Arrangement by Marty	
	Paich	
	Orchestra directed by	
	Marty Paich	

Los Angeles		**October 13, 1963**
	Arrangement by Gil Frau	
	Orchestra directed by Gus Levene	
2295	Have Yourself A Merry	Reprise 243
	Little Christmas	(edited)
	W/Chorus	Rep. RS50,001
		(unedited)

Los Angeles		**December 3, 1963**
	Arrangements by Don Costa	
2448	Talk To Me Baby	Reprise 0249
		Rep. FS1013
2449	Stay With Me (Main	Reprise 0249
	Theme From 'The	Rep. FS6167
	Cardinal')	

Los Angeles		**January 2, 1964**
	Arrangements by Nelson Riddle	
	W/Fred Waring & His Pennsylvanians	
2467	You're A Lucky Fellow Mr.	Rep. FS2020
	Smith	Rep. FS5250 (Italy)
	Arrangement by Jack	
	Halloran	
2468	The House I Live In	Rep. FS2020, 2016
2469	Early American	Rep. FS2020
		Rep. FS5283 (Italy)

Los Angeles		**January 27, 1964**
	Arrangements by Nelson Riddle	
2521	The Way You Look	Rep. FS1011
	Tonight	
2522	Three Coins In The	Rep. FS1011
	Fountain	
2523	Swinging On A Star	Rep. FS1011
2524	In The Cool, Cool, Cool	Rep. FS1011
	Of The Evening	
2525	The Continental	Rep. FS1011

Los Angeles		**January 28, 1964**
	Arrangements by Nelson Riddle	
2526	It Might As Well Be	Rep. FS1011
	Spring	
2527	Secret Love	Rep. FS1011
2528	Moon River	Rep. FS1011
2529	Days Of Wine And Roses	Rep. FS1011

2530	Love Is A Many	Rep. FS1011
	Splendoured Thing	

Los Angeles		**February 4, 1964**
	Fred Waring And His Pennsylvanians	
2470	Let Us Break Bread	Rep. FS2020
	Together	Rep. FS5283 (Italy)
	Arrangement by	
	Roy Ringwald	
	W/Bing Crosby	
2471	You Never Had It So Good	Rep. FS2020
	Arrangement by	Rep. FS5283 (Italy)
	Jack Halloran	
	W/Bing Crosby	

Los Angeles		**April 8, 1964**
	Arrangements by Nelson Riddle	
2628	My Kind Of Town	Reprise 0279
		Rep. 2FS1016
2629	I Like To Lead When	Reprise 0279
	I Dance	Rep. FS6167
2577	*I Can't Believe I'm Losing	Reprise 0380
	You	Rep. FS1013
	Arrangement by Don	
	Costa	

*Over-dubbed w/guitar March 15, 1968—released as a single—Reprise 0677.

Los Angeles		**April 10, 1964**
	Arrangements by Nelson Riddle	
2631	Style	Rep. FS2021
	W/Bing Crosby &	
	Dean Martin	
2632	Mister Booze	Rep. FS2021
	W/Bing Crosby, Dean	
	Martin, Sammy Davis Jr.	
	& Chorus	
2633	Don't Be A Do-Badder	Rep. FS2021
	W/Bing Crosby, Dean	
	Martin, Sammy Davis Jr.	
	& Chorus	

Los Angeles		**June 9, 1964**
	Arrangements by Quincy Jones	
	W/Count Basie & His Orchestra	
2809	The Best Is Yet To Come	Rep. FS1012
2810	I Wanna Be Around	Rep. FS1012
2811	I Believe In You	Rep. FS1012
2812	Fly Me To The Moon	Rep. FS1012

Los Angeles		**June 10, 1964**
	Arrangements by Quincy Jones	
	W/Count Basie & His Orchestra	
2814	Hello Dolly	Rep. FS1012
2815	The Good Life	Rep. FS1012
2816	I Wish You Love	Rep. FS1012

Los Angeles		**June 12, 1964**
	Arrangements by Quincy Jones	
	W/Count Basie & His Orchestra	
2817	I Can't Stop Loving You	Rep. FS1012
2818	More	Rep. FS1012
2819	Wives And Lovers	Rep. FS1012

Los Angeles		**June 16, 1964**
	Fred Waring & His Pennsylvanians	
2453	An Old Fashioned	Rep. FS2022
	Christmas	
	Arrangement by Nelson	
	Riddle	

2454	I Heard The Bells On Christmas Day Arrangement by Nelson Riddle	Reprise 0314 Rep. FS2022
2455	The Little Drummer Boy Arrangement by Dick Reynolds	Reprise 0314 Rep. FS2022

Los Angeles   **June 19, 1964**

Arrangements by Jack Halloran
W/Fred Waring And His Pennsylvanians

2457	Go Tell It On The Mountain W/Bing Crosby	Reprise 0317 Rep. FS2022
2458	We Wish You The Merriest Co-arranged by Harry Betts W/Bing Crosby	Reprise 0317 Rep. FS2022

Los Angeles   **July 17, 1964**

Arrangements by Ernie Freeman

2888	Softly As I Leave You W/chorus	Reprise 0301 Rep. FS1012
2889	Then Suddenly Love W/chorus	Reprise 0301 Rep. FS1013
2890	Since Marie Has Left Paree Arrangement by Billy May W/chorus	N/R
2891	Available W/chorus	Reprise 0350 Rep. FS1013

Los Angeles   **October 3, 1964**

Arrangements by Nelson Riddle

2980	Pass Me By Arrangement by Billy May W/Chorus	Rep. FS1013
2981	Emily W/Chorus	Reprise 0332 Rep. FS1013
2982	Dear Heart W/chorus	Rep. FS1013

Los Angeles   **November 11, 1964**

Arrangements by Ernie Freeman
W/Vocal Chorus

3046	Somewhere In Your Heart	Reprise 0332 Rep. FS1025
3047	Anytime At All	Reprise 0350 Rep. FS6167

Hollywood   **April 13, 1965**

Arrangements by Gordon Jenkins

H3295	Don't Wait Too Long	Rep. FS1014
H3296	September Song	Rep. FS1014
H3297	Last Night When We Were Young	Rep. FS1014
H3298	Hello Young Lovers	Rep. FS1014

Hollywood   **April 14, 1965**

Arrangements by Gordon Jenkins

H3299	I See It Now	Rep. FS1014
H3300	When The Wind Was Green	Rep. FS1014
H3301	Once Upon A Time	Rep. FS1014
H3302	How Old Am I	N/R
HX3320	Tell Her You Love Her Each Day Arrangement by Ernie Freeman W/Chorus	Reprise 0373 Rep. FS1025

HX3321	When Somebody Loves You Arrangement by Ernie Freeman W/Chorus	Reprise 0398 Rep. FS1025

Hollywood   **April 22, 1965**

Arrangements by Gordon Jenkins

H3352	It Was a Very Good Year	Reprise 0429 Rep. FS1014
H3353	The Man In The Looking Glass	Rep. FS1014
H3354	This Is All I Ask	Rep. FS1014
H3355	It Gets Lonely Early	Rep. FS1014
H3302	*How Old Am I	Rep. FS1014

*Over-dubbed w/guitar March 15, 1968—released as a single—Reprise 0677.

Los Angeles   **May 6, 1965**

Arrangement by Ernie Freeman

HX3417	Forget Domani	Reprise 0380 Rep. FS1025

Hollywood   **May 27, 1965**

Arrangement by Gordon Jenkins

H3442	The September Of My Years	Reprise 0531 Rep. FS1014

Hollywood   **August 23, 1965**

Arrangements by Torrie Zito

HX3703	Everybody Has The Right To Be Wrong! (At Least Once)	Reprise 0410 Rep. FS1015
HX3704	I'll Only Miss Her When I Think Of Her	Reprise 0410 Rep. FS1015
HX3707	Golden Moment Arrangement by Nelson Riddle	Rep. FS1015

Hollywood   **October 11, 1965**

Orchestra directed by Sonny Burke

H3767	Come Fly With Me Arrangement by Billy May	Rep. 2FS1016
H3768	I'll Never Smile Again Arrangement by Freddy Stultz W/Chorus	Rep. 2FS1016

Hollywood   **October 21, 1965**

Arrangements by Nelson Riddle

HX3728	Moment To Moment Orchestral track recorded September 14, 1965	Reprise 0429 Rep. FS5238 (Italy)
H3770	Love And Marriage Orchestral track recorded October 11, 1965	Rep. 2FS1016

Hollywood   **November 29, 1965**

Arrangements by Nelson Riddle

H3892	Moon Song	Rep. FS1018
H3893	Moon Love	Rep. FS1018
H3894	The Moon Got In My Eyes	Rep. FS1018
H3895	Moonlight Serenade	Rep. FS1018
H3896	Reaching For The Moon	Rep. FS1018

Hollywood   **November 30, 1965**

Arrangements by Nelson Riddle

H3897	I Wished On The Moon	Rep. FS1018
H3898	Moonlight Becomes You	Rep. FS1018

H3899	Moonlight Mood	Rep. FS1018
H3900	Oh You Crazy Moon	Reprise 0470
		Rep. FS1018
H3901	The Moon Was Yellow	Rep. FS1018

Las Vegas — January 26—February 1, 1966
2 shows each night

Arrangements by Quincy Jones
W/Count Basie & His Orchestra

J4097	I've Got A Crush On You	Rep. FS1019
J4098	I've Got You Under My Skin	Rep. 2FS1019
J4099	The September Of My Years	Rep. 2FS1019
J4100	Street Of Dreams	Rep. 2FS1019
J4101	You Make Me Feel So Young	Reprise 0509
		Rep. 2FS1019
J4102	The Shadow Of Your Smile	Rep. 2FS1019
J4103	Luck Be A Lady	N/R
J4104	It Was A Very Good Year	Rep. 2FS1019
J4105	Don't Worry 'Bout Me	Rep. 2FS1019
J4106	My Kind Of Town	Rep. 2FS1019
J4107	One For My Baby	Rep. 2FS1019
J4108	Fly Me To The Moon	Rep. 2FS1019
J4109	Get Me To The Church On Time	Rep. 2FS1019
J4110	Angel Eyes	Rep. 2FS1019
J4111	Where Or When	Rep. 2FS1019
J4112	Come Fly With Me	Rep. 2FS1019

NOTE: This was Sinatra's first album of concert recordings. It is a compilation of ten shows recorded at the Sands—January 26 to February 1, 1966. On November 5, 1961, Reprise recorded Sinatra's show at the Sands with the Antonio Morelli orchestra. Sinatra was displeased with the results. It has never been released. Reprise did extensive recordings of Sinatra with the Clan in 1962 and 1963. Except for a brief segment on Rep. 2FS1016, they have never been released. The comedy skits were considered too risqué in 1963.

Hollywood — April 11, 1966

Arrangement by Ernie Freeman

J4195	Strangers In The Night	Reprise 0470
		Rep. FS1017, 1025

Hollywood — May 11, 1966

Arrangements by Nelson Riddle

J4234	My Baby Just Cares For Me	Rep. FS1017
J4235	Yes Sir, That's My Baby	Rep. FS1017
J4236	You're Driving Me Crazy	Rep. FS1017
J4237	The Most Beautiful Girl In The World	Rep. FS1017

Hollywood — May 16, 1966

Arrangements by Nelson Riddle

J4238	Summer Wind	Reprise 0509
		Rep. FS1017, 1025
J4239	All Or Nothing At All	Rep. FS1017
J4240	Call Me	Rep. FS1017
J4241	On A Clear Day (You Can See Forever)	Rep. FS1017
J4242	Downtown	Rep. FS1017

Hollywood — June 10, 1966

J4363	Gunga Din (spoken word)	N/R

Hollywood — July 25, 1966

Arrangements by Ernie Freeman

J4410	She Believes In Me	N/R
J4412	That's Life	N/R

Hollywood — October 18, 1966

Arrangement by Ernie Freeman

J4569	That's Life	Reprise 05321
		Rep. FS1020, 1025

Hollywood — November 17, 1966

Arrangements by Ernie Freeman

J4661	Give Her Love	Reprise 0561
		Rep. FS1020
J4662	What Now My Love	Rep. FS1020
J4663	Somewhere My Love	Rep. FS1020
J4664	Winchester Cathedral	Rep. FS1020

Hollywood — November 18, 1966

Arrangements by Ernie Freeman

J4665	I Will Wait For You	Reprise 0561
		Rep. FS1020
J4666	You're Gonna Hear From Me	Rep. FS1020
J4667	Sand And Sea	Rep. FS1020
J4668	The Impossible Dream	Rep. FS1020

Hollywood — January 30, 1967

Arrangements by Claus Ogerman

K4807	Baubles, Bangles And Beads W/Antonio Carlos Jobim	Rep. FS1021
K4808	I Concentrate On You W/Antonio Carlos Jobim	Rep. FS1021
K4809	Dindi	Rep. FS1021
K4810	Change Partners	Rep. FS1021

Hollywood — January 31, 1967

Arrangements by Claus Ogerman

K4811	Quiet Nights Of Quiet Stars (Corcovado)	Rep. FS1021
K4812	If You Never Come To Me	Rep. FS1021
K4813	The Girl From Ipanema W/Antonio Carlos Jobim	Rep. FS1021
K4814	Meditation	Rep. FS1021

Hollywood — February 1, 1967

Arrangements by Claus Ogerman

K4815	Once I Loved	Rep. FS1021
K4816	How Insensitive W/Antonio Carlos Jobim	Rep. FS1021
K4817	Drinking Again	Rep. FS1022
K4818	Somethin' Stupid Arrangement by Billy Strange W/Nancy Sinatra	Reprise 0561
		Rep. FS1022, 1025

New York City — June 29, 1967

K5296	You Are There Arrangement by Gordon Jenkins	Reprise 0610
		Rep. FS1022
K5297	The World We Knew Arrangement by Ernie Freeman	Reprise 0610
		Rep. FS1022, 1025
K5298	This Town Arrangement by Billy Strange	N/R

Hollywood — July 24, 1967

K6108	Born Free Arrangement by Gordon Jenkins	Rep. FS1022
K6109	This Is My Love Arrangement by Gordon Jenkins	Reprise 0631
		Rep. FS1022

K6110	This Is My Song Arrangement by Ernie Freeman	Rep. FS1022
K6111	Don't Sleep In The Subway Arrangement by Ernie Freeman W/Chorus	Rep. FS1022
K6112	Some Enchanted Evening Arrangement by H. B. Barnum	Rep. FS1022
K6113	This Town Arrangement by Billy Strange	Reprise 0631 Rep. FS1022, 1025

Hollywood September 20, 1967
Arrangement by Billy Strange

K6159	Younger Than Springtime	Rep. RS6277 Rep. FS5250 (Italy)

Hollywood December 11, 1967
Arrangements by Billy May
W/Duke Ellington And His Orchestra

K6319	All I Need Is The Girl	Rep. FS1024
K6320	Yellow Days	Rep. FS1024
K6321	Indian Summer	Rep. FS1024
K6322	Come Back To Me	Rep. FS1024

Hollywood December 12, 1967
Arrangements by Billy May
W/Duke Ellington And His Orchestra

K6324	Sunny	Rep. FS1024
K6326	Follow Me	Rep. FS1024
K6325	I Like The Sunrise	Rep. FS1024
K6323	Poor Butterfly	Rep. FS1024

New York City July 24, 1968
Arrangements by Don Costa

L5401	My Way Of Life	Reprise 0764 Rep. FS1027
L5402	Cycles	Reprise 0764 Rep. FS1027, 1034
L5403	Whatever Happened To Christmas	Reprise 0790 Rep. FS1026

Hollywood August 12, 1968
Arrangements by Nelson Riddle

L6755	The Twelve Days Of Christmas W/Frank Jr., Nancy and Tina	Rep. FS1026
L6756	The Bells Of Christmas (Greensleeves) W/Frank Jr., Nancy and Tina	Rep. FS1026
L6757	I Wouldn't Trade Christmas W/Frank Jr., Nancy and Tina	Rep. 0790 Rep. FS1026
L6758	The Christmas Waltz	Rep. FS1026

Hollywood November 11, 1968
Arrangements by Nelson Riddle

L6927	Blue Lace	Reprise 0817 Rep. FS1032 (England)
L6928	Star	Reprise 0798 Rep. FS1034

Hollywood November 12, 1968
Arrangements by Don Costa
Orchestra directed by Bill Miller

L6929	Little Green Apples	Rep. FS1027

L6930	Gentle On My Mind	Rep. FS1027
L6931	By The Time I Get To Phoenix	Rep. FS1027

Hollywood November 13, 1968
Arrangements by Don Costa
Orchestra directed by Bill Miller

L6932	Moody River	Rep. FS1027
L6933	Pretty Colours	Rep. FS1027

Hollywood November 14, 1968
Arrangements by Don Costa
Orchestra directed by Bill Miller

L6934	Rain In My Heart	Reprise 0798 Rep. FS1027
L6935	Wandering	Rep. FS1027
L6937	From Both Sides Now	Rep. FS1027

Hollywood December 30, 1968
Arrangement by Don Costa

L7053	My Way	Reprise 0817 Rep. FS1029, 1034

Hollywood February 11, 1969
Arrangements by Eumir Deodato
Orchestra directed by Morris Stoloff

M7141	One Note Samba W/Antonio Carlos Jobim	Rep. FS1033
M7142	Don't Ever Go Away	Rep. FS1033
M7143	Wave	Rep. FS1033
M7145	Bonita	Rep. K64039 (England)

Hollywood February 12, 1969
Arrangements by Eumir Deodato
Orchestra directed by Morris Stoloff

M7162	Someone To Light Up My Life	Rep. FS1033
M7163	Desafinado (Off Key) W/Antonio Carlos Jobim	N/R
M7164	Drinking Water (Aqua De Beber) W/Antonio Carlos Jobim	Rep. FS1033

Hollywood February 13, 1969
Arrangements by Eumir Deodato
Orchestra directed by Morris Stoloff

M7165	Song Of The Sabia	Reprise 0970 Rep. K64039 (England)
M7166	This Happy Madness W/Antonio Carlos Jobim	Rep. FS1033
M7167	Triste	Rep. FS1033
M7180	All My Tomorrows Arrangement by Don Costa	Rep. FS1029
M7181	Didn't We Arrangement by Don Costa	Rep. FS1029

Hollywood February 20, 1969
Arrangements by Don Costa

M7182	A Day In The Life Of A Fool	Rep. FS1029
M7183	Yesterday	Rep. FS1029
M7220	If You Go Away	Rep. FS1029

Hollywood February 24, 1969
Arrangements by Don Costa

M7221	Watch What Happens	Rep. FS1029
M7222	For Once In My Life	Rep. FS1029
M7223	Mrs. Robinson	Rep. FS1029
M7224	Hallelujah, I Love Her So	Rep. FS1029

Hollywood		February 25, 1969
	Arrangement by Don Costa	
RA3401-Z	Shadow Of The Moon	Rep. FS5283 (Italy)
		Rep. W54093 (Italy)

Hollywood		March 19, 1969
	Arrangements by Don Costa	
M7263	I've Been To Town	Rep. FS1030
M7264	Empty Is	Rep. FS1030
M7265	The Single Man	Rep. FS1030
M7266	Lonesome Cities	Rep. FS1030

Hollywood		March 20, 1969
	Arrangements by Don Costa	
M7267	The Beautiful Strangers	Rep. FS1030
M7268	A Man Alone	Reprise 0852
		Rep. FS1030, 1034
M7269	A Man Alone (Reprise)	Rep. FS1030
M7270	Love's Been Good To Me	Reprise 0852
		Rep. FS1030, 1034

Hollywood		March 21, 1969
	Arrangements by Don Costa	
M7271	Out Beyond The Window	Rep. FS1030
M7272	Night	Rep. FS1030
M7273	Some Travelling Music	Rep. FS1030
M7274	From Promise To Promise	Rep. FS1030

New York City		July 14, 1969
	Arrangements by Joseph Scott & Bob Gaudio	
M51586	I Would Be In Love (Anyway)	Reprise 0895
		Rep. FS1031
M51587	The Train	Reprise 0920
		Rep. FS1031
M51588	Goodbye	Rep. FS1031

New York City		July 15, 1969
	Arrangements by Charles Calello	
M51589	Watertown	Reprise 0895
		Rep. FS1031
M51591	Elizabeth	Rep. FS1031
M51592	Michael And Peter	Rep. FS1031

New York City		July 16, 1969
	Arrangements by Bob Gaudio and Joseph Scott	
M51594	She Says W/Chorus	Rep. FS1031
M51596	What's Now Is Now	Reprise 0920
		Rep. FS1031

New York City		July 17, 1969
	Arrangements by Charles Calello	
M51636	For A While	Rep. FS1031
M51637	Lady Day	N/R
M51638	What A Funny Girl (You Used To Be)	Rep. FS1031

Hollywood		August 18, 1969
	Arrangements by Don Costa	
M17431	Forget To Remember	Reprise 0865
		Rep. FS5240 (Italy)
M17432	Goin' Out Of My Head	Reprise 0865
		Rep. FS1034

New York City		October 13, 1969
	Arrangement by Charles Calello	
M161493	Lady Day	N/R

Hollywood		November 7, 1969
	Arrangement by Don Costa	
M17803	Lady Day	Reprise 0970
		Rep. FS1033

Hollywood		October 26, 1970
	Arrangements by Don Costa	
N19254	I Will Drink The Wine	Rep. FS1033
N19255	Bein' Green	Reprise 0981
		Rep. FS1033, 1034
N19256	My Sweet Lady	Rep. FS1033

Hollywood		October 27, 1970
	Arrangement by Don Costa	
N19261	Sunrise In The Morning	Rep. FS1033

Hollywood		October 28, 1970
	Arrangements by Lenny Hayton	
N19267	I'm Not Afraid	Reprise 1011
		Rep. FS1034
N19268	Something	Reprise 0981
		Rep. FS1034

Hollywood		October 29, 1970
	Arrangements by Don Costa	
N19269	Leaving On A Jet Plane	Rep. FS1033
N19270	Close To You	Rep. FS1033

Hollywood		November 2, 1970
	Arrangements by Don Costa	
N19276	Feelin' Kinda Sunday W/Nancy Sinatra	Reprise 0980
		Rep. FS5250 (Italy)
N19277	Life's A Trippy Thing W/Nancy Sinatra	Reprise 1011
		Rep. FS5250 (Italy)

NOTE: N19279 'The Game Is Over' was not recorded. Sinatra rehearsed the song with Bill Miller but declined to record it (11/2/70).

Hollywood		April 29, 1973
	Hurt Doesn't Go Away/ Nobody Wins/Noah	Masters Destroyed

Hollywood		June 4, 1973
	Arrangements by Gordon Jenkins	
RCA4011	Bang, Bang	N/R
RCA4012	You Will Be My Music	Reprise S1190
		Rep. FS2155
RCA4013	Noah W/Chorus	Rep. FS2155

Hollywood		June 5, 1973
	Arrangements by Gordon Jenkins	
RCA4014	Nobody Wins	Rep. FS2155
RCA4015	The Hurt Doesn't Go Away	Reprise S1327
		Rep. W54093 (Italy)

Hollywood		June 21, 1973
	Arrangements by Don Costa	
	Orchestra directed by Gordon Jenkins	
RCA4026	Winners	Reprise S1190
		Rep. FS2155
RCA4027	Let Me Try Again	Reprise S1181
		Rep. FS2155

Hollywood		June 22, 1973
	Arrangements by Gordon Jenkins	
RCA4028	Empty Tables	Reprise S1343
		Rep. W54093 (Italy)
RCA4029	Walk Away	N/R
RCA4030	Send In The Clowns	Reprise S1181
		Rep. FS2155
RCA4031	There Used To Be A Ballpark	Rep. FS2155

Hollywood		August 20, 1973
	Orchestra directed by Gordon Jenkins	
RCA4188	You're So Right (For What's Wrong In My Life) Arrangement by Gordon Jenkins	Rep. FS2155
RCA4189	Dream Away Arrangement by Don Costa	Rep. FS2155

Hollywood		December 10, 1973
	Arrangements by Don Costa	
RCA4523	Bad, Bad Leroy Brown	Reprise S1196 Rep. FS2195
RCA4524	I'm Gonna Make It All The Way	Reprise S1196 Rep. FS2195

Hollywood		May 7, 1974
	Arrangements by Gordon Jenkins	
SCA4720	Empty Tables	N/R
SCA4721	If	Rep. FS2195
SCA4722	The Summer Knows	Rep. FS2195

Hollywood		May 8, 1974
	Arrangements by Don Costa	
SCA4840	Sweet Caroline	Rep. FS2195
SCA4841	You Turned My World Around	Reprise S1208 Rep. FS2195

Hollywood		May 9, 1974
	Arrangement by Don Costa	
SCA4842	You Are The Sunshine Of My Life	N/R

Hollywood		May 21, 1974
	Arrangements by Don Costa	
SCA4849	What Are You Doing The Rest Of Your Life	Rep. FS2195
SCA4850	Tie A Yellow Ribbon Round The Ole Oak Tree	Rep. FS2195
SCA4851	Satisfy Me One More Time	Reprise S1208 Rep. FS2195
SCA4852	If You Could Read My Mind	N/R

Hollywood		May 24, 1974
	Arrangement by Don Costa	
SCA4842	You Are The Sunshine Of My Life Orchestral track recorded May 21, 1974	Rep. FS2195

Hollywood		September 24, 1974
	Arrangements by Gordon Jenkins	
SCA5051	The Saddest Thing Of All	N/R
SCA5052	Everything Happens To Me	N/R
SCA5053	Just As Though You Were Here	N/R N/R

New York City		October 13, 1974
	Orchestra directed by Bill Miller W/Woody Herman And The Young Thundering Herd	
SXX0163	The Lady Is A Tramp Arrangement by Billy Byers	Rep. FS2207
SXX0164	I Get A Kick Out Of You Arrangement by Nelson Riddle Verse is taken from Philadelphia Concert, October 7, 1974. Chorus is from Main Event, October 13, 1974	Rep. FS2207

SXX0165	Let Me Try Again Arrangement by Don Costa	Rep. FS2207
SXX0166	Autumn In New York Arrangement by Billy May Taken from New York City Concert, October 12, 1974	Rep. FS2207
SXX0167	I've Got You Under My Skin Arrangement by Nelson Riddle Taken from Buffalo Concert, October 4, 1974	Rep. FS2207
SXX0168	Bad, Bad Leroy Brown Arrangement by Don Costa	Rep. FS2207
SXX0169	Angel Eyes Arrangement by Nelson Riddle Taken from Buffalo Concert, October 4, 1974	Rep. FS2207
SXX0170	You Are The Sunshine Of My Life Arrangement by Don Costa	Rep. FS2207
SXX0171	The House I Live In Arrangement by Nelson Riddle Taken from Boston Concert, October 2, 1974	Rep. FS2207
SXX0172	My Kind Of Town Arrangement by Nelson Riddle	Rep. FS2207
SXX0173	My Way Arrangement by Don Costa Taken from Boston Concert, October 2, 1974	Rep. FS2207

Hollywood		February 20, 1975
	Arrangement by Don Costa Orchestra directed by Bill Miller	
TCA5325	The Only Couple On The Floor	N/R

Hollywood		March 3, 1975
	Arrangements by Don Costa Orchestra directed by Bill Miller	
TCA5292	Anytime (I'll Be There) W/Chorus	Reprise S1327 Rep. W54093 (Italy)
TCA5325	The Only Couple On The Floor W/Chorus	Reprise S1335 Rep. W54093 (Italy)
TCA5326	I Believe I'm Gonna Love You Arrangement by Al Capps W/Chorus	Reprise S1335 Rep. W54093 (Italy)
TCA5327	Grass W/Chorus	N/R

Hollywood		March 12, 1975
	Arrangements by Don Costa	
TCA5342	Oh, Babe, What Would You Say	N/R
TCA5343	You Are The Sunshine Of My Life	N/R
TCA5344	That Old Black Magic	N/R

New York City		August 18, 1975
	Arrangement by Gordon Jenkins	
TCA5601	The Saddest Thing Of All	Reprise S1343
	Orchestral track recorded August 4, 1975	Rep. W54093 (Italy)

Hollywood		October 24, 1975
	Arrangements by Don Costa	
TCA5717	A Baby Just Like You	Reprise S1342
	W/Chorus	Rep. W54093 (Italy)
TCA5718	Christmas Mem'ries	Reprise S1342
	W/Chorus	Rep. W54093 (Italy)

Hollywood		February 5, 1976
	Arrangements by Don Costa Orchestra directed by Bill Miller	
UCA5873	I Sing The Songs (I Write The Songs)	Reprise S1347 Rep. W54093 (Italy)
UCA5874	Empty Tables W/Bill Miller, piano	Reprise S1347 Rep. W54101 (Italy) Rep. K64039 (England)
UCA5875	Send In The Clowns W/Bill Miller, piano Spoken introduction by Sinatra	Reprise S1382 Rep. W54101 (Italy)

NOTE: Reprise recorded Sinatra at Caesar's Palace, January 21, 1976—second show. The recorded segment included three songs from this session. Sinatra was not satisfied with the results and the above session was scheduled.

Hollywood		June 21, 1976
UCA6205	The Best I Ever Had Arrangement by Billy May Saxophone solo by Sam Butera	Reprise S1364 Rep. W54101 (Italy)
UCA6206	Stargazer Arrangement by Don Costa Orchestra directed by Bill Miller Saxophone solo by Sam Butera	Reprise S1364 Rep. W54101 (Italy) Rep. K64039 (England)

New York City		September 27, 1976
UCA6251	*Dry Your Eyes Arrangements by Don Costa Orchestra directed by Bill Miller	Reprise S1377 Rep. W54101 (Italy)
UNY1180	Like A Sad Song Arrangement by Claus Ogerman	Reprise S1377 Rep. W54101 (Italy)

*Orchestral track recorded June 21, 1976 in Hollywood.

Hollywood		November 12, 1976
	Arrangements by Nelson Riddle	
UCA6590	I Love My Wife	Reprise S1382 Rep. W54101 (Italy)
UCA6591	Evergreen	N/R

Hollywood		January 19, 1977
	Arrangements by Charles Calello	
VLA1288	Everybody Ought To Be In Love Orchestral track recorded on January 7, 1977	N/R

New York City		February 16, 1977
	Arrangements by Joe Beck	
UNY1197	Night And Day Orchestral track recorded February 15, 1977	Reprise S1386 Rep. W54101 (Italy)
UNY1198	All Or Nothing At All	N/R
VNY1288	Everybody Ought To Be In Love Arrangement by Charles Calello Orchestral track recorded February 15, 1977	Reprise S1386 Rep. W54101 (Italy)

Hollywood		March 9, 1977
	Arrangements by Nelson Riddle	
VCA6842	Nancy	N/R
VCA6844	Stella By Starlight	N/R
VCA6845	Emily	N/R

Hollywood		March 14, 1977
	Arrangements by Nelson Riddle	
VCA6840	Linda Orchestral track recorded March 13, 1977	N/R
VCA6841	Sweet Lorraine Orchestral track recorded March 13, 1977	N/R
VCA6848	Barbara Orchestral track recorded March 11, 1977	N/R

Hollywood		July 17, 1978
	Arrangements by Don Costa	
WCA8129	That's What God Looks Like	N/R
WCA8130	Remember	N/R
WCA8131	You And Me	N/R

Los Angeles		July 16, 1979
	Arrangements by Billy May	
XCA-9299	Street Of Dreams	N/R
XCA-9302	More Than You Know W/Chorus	N/R
XCA-9300	My Shining Hour W/Chorus	N/R

Los Angeles		July 17, 1979
	Arrangements by Billy May	
XCA-9295	But Not For Me W/Chorus	N/R
XCA-9303	They All Laughed	N/R
SCA-9294	The Song Is You	N/R

Los Angeles		July 18, 1979
	Arrangements by Billy May	
XCA-9296	I Had The Craziest Dream W/Chorus	Rep. 3FS2300
XCA-9297	It Had To Be You	Rep. 3FS2300
XCA-9298	Let's Face The Music & Dance	N/R

New York		August 20, 1979
	Arrangements by Don Costa	
XNY-2099	You & Me	RPS49517 Rep. 3FS2300
XNY-2104	Summer Me, Winter Me	Rep. 3FS2300
XNY-2102	McArthur Park	Rep. 3FS2300

New York		**August 21, 1979**
Arrangements by Don Costa		
XNY-2106	For The Good Times W/Eileen Farrell & Chorus	Rep. 3FS2300
XNY-2101	What God Looks Like To Me	Rep. RPS49233 Rep. 3FS2300
XNY-2107	Love Me Tender W/Chorus	Rep. 3FS2300

New York		**August 22, 1979**
Arrangements by Don Costa		
XNY-2109	Isn't She Lovely? W/Chorus	N/R
XNY-2100	Just The Way You Are	Rep. 3FS2300
XNY-2105	Song Sung Blue W/Chorus	Rep. 3FS2300

Los Angeles		**September 17, 1979**
Arrangements by Billy May		
XCA-9301	All Of You	Rep. 3FS2300
XCA-9300	My Shining Hour W/Chorus	Rep. 3FS2300
XCA-9302	More Than You Know W/Chorus	Rep. 3FS2300

Los Angeles		**September 18, 1979**
Arrangements by Billy May		
XCA-9294	The Song Is You	Rep. 3FS2300
XCA-9295	But Not For Me W/Chorus	Rep. 3FS2300
XCA-9299	Street Of Dreams	Rep. 3FS2300
XCA-9303	They All Laughed	Rep. 3FS2300

Los Angeles		**September 19, 1979**
Arrangement by Billy May		
XCA-9298	Let's Face The Music & Dance	Rep. 3FS2300
Arrangement by Don Costa		
Orchestra conducted by Vinnie Falcone		
XNY-2103	New York, New York	Rep. RPS49233 Rep. 3FS2300

Los Angeles		**December 3, 1979**
Arrangement by Nelson Riddle		
Orchestra conducted by Vinnie Falcone		
XNY-2108	Something	Rep. 3FS2300

Los Angeles		**December 17, 1979**
Arrangements by Gordon Jenkins		
W/Chorus and LA Philharmonic Symphony Orchestra		
XCA-9306	The Future	Rep. 3FS2300
XCA-9307	I've Been There	Rep. RPS49517 Rep. 3FS2300
XCA-9308	Song Without Words	Rep. 3FS2300

Los Angeles		**December 18, 1979**
Arrangements by Gordon Jenkins		
W/Chorus and LA Philharmonic Symphony Orchestra		
XCA-9309	Before The Music Ends	Rep. 3FS2300
XCA-9304	What Time Does The Next Miracle Leave	Rep. 3FS2300
XCA-9305	World War None	Rep. 3FS2300

Hollywood		**April 8, 1981**
Arranged and Conducted by Gordon Jenkins		
ZLA-1030	Bang Bang	Rep. FS2305
ZLA-1031	Everything Happens To Me	N/R
Arrangement by Nelson Riddle		
Orchestra conducted by Vinnie Falcone		

Z-1032	The Gal That Got Away/ It Never Entered My Mind	Rep. FS2305

New York		**July 20, 1981**
Arranged and conducted by Gordon Jenkins		
ZNY-2619	Thanks For The Memory	Rep. FS2305
ZNY-2620	I Love Her	Rep. FS2305
ZNY-2621	A Long Night	Rep. FS2305

New York		**July 21, 1981 (day)**
Arranged and conducted by Don Costa		
ZNY-2623	Say Hello	Rep. RPS49827

New York		**July 21, 1981 (night)**
Arranged and conducted by Gordon Jenkins		
ZNY-2622	South to a Warmer Place	Rep. FS2305

New York		**August 19, 1981**
Arranged and conducted by Don Costa		
ZNY-2624	Good Thing Going	Rep. RPS49827 Rep. FS2305

New York		**September 10, 1981**
Arranged and conducted by Gordon Jenkins		
ZNY-2634	Monday Morning Quarterback	Rep. FS2305
ZNY-2635	Hey Look, No Crying (Edited version released)	Rep. FS2305

Los Angeles		**December 3, 1981**
Arrangement by Don Costa		
Orchestra conducted by Vinnie Falcone		
ZCA1518S	Foster Grandparents Recording Love a Child	Rep. 7-29903

New York		**August 17, 1982**
Arrangement by Don Costa		
Orchestra conducted by Vinnie Falcone		
N/A	Searchin'	N/R
Arrangement by Billy May		
N/A	Love Makes Us	N/R

New York		**January 19, 1983**
Arrangement by Don Costa		
Orchestra conducted by Joe Parnello		
N/A	Searchin'	N/R
Arrangement by Tony Mottola		
N/A	It's Sunday	N/R
Arrangement by Billy May		
N/A	Love Makes Us Here's to the Band (run-through)	N/R

New York		**January 25, 1983**
Arranged and conducted by Joe Parnello		
BNY 3126S	Here's to the Band	7-29677
N/A	All the Way Home	N/R

Los Angeles		**February 28, 1983**
Guitar arrangement played by Tony Mottola		
BNY 3127S	It's Sunday	7-29677

Los Angeles		**March 16, 1983**
Arranged and conducted by Joe Parnello		
N/A	How D'Ya Keep the Music Playin'	N/R

THE FILMS

Las Vegas Nights—Paramount 1941
I'll Never Smile Again—W/Tommy Dorsey And His Orchestra

Ship Ahoy—Metro Goldwyn-Mayer—1942
 The Last Call For Love—W/Tommy Dorsey And His Orchestra
 Poor You—W/Tommy Dorsey And His Orchestra, Red Skelton, Eleanor Powell
 Moonlight Bay—W/Tommy Dorsey And His Orchestra And The Pied Pipers

Reveille With Beverly—Columbia—1943
 Night And Day

Higher And Higher—RKO—1943
 I Couldn't Sleep A Wink Last Night
 The Music Stopped
 I Saw You First—W/Marcy McGuire
 A Lovely Way To Spend An Evening
 You're On Your Own

The Shining Future—Warner Bros.—1944
 There'll Be A Hot Time In The Town Of Berlin

Step Lively—RKO—1944
 Come Out, Come Out, Wherever You Are—W/Gloria Haven And Chorus
 As Long As There's Music
 Where Does Love Begin?—W/Anne Jeffreys
 Some Other Time—W/Gloria Haven

All-Star Bond Rally—20th Century Fox—1945
 Saturday Night—W/Harry James And His Orchestra

The House I Live In—RKO—1945
 If You Are But A Dream
 House I Live In

Anchors Aweigh—Metro-Goldwyn-Mayer—1945
 We Hate To Leave—W/Gene Kelly And Chorus
 Brahms Lullaby
 I Begged Her—W/Gene Kelly
 If You Knew Susie—W/Gene Kelly
 What Makes The Sunset?
 Tonight We Love
 The Charm Of You
 I Fall In Love Too Easily

Christmas Trailer (Short Subject-3 minutes)—Metro-Goldwyn-Mayer-1945
 Silent Night

Till The Clouds Roll By—Metro-Goldwyn-Mayer—1946
 Ol' Man River

It Happened In Brooklyn—Metro-Goldwyn-Mayer—1947
 Whose Baby Are You?
 The Brooklyn Bridge
 I Believe—W/Jimmy Durante And Billy Roy
 Time After Time
 The Song's Gotta Come From The Heart—W/Jimmy Durante
 La Ci Darem La Mano—W/Kathryn Grayson (alternate take in M-G-M's vault)
 It's The Same Old Dream—W/Chorus

Lucky Strike Promo Film—1948-Salesman's Movie-American Tobacco Co.
 Embraceable You—W/The Lucky Strike Quartette And The Hit Parade Orchestra

The Miracle Of The Bells—RKO—1948
 Ever Homeward

The Kissing Bandit—Metro-Goldwyn-Mayer—1948
 What's Wrong With Me?
 If I Steal A Kiss
 Siesta
 Senorita—W/Kathryn Grayson

Take Me Out To The Ball Game—Metro-Goldwyn-Mayer—1949
 Take Me Out To The Ball Game—W/Gene Kelly
 Yes Indeedy—W/Gene Kelly, Jules Munshin And Chorus
 O'Brien To Ryan To Goldberg—W/Gene Kelly and Jules Munshin
 She's The Right Girl For Me
 Boys And Girls Like You And Me—deleted from film
 It's Fate, Baby, It's Fate—W/Betty Garrett
 Strictly U.S.A.—W/Gene Kelly, Jules Munshin, Esther Williams, Betty Garrett And Chorus

On The Town—Metro-Goldwyn-Mayer—1949
 New York, New York—W/Gene Kelly And Jules Munshin
 Prehistoric Man—W/Gene Kelly, Jules Munshin And Ann Miller
 Come Up To My Place—W/Betty Garrett
 You're Awful—W/Betty Garrett
 On The Town—W/Gene Kelly, Jules Munshin, Betty Garrett, Ann Miller And Vera Ellen
 Count On Me—W/Jules Munshin, Betty Garrett, Ann Miller And Alice Pearce

Double Dynamite—RKO—1951
 It's Only Money—W/Groucho Marx
 Kisses And Tears—W/Jane Russell

Meet Danny Wilson—Universal-International—1951
 You're A Sweetheart
 Lonesome Man Blues
 She's Funny That Way
 That Old Black Magic
 When You're Smiling
 All of Me
 A Good Man Is Hard To Find—W/Shelley Winters
 I've Got A Crush On You
 How Deep Is The Ocean?

Young At Heart—Warner Bros.—1955
 Young At Heart
 Someone To Watch Over Me
 Just One Of Those Things—issued on Warner Bros.—Fifty Years of Film Music-WB3XX2736
 One For My Baby
 You My Love—W/Doris Day

Guys And Dolls—Metro-Goldwyn-Mayer—1955
 The Oldest Established Permanent Floating Crap Game In New York—W/Stubby Kaye And Johnny Silver
 Guys And Dolls—W/Stubby Kaye, Johnny Silver And Chorus
 Adelaide
 Sue Me—W/Vivian Blaine

The Tender Trap—Metro-Goldwyn-Mayer—1955
 The Tender Trap
 The Tender Trap—W/Debbie Reynolds, Celeste Holm And David Wayne

The Man With The Golden Arm—United Artists—1955
 The Man With The Golden Arm— deleted from film

High Society—Metro-Goldwyn-Mayer—1956
 Sinatra's recordings from this film have been released commercially on Capitol SW750—'High Society'

The Joker Is Wild—Paramount—1957
 At Sundown
 I Cried For You
 If I Could Be With You
 Chicago—deleted from film
 All The Way

150

Out Of Nowhere (Parody)
Swingin' On A Star (Parody)
All The Way (Parody)
Martha, Martha (Parody)

Pal Joey—Columbia—1957
I Didn't Know What Time It Was
There's A Small Hotel
I Could Write A Book—W/Kim Novak
The Lady Is A Tramp
Bewitched
What Do I Care For A Dame?—available on Capitol Soundtrack-
SW912

A Hole In The Head—United Artists—1959
All My Tomorrows
High Hopes—W/Eddie Hodges

Can-Can—20th Century Fox—1960
Sinatra's recordings for this film have been released commercially on Capitol SW1301—'Can-Can'

World Tour—Sinatra Enterprises—1962
In The Still Of The Night (London)
At Long Last Love (Israel)
All The Way (Jerusalem)
Lady Is A Tramp (Paris)
I Could Have Danced All Night (Athens)

Sinatra In Israel—Israel Foundation of Histadruth—1962
In The Still Of The Night (Tel Aviv)
Without A Song (Israel)

Come Blow Your Horn—Paramount—1963
Come Blow Your Horn

Robin And The Seven Hoods—Warner Bros.—1964
I Like To Lead When I Dance—deleted from the film
Style—W/Bing Crosby And Dean Martin
Mister Booze—W/Bing Crosby, Dean Martin, Sammy Davis Jr.
And Chorus
My Kind of Town
Don't Be A Do-Badder—W/Bing Crosby, Dean Martin, Sammy
Davis Jr. and Chorus

UNRELEASED SOUNDTRACKS

Music At War—RKO—1943
The Song Is You

**Finian's Rainbow—Distributors Corporation Of America—
1954-55**
Animated cartoon soundtrack-never completed
If This Isn't Love/W/Ella Logan And Chorus
Ad Lib Blues—W/Louis Armstrong
Necessity
Old Devil Moon—W/Ella Logan (running time 7 mins. & 57
secs.)
Necessity—W/Ella Fitgerald
Great Come And Get It Day

Carousel—20th Century Fox—1955
Sinatra was scheduled to appear in the film as Billy Bigelow. A
dispute developed with 20th Century and he dropped out, but
not before he had recorded three songs for the film.

Soliloquy
If I Loved You—W/Shirley Jones
Untitled duet—W/Cameron Mitchell
This song was dropped from the film

SINATRA'S VOICE ON THE SOUNDTRACK
(Sinatra did not appear in these films)

A Thousand And One Nights—1945
All Or Nothing At All

Adam's Rib—1949
Farewell Amanda—written by Cole Porter-the running time was
1 min. and 27 secs. Only a brief segment is heard in the film.

Three Coins In The Fountain—1954
Three Coins In The Fountain

Advise And Consent—1962
Loser's Song

The Victors—1963
Have Yourself A Merry Little Christmas
(available on Colpix SCP 516)

A New Kind Of Love—1963
You Brought A New Kind Of Love To Me—Reprise recording

Paris When It Sizzles—1964
The Girl Who Stole The Eiffel Tower—brief segment is heard in
film

The Silencers—1966
Come Fly With Me—Reprise recording

The Ambushers—1967
Strangers In The Night—Reprise recording

Carnal Knowledge—1971
Dream—Columbia recording

The Front—1976
Young At Heart—Capitol recording

Looking For Mr. Goodbar—1977
All Of Me—Capitol recording

The End—1978
My Way—Reprise Recording

Raging Bull—1980
All Or Nothing At All—Columbia recording
Come Fly With Me—Capitol recording

S.O.B.—1981
All The Way—Reprise recording

Inside Moves—1982
Put Your Dreams Away—Reprise recording

They All Laughed—1982
New York, New York—Reprise recording
You and Me—Reprise recording
More Than You'll Ever Know—Reprise recording
They All Laughed—Reprise recording

Diner—1982
I've Got You Under My Skin—Capitol recording

V DISCS

Studio recordings by Frank Sinatra for the United States
Government's Overseas Victory Disc Programme—1943 to 1949.
(The radio air checks that were issued on V-Discs are not listed)

New York City   January 20, 1941
Arrangement by Sy Oliver with the Tommy Dorsey Orchestra
CS060349-2   Without A Song   V-Disc 33-B (Army)
VP126-D3MC   Victor 36396 (12
180   inch) com. issue

New York City   **February 7, 1941**

The Pied Pipers with the Tommy Dorsey Orchestra

BS060626-1   Do I Worry   N/R on V-Disc
VP673-D4TC   Victor 27338-com.
173   issue

New York City   **July 15, 1941**

Arrangement by Harry Rodgers with Band Chorus
And the Tommy Dorsey Orchestra

BS066923-1   Blue Skies   V-Disc 1-B (Army)
DBHC 152   Victor 27566-com.
                                      issue

New York City   **September 26, 1941**

The Tommy Dorsey Orchestra

BS067653-2   The Sunshine Of Your V-Disc 434-B
VP762-D4TC   Smile   (Army)
229   214-B (Navy)
                                      Victor 27638-com.
                                      issue

Hollywood   **January 19, 1942**

Arrangements by Axel Stordahl

PBS072042-1   The Night We Called It A   N/R on V-Disc
VP709-D4TC   Day   Bluebird 11463-
204   com. issue
PBS072043-1   The Lamplighter's   V-Disc 434-B
VP762-D4TC   Serenade   (Army)
229   214-B (Navy)
                                      Bluebird 11515
PBS072044-1   The Song Is You   V-Disc 25-B (Army)
VP74-D3MC   Bluebird 11515-
137   com. issue
PBS072045-1   Night And Day   V-Disc 25-A
VP65-D3MC   (Army)
128   Bluebird 11463-
                                      com. issue

Hollywood   **March 9, 1942**

Arrangement by Sy Oliver with the Tommy Dorsey Orchestra

PBS072171-1   Somewhere A Voice Is N/R on V-Disc
VP658-D4TC   Calling   Victor 27887-20-
160   2006-com. issue

New York City   **June 17, 1942**

Arrangement by Axel Stordahl with the Tommy Dorsey Orchestra

BS075282-1   In The Blue Of Evening   V-Disc 18-A
VP23-D3MC   (Army)
114   Victor 27947-20-
                                      1530-com. issue

New York City   **October 17, 1943**

Broadway Bandbox—dress rehearsal-CBS
Arrangements by Axel Stordahl

VP245-D3MC   I Only Have Eyes For V-Disc 72-A
268   You—spoken intro.   (Army)
                W/Bobby Tucker Singers
VP246-D3MC   Kiss Me Again   V-Disc 72-B (Army)
269   103-B (Navy)
VP246-D3MC   Hot Time In The Town Of   V-Disc 72-B
269   Berlin (There's Gonna   103-B (Navy)
                Be)

New York City   **November 14, 1943**

Songs By Sinatra—dress rehearsal—CBS
Arrangement by Axel Stordahl

VP282   The Music Stopped   V-Disc 116-A
                                      (Army)

New York City   **November 21, 1943**

Songs By Sinatra—dress rehearsal—CBS

VP283   I Couldn't Sleep A Wink   V-Disc 116-B
                Last Night

Arrangement by Alec
Wilder

VP283   The Way You Look   V-Disc 116-B
                Tonight
                Arrangement by
                Axel Stordahl
                W/Bobby Tucker Singers
VP375-D3MC   I'll Be Around   V-Disc 124-A
452   Arrangement by Alec   (Army)
                Wilder
VP375-D3MC   You've Got A Hold On Me   V-Disc 124-A
452   Arrangement by Axel   (Army)
                Stordahl
VP376-D3MC   A Lovely Way to Spend V-Disc 124-B
453   An Evening   (Army)
                Arrangement by Axel
                Stordahl
VP376-D3MC   She's Funny That Way V-Disc 124-B
453   Arrangement by   (Army)
                Axel Stordahl

New York City   **December 5, 1943**

Songs By Sinatra—dress rehearsal—CBS
Arrangement by Axel Stordahl

VP448   Speak Low   V-Disc 154-A
                                      (Army)

New York City   **December 26, 1943**

Songs By Sinatra—dress rehearsal
Arrangement by Axel Stordahl—W/Bobby Tucker Singers

VP448   Close To You   V-Disc 154-A
                                      (Army)

Hollywood   **January 12, 1944**

Vimms Vitamins Show—CBS
Arrangement by Axel Stordahl

VP498-D4TC   My Shining Hour   V-Disc 166-B
56   (Army)

Hollywood   **February 9, 1944**

Vimms Vitamins Show—CBS
Arrangement by Axel Stordahl

VP498-D4TC   Long Ago And Far Away V-Disc 166-B
56   (Army)

New York City   **May 16, 1944**

Vimms Vitamins Show—CBS—dress rehearsal
Arrangements by Axel Stordahl

VP681-D4TC   Some Other Time   V-Disc 241-B
185   (Army)
                                      21-B (Navy)
VP681-D4TC   Come Out Wherever You V-Disc 241-B
185   Are   (Army)
                                      21-B (Navy)

Hollywood   **May 24, 1944**

Vimms Vitamins Show—CBS
Arrangements by Axel Stordahl

VP742-D4TC   Put Your Dreams Away V-Disc 262-A
217   (Dress Rehearsal)   (Army)
                                      42-A (Navy)
VP242-D4TC   And Then You Kissed Me   V-Disc 262-A
217   (Army)
                                      42-A (Navy)

Hollywood   **July 8, 1944**

V-Disc Recording Session
Arrangements by Axel Stordahl

VP818-D4TC   All The Things You Are V-Disc 287-B
262   (Army)
                                      67-B (Navy)

VP818-D4TC 262	All Of Me	V-Disc 287-B (Army) 67-B (Navy)
VP823-D4TC 267	Nancy	V-Disc 323-A (Army) 103-A (Navy)
VP824-D4TC 268	Mighty Lak'A Rose	V-Disc 310-A (Army) 90-A (Navy)
VP919-D4TC 426	If Loveliness Were Music	N/R on V-Disc
VP1148-XP 34237	Brahms' Lullaby	N/R on V-Disc
VP1148-XP 34237	I'll Follow My Secret Heart	N/R on V-Disc
VP1332-D5TC 295	Falling In Love With Love	V-Disc 467-A (Army) 247-A (Navy)
VP1399-D5TC 515	Brahms' Lullaby	V-Disc 506-A (Army) 266-A (Navy)
VP1399-D5TC 515	I'll Follow My Secret Heart	V-Disc 506-A (Army) 266-A (Navy)

New York City   **October 11, 1944**
Vimms Vitamins Show—dress rehearsal
Arrangements by Alex Stordahl

VP941-D4MC 443	There's No You	V-Disc 378-A (Army) 155-A (Navy)
VP941-D4MC 443	Someone To Watch Over Me W/Chorus	V-Disc 378-A (Army) 155-A (Navy)

New York City   **October 18, 1944**
Vimms Vitamins Show—dress rehearsal
Arrangements by Axel Stordahl

VP976-D4TC 474	Let Me Love You Tonight	V-Disc 351-A (Army) 131-A (Navy)
VP976-D4TC 474	Just Close Your Eyes	V-Disc 351-A (Army) 131-A (Navy)

New York City   **October 23, 1944**
For the Record—NBC
Arrangements by Raymond Paige

None	If You Are But A Dream	N/R on V-Disc
None	Sunday, Monday Or Always—parody	N/R on V-Disc
None	Brahms' Lullaby	N/R on V-Disc

New York City   **November 14, 1944**
Arrangements by Axel Stordahl

C033808-2 VP1030-XP 33905	If You Are But A Dream	V-Disc 393-A (Army) 173-A (Navy) Col. 36756, 36814-com. issue
C033809-1 VP1030-XP 33905	Saturday Night	V-Disc 393-A (Army) 173-A (Navy) Col. 36762, 50069-com. issue

Buffalo, N.Y.   **November 16, 1944**
Kraft Music Hall—W/Bing Crosby
Arrangement by John Scott Trotter

None	These Foolish Things W/Bing Crosby	N/R on V-Disc

New York City   **December 1, 1944**
Arrangements by Axel Stordahl

C033929-1 V P 1 1 3 8 - X P 34193	I Begged Her W/The Ken Lane Singers	V-Disc 405-A (Army) 185-A (Navy) Col. 36774-com. issue
C033930-2 V P 1 1 3 8 - X P 34193	What Makes The Sunset	V-Disc 405-A (Army) 185-A (Navy) Col. 36774-com. issue

New York City   **December 3, 1944**
Arrangement by Axel Stordahl

C033936-1 VP1496-D5TC 596	The Charm Of You	V-Disc 537-A (Army) Col. 36830-com. issue

Hollywood   **December 19, 1944**
Arrangements by Axel Stordahl

HC01184-1 VP1332-D5TC 295	When Your Lover Has Gone	V-Disc 467-A (Army) 247-A (Navy) Col. 36791-com. issue

Hollywood   **January 3, 1945**
Max Factor Show—Starring Frank Sinatra
Arrangement by Axel Stordahl

VP1343-D5TC 410	None But The Lonely Heart W/chorus	V-Disc 494-A (Army)

Hollywood   **April 4, 1945**
Max Factor Show—Starring Frank Sinatra
Arrangement by Axel Stordahl

VP1273-XP 34648	Ol' Man River	V-Disc 460-A (Army) 240-A (Navy)

Hollywood   **May 1, 1945**
Arrangement by Axel Stordahl

HC01379-1 VP1496-D5TC 596	You'll Never Walk Alone W/Ken Lane Singers	V-Disc 537-A (Army) Col. 36825, 50066-com. issue

New York City   **May 24, 1945**
Arrangements by Xavier Cugat

VP1489-XP35091	Stars In Your Eyes	N/R on V-Disc
VP1489-XP 35091	My Shawl	N/R on V-Disc
C034817-1 VP1491-D5TC 587	Stars In Your Eyes	V-Disc 521-B (Army) Col. 36842-com. issue
C034818-1 VP1491-D5TC 587	My Shawl	V-Disc 521-B (Army) Col. 36842-com. issue

Hollywood   **July 30, 1945**
Arrangements by Axel Stordahl

HC01499-1 JDB179-JBB179-D6TC 6025	Someone To Watch Over Me	V-Disc 711-B (Army) Col. 36921, 38220-com. issue

HC01500-1 JDB172-D6TC 6018	You Go To My Head	V-Disc 700-B (Army) Col. 36918-com. issue
HC01501-1 J180-JDB180- D6TC 6026	These Foolish Things	V-Disc 822-A (Army) Col. 36919-com. issue
HC01502-1 JDB179- JBB179-D6TC 6025	I Don't Know Why	V-Disc 711-B (Army) Col. 36918-com. issue

Hollywood   **September 26, 1945**
Frank Sinatra Old Gold Show
Arrangements by Axel Stordahl

VP1586-D5TC 1409	Homesick That's All	V-Disc 564-A (Army)
VP1586-D5TC 1409	The Night Is Young And You're So Beautiful W/Dinah Shore	V-Disc 564-A (Army)

Hollywood   **October 3, 1945**
Frank Sinatra Old Gold Show
Arrangements by Axel Stordahl

VP1597-D5TC 1423	Aren't You Glad You're You (Spoken intro)	V-Disc 594-A (Army)
VP1597-D5TC 1423	You Brought A New Kind Of Love To Me	V-Disc 594-A (Army)

New York City   **October 24, 1945**
Frank Sinatra Old Gold Show—dress rehearsal
Arrangements by Axel Stordahl—with Tommy Dorsey

VP1623-D5TC 1449	I'll Never Smile Again W/The Pied Pipers	V-Disc 582-A (Army)
VP1623- D5TC-1449	Without A Song	V-Disc 582-A (Army)

New York City   **November 15, 1945**
Arrangement by Mitch Miller

C035426-1 JDB VP1708- D5TC 1540	Old School Teacher	V-Disc 614-A (Army) N/R

New York City   **November 14, 1945**
Frank Sinatra Old Gold Show—dress rehearsal
Arrangement by Axel Stordahl

JDB VP1708- D5TC 1540	Oh What It Seemed To Be	V-Disc 614-A (Army)

New York City   **November 30, 1945**
Arrangement by Axel Stordahl

C035484-1 JDB41-D6TC 5081	I Have But One Heart (Spoken intro)	V-Disc 625-A (Army) Col. 37554-com. issue

New York City   **December 19, 1945**
Frank Sinatra Old Gold Show—dress rehearsal
Arrangements by Axel Stordahl

JDB VP1761- D5TC 1819	Oh Little Town of Bethlehem W/Mitchell Boys Choir	V-Disc 652-B (Army)
	White Christmas W/Mitchell Boys Choir	V-Disc 652-B (Army)
JDP VP1761- D5TC 1819		

NOTE: (1) 'Joy To The World' appears on V-Disc 652-B-Choral
Group only.

(2) December 5 and 10, 1945, Sinatra conducted the
Columbia String Orchestra. They recorded six Alec Wilder Songs
which were issued on Columbia. Four of the songs were issued on
V-Discs 635-A and B642-A and B. There were no vocals.

New York City   **January 2, 1946**
Frank Sinatra Old Gold Show—dress rehearsal
Arrangement by Axel Stordahl

J180-JDB180- D6TC 6026	Over The Rainbow W/Chorus	V-Disc 822-A (Army)

Hollywood   **January 16, 1946**
Frank Sinatra Old Gold Show
Arrangement by Axel Stordahl

JB118-D6TC 5297	Where Is My Bess? spoken coda by Sinatra	V-Disc 789-B (Army)

Hollywood   **Februaary 13, 1946**
Frank Sinatra Old Gold Show—dress rehearsal
Arrangement by Axel Stordahl

JDB145-D6TC 5962	The Song Is You spoken intro. by Bob Hope	V-Disc 689-A (Army)

Hollywood   **February 24, 1946**
Arrangements by Axel Stordahl

HC01735-1 JBB217-D6TC 6079	Begin The Beguine	V-Disc 722-B (Army) Col. 37064-com. issue
HC01736-1 JDB136-D6TC 5945	Something Old, Something New	V-Disc 679-B (Army) Col. 36987-com. issue

Hollywood   **February 27, 1946**
Frank Sinatra Old Gold Show
Arrangement by Axel Stordahl

JDB70-B 45220	Should I W/The Pied Pipers Spoken coda by Sinatra— no vocal	V-Disc 663-B (Army)

Hollywood   **March 10, 1946**
Arrangements by Axel Stordahl

HC01749-1 JBB217-D6TC 6079	That Old Black Magic Spoken intro.	V-Disc 722-B (Army) Col. 37257-com. issue
HC01750-1 JDB136-D6TC 5945	That Girl That I Marry	V-Disc 679-B (Army) Col. 36975-com. issue

New York City   **April 7, 1946**
Arrangement by Axel Stordahl

XC036056-1 JB 339-D7TC 7117	Soliloquy Part 1	V-Disc 749-A (Army) Col. 2L6-com. issue
XC036057-1 JB 340-D7TC 7118	Soliloquy Part 2	V-Disc 749-B (Army) Col. 2L6 com. issue

New York City   **April 10, 1946**
Frank Sinatra Old Gold Show—dress rehearsal
Arrangement by Axel Stordahl

JB118-D6TC 5297	I Fall In Love With You Everyday	V-Disc 789-B (Army)

New York City   **April 24, 1946**
Frank Sinatra Old Gold Show—dress rehearsal
Arrangements by Axel Stordahl

JDB110-D6TC 5290	They Say It's Wonderful	V-Disc 670-A (Army)

JDB110-D6TC 5290	You Are Too Beautiful	V-Disc 670-A (Army)

Hollywood June 5, 1946
Frank Sinatra Old Gold Show
Arrangement by Axel Stordahl

JDB172-D6TC 6018	Come Rain Or Come Shine	V-Disc 700-B (Army)

Hollywood August 8, 1946
Arrangement by Axel Stordahl

HC01946-1 J638-1068	Lost In The Stars	V-Disc 879-A (Army) Col. 38650-com. issue

Hollywood November 7, 1946
Arrangment by Axel Stordahl

HC02137-1 JDB46-D6TC 5092	My Romance W/Dinah Shore	V-Disc 645-A (Army) N/R

New York City December 15, 1946
Arrangements by Axel Stordahl

C037162-1 JB343-D7TC 7121	I Want To Thank Your Folks Spoken intro by George Simon	V-Disc 763-A (Army) Col. 37251.-com. issue
C037164-1 JB343-D7TC 7121	You Can Take My Word For It Baby Arrangement by Page Cavanaugh W/The Page Cavanaugh Trio	V-Disc 763-A (Army) Col. 40229-com. issue
C037177-1 JB342-D7TC 7120	Sweet Lorraine spoken intro by George Simon Arrangement by Sy Oliver W/The Metronome All Stars	V-Disc 754-B (Army) Col. 37293-com. issue

Hollywood August 11, 1947
Arrangements by Axel Stordahl

HC02519-1 J540-USS 1011	That Old Feeling spoken intro	V-Disc 851-A (Army) Col. 902-com. issue
HC02522-1	One For My Baby	V-Disc 831-A (Army) Col. 38474-com. issue

Hollywood September 1947
Special V-Disc recording—unknown location
Arrangement by Axel Stordahl

J539-ND7TC 1443	Stormy Weather spoken intro	V-Disc 839-A (Army)

New York City December 8, 1947
Arrangement by Axel Stordahl

C038498-1 J574-USS 1028	Ever Homeward	V-Disc 859-B (Army) Col. 38151-com. issue

Hollywood May, 1948
Special V-Disc recordings—unknown location
Arrangements by Axel Stordahl

J616-USS 1046	Silent Night spoken intro. W/Chorus	V-Disc 868-A (Army)
J616-USS 1046	Adeste Fideles	V-Disc 868-A (Army)
J616-USS 1046	Oh Little Town Of Bethlehem W/Chorus	V-Disc 868-A (Army)
J617-USS 1047	It Came Upon The Midnight Clear W/Chorus	V-Disc 868-B (Army)
J617-USS 1047	Jingle Bells W/Chorus	V-Disc 868-B (Army)
J617-USS 1047	Santa Claus Is Comin' To Town	V-Disc 868-B (Army)

Hollywood December 16, 1948
Arrangement by Axel Stordahl

HC03467-1 J689-1119	Sunflower spoken intro	V-Disc 904-B (Army) Col. 38391-com. issue

SINATRA
V-DISCS ON ALBUMS

Sinatra—The Early Years **Windmill WMD240**
(England)

Side 1
1. All The Things You Are
2. All Of Me
3. Mighty Lak' A Rose
4. Nancy
5. There's No You
6. Someone To Watch Over Me

Side 2
1. Ol' Man River
2. When Your Lover Has Gone
3. Falling In Love With Love
4. None But The Lonely Heart
5. I'll Never Smile Again
6. Without A Song

Sinatra For The Collector: Volume 1—The V Disc Years
My Way MW1001
(Canada)

Side 1
1. Sunflower
2. A Lovely Way to Spend An Evening
3. She's Funny That Way
4. There's No You
5. Come Out Wherever You Are
6. Some Other Time
7. You've Got A Hold On Me

Side 2
1. Soliloquy
2. Aren't You Glad You're You
3. I'll Be Around
4. You Brought A New Kind Of Love To Me
5. Someone To Watch Over Me
6. One For My Baby

Sinatra For the Collector: Volume 2—The V Disc Years
My Way MW1002
(Canada)

Side 1
1. I Only Have Eyes For You
2. A Hot Time In The Town Of Berlin
3. Let Me Love You Tonight
4. Ol' Man River
5. I'll Follow My Secret Heart
6. When Your Lover Has Gone
7. All The Things You Are

Side 2
1. Falling In Love With Love
2. The Night Is Young And You're So Beautiful W/Dinah Shore
3. All Of Me
4. Nancy
5. Old School Teacher
6. Just Close Your Eyes
7. Put Your Dreams Away
8. And Then You Kissed Me

Frank Sinatara On V-Disc

Dan Records VC-5019
(Japan)

Side 1
1. Sunflower
2. None But The Lonely Heart
3. My Romance
   W/Dinah Shore
4. The Night Is Young And
   You're So Beautiful
   W/Dinah Shore
5. I'll Never Smile Again
6. Without A Song
7. Should I
8. One For My Baby

Side 2
1. Old School Teacher
2. Aren't You Glad You're You
3. I'll Follow My Secret Heart
4. Come Rain Or Come Shine
5. All The Things You Are
6. When Your Lover Has Gone
7. White Christmas
8. Ol' Man River

Frank Sinatra On V-Disc Volume 1

APEX AX1
(England)

Side 1
1. I Only Have Eyes For You
2. Kiss Me Again
3. A Hot Time In The Town
   Of Berlin
4. The Music Stopped
5. I Couldn't Sleep A Wink
   Last Night
6. The Way You Look Tonight
7. I'll Be Around
8. You've Got A Hold On Me

Side 2
1. A Lovely Way To Spend
   An Evening
2. She's Funny That Way
3. Speak Low
4. Close To You
5. My Shining Hour
6. Long Ago And Far Away
7. Some Other Time
8. Come Out Wherever You
   Are

SINATRA LPs ON THE BILLBOARD CHARTS 1945–82

DATE	POS	WKS	TITLE	LABEL
3-14-46	1	18	The Voice Of Frank Sinatra	Col. 112
5-9-47	2	7	Songs By Sinatra	Col. 124
12-24-48	7	1	Christmas Songs By Sinatra	Col. 167
2-27-54	3	20	Songs For Young Lovers	Cap. 488
9-4-54	3	20	Swing Easy	Cap. 528
5-28-55	2	29	In The Wee Small Hours	Cap. 581
3-31-56	2	66	Songs For Swingin' Lovers	Cap. 653
12-22-56	8	25	This Is Sinatra	Cap. 768
3-2-57	5	14	Close To You	Cap. 789
5-18-57	2	42	A Swingin' Affair	Cap. 803
9-14-57	3	29	Where Are You?	Cap. 855
12-21-57	18	2	A Jolly Christmas	Cap. 894
1-25-58	1	71	Come Fly With Me	Cap. 920
4-19-58	8	7	This Is Sinatra, Vol. 2	Cap. 982
5-24-58	12	1	The Frank Sinatra Story	Col. 2L 6
9-20-58	1	120	Only The Lonely	Cap. 1053
1-31-59	2	140	Come Dance With Me	Cap. 1069
6-7-59	8	15	Look To Your Heart	Cap. 1164
8-23-59	2	73	No One Cares	Cap. 1221
8-21-60	1	86	Nice N' Easy	Cap. 1417
2-19-61	3	36	Sinatra's Swingin' Session	Cap. 1491
4-16-61	4	60	All The Way	Cap. 1538
5-7-61	6	35	Ring-A-Ding Ding	Rep. 1001
8-20-61	8	39	Come Swing With Me	Cap. 1594
8-20-61	6	22	Sinatra Swings	Rep. 1002
11-12-61	3	42	I Remember Tommy	Rep. 1003
3-17-62	8	31	Sinatra And Strings	Rep. 1004
4-21-62	19	29	Point Of No Return	Cap. 1676
8-18-62	15	18	Sinatra Sings . . . Of Love And Things	Cap. 1729
9-1-62	18	16	Sinatra And Swinging' Brass	Rep. 1005
11-10-62	25	17	All Alone	Rep. 1007
12-22-62	120	2	A Jolly Christmas	Cap. 894
2-2-63	5	42	Sinatra—Basie	Rep. 1008
6-2-63	6	35	The Concert Sinatra	Rep. 1009
9-28-63	129	4	Tell Her You Love Her	Cap. 1919
10-5-63	8	43	Sinatra's Sinatra	Rep. 1010
4-11-64	10	24	Days Of Wine & Roses, Moon River & Other Academy Award Winners	Rep. 1011
5-30-64	116	7	F/Sinatra/B. Crosby/ F. Waring—America I Hear You Singing	Rep. 2020
8-22-64	13	31	It Might As Well Be Swing	Rep. 1012
12-19-64	19	28	Softly As I Leave You	Rep. 1013
7-3-65	9	44	Sinatra '65	Rep. 6167
8-21-65	5	69	September Of My Years	Rep. 1014
12-25-65	9	32	A Man & His Music	Rep. 1016
12-25-65	30	16	My Kind Of Broadway	Rep. 1015
4-23-66	34	14	Moonlight Sinatra	Rep. 1018
6-18-66	1	73	Strangers In The Night	Rep. 1017
8-20-66	9	44	Sinatra At The Sands	Rep. 1019
12-31-66	6	61	That's Life	Rep. 1020
4-15-67	19	28	F. A. Sinatra & A. C. Jobim	Rep. 1021
7-29-67	195	2	The Movie Songs	Cap. 2700
9-16-67	24	23	Frank Sinatra	Rep. 1022
2-24-68	78	13	Francis A. & Edward K.	Rep. 1024
9-7-68	55	25	Frank Sinatra's Greatest Hits	Rep. 1025
12-28-68	18	28	Cycles	Rep. 1027
5-10-69	11	19	My Way	Rep. 1029
8-23-69	186	3	Close-Up	Cap. 254
9-6-69	30	16	A Man Alone	Rep. 1030
4-11-70	101	10	Watertown	Rep. 1031
4-24-71	73	15	Sinatra & Company	Rep. 1033
6-10-72	88	17	Sinatra's Greatest Hits Vol. 2	Rep. 1034
10-13-73	13	22	Ol' Blue Eyes Is Back	Rep. 2155
7-13-74	48	11	Some Nice Things I've Missed	Rep. 2195
11-16-74	37	12	The Main Event	Rep. 2207
1-11-75	170	3	Round One	Cap. 11357
4-12-80	16	22	Trilogy	Rep. 3FS2300
11-13-81	52	13	She Shot Me Down	Rep. FS2305

SINATRA ALBUMS TO MAKE CASH BOX ALBUMS CHART—1962–82

DATE	POS	WKS	TITLE	LABEL
3-3-62	5	23	Sinatra And Strings	Rep. 1004
3-31-62	14	13	Point Of No Return	Cap. 1676
8-11-62	28	9	Sinatra Sings Of Love And Things	Cap. 1729
8-25-62	14	12	Sinatra & Swingin' Brass	Rep. 1005
11-10-62	25	10	All Alone	Rep. 1007
2-2-63	6	26	Sinatra—Basie	Rep. 1008
6-15-63	7	17	The Concert Sinatra	Rep. 1009
8-24-63	40	6	Tell Her You Love Her	Cap. 1919
9-28-63	7	25	Sinatra's Sinatra	Rep. 1010
4-4-64	16	11	Academy Award Winners	Rep. 1011
6-6-64	92	5	America I Hear You Singing	Rep. 2020
8-8-64	36	7	Robin & The Seven Hoods	Rep. 2021
8-15-64	13	19	It Might As Well Be Swing	Rep. 1012
12-19-64	17	17	Softly As I Leave You	Rep. 1013
6-26-65	14	20	Sinatra '65	Rep. 6167
8-14-65	5	48	September Of My Years	Rep. 1014
12-11-65	72	13	Sinatra '65	Rep. 6167*

12-11-65	40	16	My Kind Of Broadway	Rep. 1015	
12-18-65	16	25	A Man And His Music	Rep. 1016	
4-23-66	19	14	Moonlight Sinatra	Rep. 1018	
6-18-66	1	35	Strangers In The Night	Rep. 1017	
8-20-66	12	22	Sinatra At The Sands	Rep. 1019	
12-24-66	5	42	That's Life	Rep. 1020	
4-8-67	7	24	Sinatra & Jobim	Rep. 1021	
9-9-67	24	22	The World We Knew	Rep. 1022	
2-10-68	43	16	Francis A. & Edward K.	Rep. 1024	
8-24-68	56	17	Greatest Hits	Rep. 1025	
12-21-68	12	22	Cycles	Rep. 1027	
5-3-69	7	23	My Way	Rep. 1029	
8-23-69	18	24	A Man Alone	Rep. 1030	
4-11-70	87	11	Watertown	Rep. 1031	
5-1-71	62	14	Sinatra & Company	Rep. 1033	
6-17-72	79	10	Greatest Hits—Vol. 2	Rep. 1034	
10-27-73	7	22	Ol' Blue Eyes Is Back	Rep. 2155	
8-3-74	48	14	Some Nice Things I've Missed	Rep. 2195	
12-14-74	55	7	The Main Event	Rep. 2207	
1-18-75	174	2	Round One	Cap. 11357	
4-12-80	10	22	Trilogy	Rep. 3FS2300	
11-13-81	42	13	She Shot Me Down	Rep. FS2305	

*Returned to charts

SINATRA SINGLES TO MAKE BILLBOARD'S SINGLES CHART

Date—indicates date record first made chart
Pos—indicates highest position attained
Wks—indicates number of weeks on survey

NOTE: The numerical size of the Billboard chart changed as follows over the years:

DATE	NUMBER OF RECORDS
7-20-40	10
11-7-47	15
6-4-48	30
11-8-53	20
5-19-54	30
6-15-55	25
11-2-55	100

DATE	POS	WKS	TITLE
7-20-40	1	15	I'll Never Smile Again
7-20-40	8	1	Imagination
9-13-40	10	4	Trade Winds
10-31-40	5	3	Our Love Affair
11-22-40	3	5	We Three
12-27-40	7	1	Stardust
2-21-41	2	12	Oh, Look At Me Now
4-3-41	4	3	Do I Worry?
4-18-41	7	2	Dolores
4-25-41	9	1	Everything Happens To Me
5-2-41	7	2	Let's Get Away From It All
10-17-41	3	16	This Love Of Mine
12-12-41	9	1	Two In Love
7-17-42	3	9	Just As Though You Were Here
9-18-42	5	3	Take Me
10-29-42	10	2	Daybreak
11-5-42	1	24	There Are Such Things
2-4-43	4	13	It Started All Over Again
6-10-43	2	18	All Or Nothing At All
7-1-43	1	17	In The Blue Of Evening
7-8-43	6	7	It's Always You
7-22-43	2	13	You'll Never Know
7-23-43	10	1	Close To You
9-9-43	9	4	Sunday, Monday Or Always
9-30-43	6	9	People Will Say We're In Love
2-3-44	5	8	I Couldn't Sleep A Wink Last Night
12-21-44	7	9	White Christmas
1-18-45	7	4	I Dream Of You
2-8-45	6	3	Saturday Night
5-24-45	7	2	Dream
11-29-45	10	1	Nancy
2-14-46	2	12	Oh! What It Seemed To Be
2-28-46	10	1	Day By Day
6-20-46	8	6	They Say It's Wonderful
8-1-46	1	18	Five Minutes More
10-18-46	10	1	The Coffee Song
12-27-46	8	1	White Christmas
5-9-47	6	4	Mam'selle
5-28-48	18	4	Nature Boy
4-20-49	25	1	Sunflower
6-10-49	10	14	The Huckle Buck
6-17-49	25	2	Some Enchanted Evening
7-29-49	30	1	Bali Ha'i
10-7-49	21	8	Don't Cry Joe
12-16-49	21	7	Old Master Painter
3-10-50	24	1	Chattanoogie Shoe Shine Boy
7-28-50	12	9	Goodnight Irene
9-7-51	26	2	Castle Rock
2-13-54	2	22	Young At Heart
5-19-54	28	2	Don't Worry 'Bout Me
5-26-54	7	13	Three Coins In The Fountain
5-4-55	2	20	Learnin' The Blues
11-2-55	65	4	Same Old Saturday Night
11-2-55	5	17	Love And Marriage
11-23-55	23	15	The Tender Trap
11-2-55	65	4	Same Old Saturday Night
11-2-55	5	17	Love And Marriage
11-23-55	23	15	The Tender Trap
2-15-56	35	13	Flowers Mean Forgiveness
2-22-56	67	5	You'll Get Yours
5-9-56	30	14	How Little We Know
5-23-56	73	3	Five Hundred Guys
7-4-56	52	15	You're Sensational
7-18-56	75	5	Wait For Me
10-17-56	6	19	Hey, Jealous Lover
1-9-57	20	19	Can I Steal A Little Love
1-9-57	60	8	Your Love For Me
4-17-57	60	4	Crazy Love
4-17-57	74	5	So Long My Love
10-19-57	84	5	Chicago
10-26-57	15	30	All The Way
1-25-58	20	16	Witchcraft
5-17-58	97	1	How Are Ya' Fixed For Love?
11-2-58	41	11	Mr. Success
4-5-59	61	7	French Foreign Legion
6-21-59	30	17	High Hopes
10-15-59	38	11	Talk To Me
6-5-60	82	2	River Stay From My Door
9-4-60	60	6	Nice 'N' Easy
11-13-60	25	9	Ol' MacDonald
3-15-61	99	1	The Moon Was Yellow
3-22-61	50	7	Second Time Around

DATE	POS	WKS	TITLE
7-9-61	64	4	Granada
10-22-61	58	7	I'll Be Seeing You
12-24-61	34	8	Pocketful Of Miracles
3-24-62	98	1	Stardust
4-7-62	75	2	Everybody's Twistin'
4-6-63	78	8	Call Me Irresponsible
1-18-64	81	3	Stay With Me
9-5-64	27	11	Softly As I Leave You
12-19-64	32	10	Somewhere In Your Heart
3-13-65	46	6	Anytime At All
5-22-65	57	6	(Tell Her) You Love Her
6-26-65	78	7	Forget Domani
12-25-65	28	8	It Was A Very Good Year
5-7-66	1	15	Strangers In The Night
9-3-66	25	7	Summer Wind
11-19-66	4	11	That's Life
3-18-67	1	13	Something Stupid
8-5-67	30	7	World We Knew
10-28-67	53	5	This Town
4-13-68	60	5	I Can't Believe I'm Losing You
8-31-68	64	6	My Way Of Life
10-12-68	23	10	Cycles
1-4-69	62	6	Rain In My Heart
3-29-69	27	8	My Way
9-13-69	75	4	Love's Been Good To Me
1-29-69	79	4	Goin' Out Of My Head/ Forget To Remember
3-21-70	88	3	I Would Be In Love Anyway
11-10-73	63	10	Let Me Try Again
4-6-74	83	7	Bad, Bad Leroy Brown
8-3-74	83	5	Your Turned My World Around
4-19-75	75	6	Anytime
8-2-75	47	6	I Believe I'm Gonna Love You
5-3-80	32	12	New York, New York
12-8-62	79	5	Me And My Shadow
4-13-63	62	8	Call Me Irresponsible
6-15-63	92	3	Come Blow Your Horn
9-19-64	38	10	Softly As I Leave You
12-26-64	32	7	Somewhere In Your Heart
3-13-65	54	5	Anytime At All
5-29-65	87	2	Tell Her You Love Her
6-26-65	58	5	Forget Domani
12-18-65	33	8	It Was A Very Good Year
5-7-66	1	15	Strangers In The Night
9-3-66	26	8	Summer Wind
11-12-66	5	13	That's Life
3-18-67	1	14	Something Stupid
8-5-67	22	8	The World We Knew
10-28-67	41	5	This Town
4-6-68	63	7	I Can't Believe I'm Losing You
8-24-68	60	4	My Way Of Life
9-21-68	88	2	Cycles
10-26-68	41	7	Cycles*
12-28-68	51	7	Rain In My Heart
3-22-69	29	10	My Way
9-6-69	61	6	Love's Been Good To Me
11-22-69	96	1	Goin' Out Of My Head
11-17-73	61	6	Let Me Try Again
4-26-75	93	2	Anytime
8-2-75	52	6	I Believe I'm Gonna Love You
5-3-80	21	12	New York, New York

*Returned to charts

SINATRA SINGLES TO MAKE CASH BOX SINGLES CHART—1962–80

DATE	POS	WKS	TITLE
12-23-61	26	9	Pocketful Of Miracles
3-31-62	81	4	Everybody's Twistin'

AUTHOR'S NOTE: Another invaluable listing of Frank Sinatra's recordings as well as his radio, television, concert and film appearances has been compiled by John Ridgway, the British representative of The Sinatra Society of Australia. Entitled *The Sinatra Files*, these authoritative works are issued in three volumes: 1. Radio, Television and Concert Appearances; 2. Recordings; 3. Films; and copies of all or any individual editions are available from Mr. Ridgway at 'Miramar', Rowney Green Lane, Alvechurch, Birmingham B48 7QF.

The Sinatra Societies

UNITED STATES
Sinatra Society of America,
Post Office Box 10512,
Dallas,
Texas 75207.

The Sinatra Social Club (Philadelphia),
Carol Summa,
3404, Edgemont,
Brookhaven,
Philadelphia 19015.

GREAT BRITAIN
Sinatra Music Society,
Roy Palphryman Esq.,
58, Elston Lane,
Bushbury,
Wolverhampton WV10 9HA.

AUSTRALIA
The Sinatra Society of Australia,
Bill Weeden,
32, Stockdale Avenue,

Clayton,
Victoria 3168.

(UK/Representative: John Ridgway,
'Miramar', Rowney Green Lane,
Alvechurch, Birmingham B48 7QF.)

(American Representative: Garry Doctor,
Post Office Box 254, Getzville, New
York, N.Y.14068.)

EUROPE
The Sinatra Society of Belgium,
Ed Vanhellemont,
Diksmuidelaan 200,
2600 Berchem (Antwerp),
Belgium.

JAPAN
The Sinatra Society of Japan,
Yasuo Sangu,
2-40-13 Honmachi,
Shibuya-Ku,
Tokyo 151.

Frank greets members of the Sinatra Music Society in London.

PERFECTLY FRANK

The Journal of the
SINATRA MUSIC SOCIETY

APRIL 1980 ISSUE No. 160

SINATRA SOCIETY
A FAN CLUB
LAS VEGAS

NOVEMBER, 1980   A NON PROFIT ORGANIZATION

Special 25th Year Issue

25

UNIVERSITY OF NEVA

The *Sinatra Society*
of *Australia*

FOR PRIVATE

CIRCULATION ONLY

Albert.

NEWSLETTER

Sinatra Society of America

40th Anniversary Issue
September 1, 1979   No. 14